£2.25p

INDUSTRIAL SOCIETY IN ENGLAND

TOWARDS THE END OF THE EIGHTEENTH CENTURY

Industrial Society in England towards the end of the Eighteenth Century

WITT BOWDEN

SECOND EDITION

FRANK CASS & CO. LTD.
1965

First Edition published in 1925
by The Macmillan Company, New York.

Second Edition published by
Frank Cass & Co. Ltd., 10 Woburn Walk, London W.C.1.

First Edition   1925
Second Edition 1965

Printed in Great Britain by
Thomas Nelson (Printers) Ltd., London and Edinburgh

To

MARY EDITH MYERS BOWDEN

INTRODUCTION TO THE
SECOND EDITION

This book, published four decades ago, explores the eighteenth-century transitional stages of our era of rapid and almost constantly accelerating technical change. It ascribes the beginnings of our industrial society to those early transformations of the instruments and organization of production. Republication gives occasion for some reflections on later trends.

Students of the past have often noted that two hundred years ago the manner of producing and transporting and distributing goods and the modes of travel and communication and the basic ideas of social status and relations between peoples had undergone from time out of mind only a slow and gradual change. The inventors in the later decades of the eighteenth century, the organizers of industry, and industrial workers with their emerging awareness and ambitions, were pioneers in worlds far more expansive than was the New World of geographical discovery and exploration and colonization. The frontiers of the New World were extended by methods essentially traditional, and the limits of expansion were fixed by earth itself; in contrast, as long as men are moved by scientific curiosity and the eighteenth-century spirit of innovation, the advancing frontiers of technology are virtually unconfined.

The technological changes of that period were in their effects uniquely significant; in nature, however, in comparison with later changes, they seem simple, elementary. They aroused at the time a sense of the marvellous that to later sophisticates may seem somewhat naive. Today we open doors to nature's secrets men had thought to be forever hidden; we control incredibly potent forces. Our exploits range from outer-space vistas, satellites, communication, even travel, to undreamed of advances in understanding and controlling the marvellously minute and complex worlds of atoms and living cells. It was the late eighteenth century, however, that marked the decisive beginnings, the epochal successes, of modern technology.

Some in our generation, pridefully exulting in the power of modern technique, endanger sanity by " the intoxication of power," viewed by Bertrand Russell as " the greatest danger of our time." Nevertheless, there is an increasing, and hopeful, awareness of the ominous as well as auspicious potential of the scientific unlocking of doors long barred and the technological mastery of the world about us. Men disturbed by human frailties in the use of seemingly superhuman powers wonder if the end may come in the unwitting or the wilful setting off of a general nuclear holocaust. Assuming survival, some fear that the machine may become a Frankenstein monster in the fictional image of the early era of mechanization. Others view the cybernation revolution as making of most men mere automatons or unproductive appendages. Others still are fearful that men at large will increasingly become the victims of the quickening pace of highly specialized technology attended as it seems to have been by the snail's pace of general education, awareness, adaptability, the collective command and humanizing of the forces of change.

Twentieth-century sophisticates are wont to think of men of the eighteenth century as having had a naive faith in their rational faculties and in the certainty of progress. Men seem, indeed, in that relatively uncomplicated and perhaps unduly optimistic time to have suffered few misgivings. Recent generations, in contrast, have been deluged by disturbing and disillusioning doctrines. These, in turn, have reflected the accelerated tempo, and the often disruptive effects, of the changes initiated by the earlier industrial society.

That contrast is apparent from a brief recalling of some of the epochal changes in ideas since the eighteenth century. Those changes illuminate the interactions of material and cultural forces and the difficulties even Englishmen, pragmatically facile in adjustment, have experienced in maintaining the traditional continuity of their society.

Even in the closing years of the eighteenth century, the Rev. T. R. Malthus, " classical pessimist," saw little chance for any save calamitously enforced restraints on procreation as keeping population within bounds. When he was formulating his gloomy ideas or " principles," he was impressed, he tells us, by the " prodigious rapidity " of growth of industry and the industrial population and by the " sudden check to population " during periods of unemployment and destitution attending fluctuations in the demands for manufactures. David Ricardo and other professors of the " dismal science " played further havoc with optimism by proclaiming such " laws " as " the iron law of wages " and giving the new industrial employers a seemingly flawless basis for laissez-faire.

The doctrines of Charles Darwin were profoundly disturbing to men who held traditional ideas of man's nature and of divine revelation; they were also disruptive because they were applied, as "social Darwinism," to industry and public policy. Men of smaller minds but even wider momentary influence, notably Herbert Spencer, converted the generally valid concepts of organic evolution into devastating errors. These gave pseudo-scientific reinforcement to the laissez-faire doctrines of the economists: public intervention in aid of human "weaklings," and even in recognition of the generally acceptable right of association when wage workers claimed the right in dealing with employers, would be contrary to "the order of nature" and would "neutralize," among men, the "beneficent working of the survival of the fittest."

A radically different and even more violently revolutionary view of man's nature and destiny, the Marxian dogma, was crucially influenced by the observations, by Karl Marx and Friedrich Engels, of English industrialism in its rawest, least humane era. Marx, in a peculiar use of the earlier mild conception of the inevitability of progress, combined with selected phases of Ricardian economics and Hegelian philosophy, developed an almost puppet-like dogma of economic determinism. He at least allowed to some of the human puppets, the exploited workers, their historically destined role of expropriating the exploiters and setting up the dictatorship of the proletariat.

The widespread acceptance of the Marxian dogma affords a remarkable example of a secular faith and of the vain search by moderns floundering in the seas of change for a refuge, as in earlier times of sluggish tempo, in dogmatic absolutes. At the opposite but not dissimilar extremes were the later not less dangerous dogmas of the far right.

Perhaps the most extreme departures from the ideas and attitudes of men of the eighteenth century are to be seen in the tendencies commonly described as Freudian. English thinkers of the seventeenth and eighteenth centuries, notably Locke and Berkeley and Hume, had explored the mind and had recognized the limitations of reason but without surrendering in the struggle for the sovereignty of reason. Few would deny that Sigmund Freud added much to the understanding of human nature. Nevertheless, Freudianism was in no small part the source of latter-day anti-intellectualism; and it would have been largely alien to the eighteenth-century ideas and attitudes of Englishmen.* At the same time, Freudian doctrines owed the extent of their influence and in part their origin to the environment of rapid tempo and of readjustment and maladjustment to change, which in turn was largely an outgrowth of eighteenth-century invention and industry.

Freud's conceptions, notably those of the subconscious, the complexes, the baleful role of libidinal inhibitions and frustrations, reflected and at the same time reinforced certain disintegrative tendencies, such as the rapid changes in occupational requirements, the shifts in residence, the uprooting of individuals and families, the increase of impersonal

---

* In a panel discussion of " The Present-Day Relevance of Eighteenth-Century Thought," reported in 1956 by the American Council of Learned Societies, a panellist, in a somewhat dubious reading of eighteenth-century minds, remarked: " If Freud had been alive in the Enlightenment, Diderot would have been his first disciple, Voltaire his first popularizer, Rousseau his first patient." Even Rousseau's need for Freudian therapy may be questioned. It is at least to be noted that no Englishman was credited (or charged) with Freudian affinity.

relations, the breakup of traditional disciplines. A narrow and literal psychological analysis of personality problems tended to obscure and to ignore both the wide range of subjective origins and the complex environmental sources of the problems. The desire to avoid neuroses and complex-forming inhibitions often seemed to excuse self-indulgence and the throwing off of elementary disciplines; self-expression with many became a warrant for disregard of standards of behaviour and canons of taste. Art and literature were extensively debased. Effusions meaningless or formless or unintegrated were often widely acclaimed; countless perversions fell to morbid levels and to wholesale market-place pandering made easy by the techniques of mass communication. Freud's doctrines and related theories, in part fanciful as they were, suffered extreme and literal-minded uses; they gave impetus to perilously disintegrative views of the unavoidable domination of behaviour by primitive, irrational, subconscious forces.

Englishmen were the main initiators of the suddenly accelerating tempo of change calling for more facility of adjustment than men at large seemed able to command. Englishmen themselves, however, have had a long tradition of assimilating their experiences and ideas with a minimum of violence and maladjustment. The early course of their readjustments to eighteenth-century changes was obstructed by the quarter century of wars and by the attendant political reaction. Nevertheless, Englishmen were able to salvage certain eighteenth-century values which contributed vitally to the maintenance of their traditional continuity. They continued to hold in high regard their rational faculties, their faith in science, careful inquiry, experimentation, for increasing knowledge and understanding and the civilized and civilizing use of power. They also maintained substantially their earlier respect for what has been called conventional wisdom or experiential wisdom as embodied in customs, amenities, implicit norms or canons of behaviour and taste and workmanship.

Englishmen, from those and perhaps other causes, have been less affected than most of their contemporaries by aberrations such as those of the economists who proclaimed their " metaphysical preconceptions " as " laws," the dogmatic deterministic Marxians, the literal-minded Freudians, the so-called modernists in literature and art and philosophy, the inflexibly intolerant and tyrannical Fascists and other extreme rightists. Those values had a vital bearing, also, on the facility of Englishmen in making their extremely difficult transition from their eighteenth-century imperial role to that of center of the British Commonwealth of Nations and membership with the former dominions in the United Nations.

Englishmen of the eighteenth century, especially those who were active in the newly rising industrial society, resembled in vital traits the prevailing types of Englishmen today. Few have ever been enamored of progress in any abstract or philosophical sense; their main interest during the earlier period as well as later was in the processes of change; their concern was in taking part in the changes and in making use of them. There was a widespread eighteenth-century optimism, to be sure, a faith in the possibilities of individual achievement and national expansion. Englishmen of the twentieth century are more keenly aware of the forces beyond their control in the make-up of the individual and in the less acquiescent, more assertive spirit of the world at large. At the same time they recognize the responsibility for making choices in areas subject to their action, a responsibility necessarily entailing the possibility of making unwise choices. Like typical Americans, they are essentially pragmatic in thinking of themselves (in terms notably set forth by John Dewey) as part of the universal process of change, in the directing of which they can best share by awareness and intelligence and good will in choosing their individual actions and their collective policies.

Their outlook, vastly enlarged beyond the already expanding horizon of the eighteenth century, embraces new conceptions of classes and peoples. The " one world " of technology, so largely eighteenth-century in its sources, must, as long as it is merely a technical unity, suffer in the nuclear age even the extreme hazard of self-destruction. Englishmen and their English-speaking kinsmen have made significant advances toward " one world " of diverse and autonomous individuals and peoples held together by mutual understanding and interests. Chiefly, perhaps, they have given substance to the ideal of substituting, in place of the age-old struggle for ascendancy in exploiting scarcity, the producing and sharing of the abundance first made possible by the inventive and creative spirit of eighteenth-century English society.

In a most vital sense, the early technological and industrial transformations made possible the profound and far-reaching changes in the status of classes and in the relations between peoples. Those changes, naturally encountering obstructions, occurred by degrees and often in painful stages.

Englishmen themselves retained for decades their faith in a neat set of hierarchies, ordained by Nature or by Providence, of classes and races and nations. Sir Thomas Smith's *Commonwealth of England* had described the masses as having "no voice nor authority in our commonwealth, and no account is made of them, but only to be ruled." Even more inclusive in the late eighteenth century than in Sir Thomas Smith's sixteenth-century world were the "common people," the "vulgar sort," those "only to be ruled." Most of Smith's sturdy yeomen, for example, had fallen by the eighteenth century into his lowest class. Even the doctrine of the public duty to maintain a subsistence wage, embodied in law and earlier practice, was widely being supplanted by poor relief as an extremely meager supplement to wages below the crudest subsistence levels. It was not until the parliamentary reform movement of the nineteenth century that even the "great new cotton lords" and their counterparts in other industries achieved formal recognition.

Twentieth-century conceptions, in contrast, call for equality of individuals before the law and the pursuit by public authorities of the ideals of equal opportunity and social security for all. No less revolutionary than recognition and attempted guarantees of the rights of personal identity and civic equality of individuals has been the acknowledgment of the ethnic awakening of peoples, their aspirations for cultural autonomy and self-expression, their demands for self-determination and self-government.

Those contrasts, however, are subject to qualifications that point to the eighteenth-century beginnings of the changes. The great industrialists took large strides in their march toward their later status. There were noteworthy advances among the factory types of industrial laborers. The rise of the workers even to a limited self-consciousness and to a disguised and rarely successful independent group activity was the more significant in the light of their extremely depressed origins and the relentless repressions attending the quarter century of wars and political reaction exemplified by the cruelly one-sided laissez-faire policy. That policy itself may be viewed in a sense as the use of delaying tactics by the " establishment " against the advance of the group described later by a member of the " establishment " as comprising " our future masters."

The areas of imperial and international relations were also profoundly affected even in the eighteenth century. The early great industrialists were more effective proponents of " the system of natural liberty " than was Adam Smith himself, who defended the Corn Laws and the Acts of Trade. When the spread of the new industrial methods reduced the competitive advantages of England, the system in application to trade became less attractive. In the meantime, however, Englishmen had pioneered in new conceptions of amity and mutuality among peoples, notably in the British Commonwealth of Nations.

It is hardly an exaggeration to say that the main achievement of eighteenth-century Englishmen was their demonstration of the possibility of substituting the technical actuality for the mythical dream of the horn of plenty. It is of more than passing interest that the international as well as the English meaning of that demonstration was envisaged at the time, notably by Sir John Sinclair in his " Plan of Agreement among the Powers of Europe and the United States of America, for the purpose of rewarding discoveries of general benefit to society." The plan, he went so far as to hope, would provide the means for ending " customary acquisitions by intrigue or conquest " in favor of the peaceful extension everywhere of invention and the benefits of progress in the useful arts.

While this book was being written a relatively recent movement was in progress for seeking out and using long-neglected surviving records and intimate sources throwing light on earlier eras of industry and labor. Noteworthy in that connection was the period dealt with in this volume. Prominent in the movement, it will be recalled, was the late Professor George Unwin. Among my pleasantest experiences while writing the book were visits in the company of Professor Unwin, not long before his untimely death, to some of the early industrial centers around Manchester, scenes not only of " local color " but also of valuable records often preserved by chance and salvaged by patient inquiry.

The study was published when I was at the University of Pennsylvania. A few years later I left academic work for service with the Federal Government. These introductory observations reflect in part my public experience and responsibility in dealing with technological changes and their human impacts, especially on wage workers.

The interval since the first publication of this book has of course been marked by additions to the detailed knowledge of the period and the subject. It is believed that these later contributions substantially confirm the views expressed in this introduction as to the uniquely germinal nature of the epoch and its bearing on succeeding generations.

Notably worth consulting are T. S. Ashton's *The Industrial Revolution, 1760–1830* (1948); the same author's *Economic History of England in the Eighteenth Century* (1955); D. Marshall, *The English People in the Eighteenth Century* (1956); N. J. Smelser, *Social Change in the Industrial Revolution* (1959); E. P. Thompson, *The Making of the English Working Class* (1963). Mention may be made of an outstanding work originally in French, P. Mantoux's *Industrial Revolution in the Eighteenth Century*, revised edition, translated by M. Vernon (1928). Useful bibliographies will be found in A. Redford's *Economic History of England, 1760–1860*, 2nd revised edition (1960). On manufacturers' associations and related groups the following may be consulted: A. Redford and others, *Manchester Merchants and Foreign Trade, 1794–1858* (1934), especially Chapter I, " Organization of Merchants before 1794 "; John Thomas, ' The Potters of Staffordshire and Their Relations with the Manchester Committee of Commerce, 1784 to 1790 ' (*Proceedings of the Manchester Statistical Society*, 1935); V. W. Bladen, ' The Association of the Manufacturers of Earthenware, 1784–86 ' (*Economic History*, a supplement to the *Economic Journal*, vol. 1, no. 3, Jan. 1928, pp. 356–67); Henry Hamilton, ' The Founding of the Glasgow Chamber of Commerce, 1783 ' (*Scottish Journal of Political Economy*, March 1954, pp. 33–48); Henry Hamilton, *An Economic History of Scotland in the Eighteenth Century* (1963), pp. 271–279 *et passim;* M. W. Beresford, *The Leeds Chambers of Commerce* (1951); J. M. Norris, ' Samuel Garbett and the Early Development of Industrial Lobbying in Great Britain ' (*Economic History Review*, 2nd series, vol. X, no. 3, 1958, pp. 450–460). W. B.

Washington, D.C.
May, 1964

PREFACE TO THE FIRST EDITION

This work is concerned with the period of English history when changes were going on which have commonly been described by the term industrial revolution. There is no agreement, however, even among historians, as to the meaning of the phrase. There is a tendency to use the term in connection with a long succession of historical events, with a continuing process that is in reality evolutionary in character.

If the word revolution is to be used at all in reference to historical phenomena, a tolerable exactness seems to demand that the history of the slow-moving evolutionary tendencies which culminate in relatively rapid and overpowering change, and of the ultimate consequences which are traceable thereto, be distinguished from the history of the crisis, the breaking of the dam, so to speak, in the current of change. In accordance with this conception, the term industrial revolution in English history may properly be confined to the initial, decisive change in England by which, in the technique of manufacturing and allied industries, power-operated machinery took the place of preeminence formerly held by the hand and the hand tool; and by which, in the organization or administration of industry, large establishments for the utilization of machinery, with an unprecedented concentration of capital and regimentation of labor, gained ascendancy over the simpler home industries, handicraft shops, and "putting-out" system.

There were minor instances of such changes before the eighteenth century; and there are today, even in England, industries which are still carried on largely in accordance with the older technique and organization. Continued improvement has been made in the major English industries since their original transformation; and in imitation of the initial changes, there has been an extension of the industrializing process—a series of industrial revolutions, if the term is to be used—by which subordinate and newly developing English industries and the industries of various other countries have come under the sway of machine technique and of factory organization. But in the more important industries of England, the essential steps in the great economic transition had been taken before the end of the eighteenth century—indeed, by the time of England's intervention in the wars of the French Revolution. It is this original and portentous change connected with the devising of machines and the building of factories in the dominant industries of England, and not the consequent extension of the new technique and the new organization, that is of unique significance in modern economic history. This fact has been recognized in a general way, but the intensive cultivation of the field has been somewhat neglected, due, perhaps, to the relative obscurity of the sources of information and to the more dramatic nature of the wars of the American and French Revolutions.

It is with this particular phase of English history that the present work is concerned. But it deals primarily not with the technical and administrative changes in themselves (wherein consisted the essence of the great economic transition, by whatever name called), but rather with the impelling forces back of the transition and with the social readjustments attending it. The causes of changing economic conditions, and the manner in which social institutions and ideas are adjusted thereto, are perhaps more significant subjects of study than the nature of the changes themselves. Any society must, indeed, have an understanding of the economic changes going on within it if its readjustments thereto are to be adequate; and the state of knowledge in late eighteenth-century England is another significant field of inquiry included in the scope of the book.

Recently, in the general field of the present study, new sources have come to light, new points of view have been reached, and several important books and articles based on original investigations in special fields have been published. In this work, older sources commonly used have been reinterpreted, newly discovered records have been examined, and the results of recent writings on related subjects have been incorporated. Such a survey of the field has inevitably placed the writer under many obligations. A general acknowledgment is far too conventional and inadequate, particularly in the case of that revered master to whom innumerable craftsmen are indebted, Professor Edward P. Cheyney. A painstaking criticism of the manuscript by Professor Frederick L. Nussbaum was notably helpful. The author's thanks are due to the *American Historical Review* for the privilege of utilizing certain passages in his articles published in that journal.

W. B.

University of Pennsylvania
September 15, 1924

CONTENTS

CHAPTER IV

THE INDUSTRIAL WORKERS

BIBLIOGRAPHY

INDUSTRIAL SOCIETY IN ENGLAND TOWARD THE END OF THE EIGHTEENTH CENTURY

CHAPTER I

THE AGE OF INVENTION

1. *Historical perspective*

THE rapid rise, since the latter part of the eighteenth century, of classes connected primarily with industry rather than with agriculture or commerce is a phenomenon familiar to all who are acquainted with economic history. But this great social transformation was in its earlier stages silent, lacking in the dramatic and the spectacular, overshadowed in contemporary imagination by politics and war. Records of the social forces of the time are meager and often remote from the main highways of historical study, and their meaning is in many cases obscure. Because of the consequent neglect, there is ample reason for further exploration of the field, and particularly of the obscure but decisive generation preceding England's engulfment in the wars of the French Revolution. It was during this earlier period that modern industrial society began to assume the distinctive forms and to acquire the peculiar significance that it has since retained.

Economic society in England, viewed in historical perspective, begins (after the obscure and primitive village and tribal economy) with the age of the great landlords.

1

Before the sixteenth century, England was much more nearly self-sufficient than during later centuries. The country as a whole depended little on other countries, and the local communities and landed estates had slight intercourse even with other parts of the country. Towns were small and widely scattered, trade was insignificant, wants and tastes were simple and crude, and most of the commodities used were produced on the farms and manors. The violence and confusion of the long period of conquest from the fifth to the eleventh century, and the turbulent and aggressive military organization of society under feudalism, involved a process of concentrating land ownership in a few powerful families, with the subjection of the masses of the people as servile workers on the land. Governmental institutions, whether associated with the crown, or with the church, or with feudalism, were dominated by the greater landlords, lay and clerical.

But during the fourteenth and fifteenth centuries, this agrarian society was undergoing transformation. Feudal landlordism was being undermined. The Black Death of the middle of the fourteenth century decimated the population and gave to the surviving laborers an economic bargaining power which the hostile, landlord-controlled government could not entirely counteract. This, combined with other factors, obscurer but perhaps more significant, enabled the servile workers to become wage laborers and in many cases free tenants and independent yeomen. The Hundred Years' War with France and the later civil wars, the Wars of the Roses, carried off, in fratricidal conflict, a large proportion of the feudal aristocracy. The strong Tudor monarchy at the end of the fifteenth century turned more and more from the older landed aristocracy and tapped sources of strength in a new aristocracy not exclusively agrarian and in the urban and commercial classes.

The second period in the history of English economic

society extends from the sixteenth century to the eighteenth, and is marked by the rise of the mercantile classes. The trading interests came into prominence at the time of the disruption of the feudal aristocracy. New wants and more elaborate tastes were introduced by the Renaissance and by the enlarged contacts of Englishmen with the Continent. The simple processes of production connected with the medieval manor no longer sufficed to gratify the expanding wants and tastes. The age of discovery and exploration gave new and powerful impetus to commercial expansion. Henry VII and later rulers, in the development of a strong national government centering around the monarchy, were no longer able to depend on feudal revenues and feudal military and political services, and were increasingly dependent on a monetary income. A money economy supplanted the older feudal economy in the conduct of public affairs. The securing of money for the maintenance of hired armies and for the carrying on of the increasingly diversified and expensive functions of government became therefore a matter of utmost urgency. The landlords were wealthy, but their wealth was in fixed capital, and in the produce of their lands, and the most effective means of increasing their taxable money was by encouraging the exportation of their surplus. The revenues of the government came to be increasingly dependent on the fluid wealth brought into the country by means of mercantile enterprises and the semi-piratical activities of the sea rovers. In consequence, the rulers came to look with increasing favor on those who were connected with maritime activities.

But when imports were greater than exports, money was going out of the country to pay the "unfavorable" balance of trade. The policy of the government came, therefore, to be fixed upon the maintenance of an excess of exports over imports. Foreigners (Venetians, Flemings, the German Hansards) who had controlled English trade were by degrees ousted in favor of Englishmen. Commercial treaties were entered into from time to time, with the object of promoting English exports. Charters were granted to numerous companies of Englishmen, the Merchant Adventurers, the Baltic company, the Muscovy, Levant, East India, Virginia, Hudson Bay companies, and various others, with monopolistic trading rights and with extensive political and military powers, for trading with various regions of the Old World and for making settlements and developing markets in the New World. A long series of navigation acts, notably those of the middle of the seventeenth century, sought to check the Dutch and other rivals and to monopolize the commerce and resources of the overseas possessions. For the maintenance and enlargement of these possessions, which were acquired in the first instances more or less by accident, an imperialistic policy was by degrees developed and worked out largely in connection with the numerous wars in which England engaged. The outstanding feature of this policy of imperialism and expansion was the maintenance of the balance of power among Continental countries—a policy which enabled England to secure control of the choicest regions of the world and to develop them advantageously while her Continental rivals were consuming their energies and resources in the waging of devastating European conflicts. The imperial aim was to develop complementary economic relations between the home country and the colonies, by which the colonies were to furnish cheap raw materials not produced in England, and to buy from England more costly manufactured goods, thus increasing the "favorable" balance of trade.

The power of the mercantile classes was further augmented by greater mobility not only of their wealth but of their intelligence. Men of varied contacts, alert, resourceful, concentrated in towns where interchange of ideas and pooling of interests and energies were relatively easy,—with such advantages, their influence in furnishing the dynamic forces and in determining the direction of progress, was out of all proportion to their numbers and their wealth.

These various tendencies and forces enabled the merchant princes to rival in power if not in social prestige the landed aristocracy of ancient lineage, and led in fact to an enlargement of the economic basis of aristocracy by the inclusion of mercantile wealth. Many of the more recently created members of the aristocracy had much in common with the classes connected immediately with trade, and the resulting alliance (an alliance out of which grew the Whig party) led to an increasing ascendancy of mercantile and imperial interests.

During the period of the rise of the mercantile classes, the manufacturers were petty in economic character, and were dominated by the merchants. Industrial capital was subordinate to commercial capital. The period since the eighteenth-century revolution in technique, by which industrial capital and the industrial classes were emancipated from mercantile domination, is the third of the major periods in the history of English economic society.

The above statement, it is to be observed, assumes a causal connection between the revolution in technique and the transition from the mercantile to the industrial era of economic society. And yet the complexity of causal relations provides in this as in most instances a perplexing and at the same time a fascinating problem of historical study. So intricate are the forces which determine human events, and so variable are the conditions under which the forces operate, that the laws of historical causation transcend the utmost reaches of knowledge yet attained by historians. The formulation of general laws of causation seems at present impossible; it is sufficiently difficult to fix upon the causes of a particular historical occurrence. We may ask the astronomer what brings about eclipses of the sun, or the meteorologist what natural forces are responsible for a storm, and the explanations appear to be definite and final. But if the historian is asked for the causes of any familiar historical phenomenon, as the rapid rise of new economic groups in England toward the end of the eighteenth century, his explanation will seem tentative and perhaps vague.

Although attainment of finality and completeness in the study of historical causation may never be possible, yet, in the case of the phenomenon mentioned,—the rise of new types of industrial society,—the problem is relatively simple. It is true that there were already in existence tendencies toward more highly organized activities in manufacturing as well as trade; and it has been assumed that the concentration of industrial capital and the regimentation of industrial labor somewhat as in the modern factory system would have come about independently of the introduction of machinery. It has been assumed that spinners (by way of illustration) would ultimately have been separated from their other employments, gathered together in large establishments, and set to work with spinning wheels under conditions not unlike those of the modern spinning factory. To this the reply may be made, by way of analogy, that if Napoleon had not assumed control in France during the later revolutionary period, probably some other commanding personality would have risen to power and directed events into substantially the same channels, because prevailing conditions were favorable. But this assumption cannot be said to nullify the important fact that it was Napoleon, and not some one else, who actually did direct affairs. It is interesting to consider what might have been the developments in English economic life had not the era of invention intervened, but it is certain that the forms actually assumed by industrial society were decisively molded by machinery.

Robert Owen in his autobiography (a priceless document of early industrialism as well as a record of a remarkable personality) gives an account of the beginning of his career as a cotton manufacturer. While employed as a common workman at Manchester in 1787, when only sixteen years old, he met a mechanic, a maker of wire frames for women's hats. Through him Owen became interested in the new spinning machinery. This mechanic, he relates, "began to tell me about great and extraordinary discoveries that were beginning to be introduced into Manchester for spinning cotton by new and curious machinery. He said he was endeavoring to see and get a knowledge of them, and that if he could succeed, he could make a very good business of it." The desired knowledge was secured, and a partnership was formed. As his share of the joint capital, Owen managed at length to get together the sum of £100. This humble beginning of the career of one of Great Britain's richest and most noted early "cotton lords" is a valid illustration of the close causal connection between the invention of machines and the rise of the new industrial capitalists. The most important, most characteristic source of this new group, ultimately the most powerful in England and indeed in the world, was in the wealth created by the "great and extraordinary discoveries" and the "new and curious machinery" by means of which Owen made his fortune.[1]

Equally noteworthy was the influence of the new industrial technique on the rise of that other distinctive group of recent times, the employees of the great industrialists. To the toiling masses of the time, as well as to the few who rose into the ranks of the great, the mechanical improvements brought economic oppor-

[1] Owen, *Life*, I, 22, ff.

tunity which vastly increased their numbers. The fears of many of the workers that labor-saving machines would take bread out of their children's mouths by robbing them of work was opposed by argument and allayed by fact. "Population," it was contended, "must go on in proportion to subsistence and in proportion to industry: now the machine eats nothing, so does not diminish subsistence," but rather, in fact, increases it, and therefore potentially creates population.[2] Such arguments, though frequently advanced, naturally made little impression on the workers. But the logic of facts prevailed, as more than one writer made haste to point out. Thus the demand for labor at Bolton was so great, as a result of the spinning factories, that the population more than doubled in a decade, and in consequence "the opposition of the populace to the use of machines for shortening labor has been quelled."[3] Similar conditions furnished convincing arguments throughout the region. Machines, "so far from tending to diminish employment, . . . must, when judiciously applied, be the means of multiplying it. . . . It is this which, almost in our own days, has expanded the villages of Lancashire into towns next to the metropolis in size."[4]

The era of invention brought to the workers new conditions of work as well as new opportunities for work —conditions which made possible a rapid process of molding the inert mass of industrial labor into mobile shape and of animating it with group life and consciousness. The new opportunities were proclaimed by many champions of mechanical methods; but the ultimate effects of the new conditions were discerned by few.[5]

While machinery has produced economic commodities

[2] Steuart, *Inquiry into the Principles of Political Economy*, I, 123.
[3] Aikin, *Description of the Country Round Manchester*, 261, 262.
[4] *Annals of Agriculture*, IX, 534, 535.
[5] There were some, however, who early observed the significance of the conditions resulting from mechanical technique in bringing

infinite in variety and in extent beyond the power of calculation or conception, it has at the same time been the decisive factor in the formation of what is far more important,—namely, the two outstanding economic groups of the modern industrialized regions. Among those who seek an understanding of present-day social forces, the age of invention is justly a subject of perennial interest.

2. The prevailing spirit of invention

In the study of the progress of invention, it would be a pleasant task to recount the lives of individual inventors, and to try to give due credit to men whose devices have as vitally influenced the lives of their fellow men as has the work of Pitt or Washington or Napoleon. But the task, however pleasant to contemplate, is impossible to perform. Most of them were humble and obscure, and the boldest and most patient of historical architects who have adventured on the task of reconstructing their careers have been rewarded with the merest fragments of materials.

A most careful search of available records rewards the student with little that is important in the personal history of most of the great inventors, but the search is extremely fruitful in showing that the individual inventors were after all merely the focal points in a well-nigh universal interest in mechanical progress. Hargreaves, Arkwright, Crompton, Cartwright, Cort, Brindley, Watt, Wedgwood,—these are the names that are commonly associated with the inventions and technical improvements that transformed the country; but while these men were engaged at their particular tasks, literally thousands of others were working with equal ardor to solve the same or similar problems. At the same time, national

about a community of interest and action on the part of industrial workers. See below, pp. 284, ff., 298.

and local societies were organized for stimulating and rewarding inventive activity; and the government paid large sums in recognition of the work of inventors, and passed laws to prevent foreigners from using English inventions. So varied and extensive was the interest in technical progress, so unprecedented was the prevailing spirit of improvement in methods of doing things, that one may properly characterize the latter part of the eighteenth century as the age of invention.

In order to appreciate the significance of this aspect of the period, it is necessary to contrast it not with the progress of more recent times but with the earlier lack of progress and absence of interest in technical improvement. The nineteenth and twentieth centuries have been kaleidoscopic in their rapidity of change. Inventions and discoveries such as would have startled the minds and revolutionized the lives of former generations are multiplied, great factories are put up and straightway rebuilt to make way for improved machinery, gigantic warships are constructed and declared obsolete well-nigh before they are manned for the trial cruise, imagined miracles of yesterday are the commonplace realities of today. The conscious aim alike of a multitude of empirical workers and of thousands of scientific investigators is to effect improvements in machinery and technique.

It was not so in the middle of the eighteenth century, when (to cite a sufficient illustration and symbol of the prevalence of primitive methods) even "Manchester goods" were transported to Bristol, to the metropolis, and to the nearby port of Liverpool by means of the ancient packhorse. Interest in technical improvement was not unknown, to be sure, but the prevailing spirit was one of conformity to methods approved by age and precedent. Workingmen with a turn for invention feared that labor-saving devices would reduce employment, as when one Lawrence Earnshaw, a north-of-England tailor's apprentice, turning mechanic, invented, about 1753, a machine to combine the operations of spinning and reeling cotton, but destroyed it, saying that "he would not be the means of taking bread out of the mouths of the poor." [6] Men of science and learning, as the faculties of the universities and the gentlemen of the Royal Society, were interested in improvements in the technique of pure science, but any idea of the application of their knowledge in the devising of inventions useful in the ordinary affairs of life was rarely entertained. Agriculture, to be sure, being the pursuit of the aristocracy, was viewed in a somewhat different light, and no less a person than Viscount Townshend was a pioneer, as early as 1730, in the introduction of technical improvements in farming by such means as seed drilling, marling, and horse hoeing. Serious efforts had also been made to improve the technique of navigation,[7]—which was directly connected not so much with "useful" economic life as with naval and imperial affairs. In general, the relation of the government to inventions was confined to the formality of issuing letters patent. Individual inventors with genius superior to that of Watt, Arkwright and Wedgwood had arisen in earlier times (asserted a popular writer), but their genius shone, "amid an ignorant and idle people, like a flambeau in a fog." The relatively inferior abilities of Watt and his contemporaries were effecting unique results because of the enlightened and active interest of the people of their time.[8]

[6] *Gentleman's Magazine,* LVII, Pt. II, 664-666, 1200.
[7] For example, see below, p. 32.
[8] Chalmers, *Estimate,* ed. 1794, Dedication, xxiv, xxv. In further reference to the contrast suggested by Chalmers, there are interesting comments and useful bibliographical notes in Dircks' *Life, Times and Scientific Labors of the Second Marquis of Worcester.* The book contains an annotated reprint of Worcester's *Century of Inventions,* as well as other documents, and lists of early works on mechanical subjects. The genius of Worcester (d. 1667) is unduly extolled; but the crude technical knowledge and the meager mechanical interests of

For the validity of the contrast between earlier times and the days of Watt and Arkwright, appeal may be made to the evidence of the patent records. Letters patent were granted in the Tudor period and in the time of James I for monopolies of various kinds, but patents for monopolies in the use of new machines and new processes were not differentiated from the general body of monopolies till late in the reign of James. Records of patents of invention since that time are fortunately accessible in the compilations made by Bennett Woodcroft of the Patent Office about the middle of the nineteenth century. Woodcroft's indexes reveal some interesting facts. The number of patents issued from 1617 to 1760, nearly a century and a half, was smaller than the number issued during the succeeding twenty-five years—697 as contrasted with 776. Though the number issued previous to 1760 varied considerably from decade to decade, there was in general a surprising uniformity. During no ten-year period preceding the year 1760 did the number exceed 100, with the sole exception of the years 1690-1699, and the number was then only 102. In the decade beginning in 1760, the number was 205, and each succeeding ten-year period was marked by a rapid increase. Going back a hundred years, to the time of the Restoration, and compiling the numbers by decades, we have the following results:

1660-1669	....	31	1730-1739	 56
1670-1679	....	51	1740-1749	 82
1680-1689	....	53	1750-1759	 92
1690-1699	....	102	1760-1769	 205
1700-1709	....	22	1770-1779	 294
1710-1719	....	38	1780-1789	 477
1720-1729	....	89		

As might naturally be expected, the momentum of inventive activity beginning about 1760 was in no whit abated

earlier times are not exaggerated. See also Price, *English Patents of Monopoly,* ch. 5.

after 1790. But the significant fact is that the momentum was acquired, the vital phase of the age of invention as evidenced by the patent records was inaugurated, during these decades.[9]

The records of the Patent Office give evidence of the new mechanical interests by indicating a greater variety as well as an increase in the number of inventions. Woodcroft's elaborate classification for use in official publications recognized 396 distinct types of inventions patented during the years 1700 to 1785, and of these, 168 types were added during the years 1760-1785.[10]

The patent records are significant in another way. In 1661 the Marquis of Worcester (reputed to have been the foremost mechanical genius of his time) secured a patent for "an invention to make a boat that roweth, draweth, or setteth even against wind or stream, yea, both, and to any part of the compass, which way soever the stream runs or wind blows, and yet the force of the wind or stream causeth its motion, nothing being required but a steersman, and whilst the boat stayeth to be loaded or unloaded, the stream or wind shall perform such work as any watermill or windmill is capable of." [11]   A patent was granted in 1692 to two men for "their new invention of taking fish by a light, which they can cause to burn some fathoms under water, with which, and a light above water, they can draw the fish which are in the compass of a league in the sea to one place." [12]   These two cases are cited because they illustrate the fact that the early patents were issued in many cases not for definite, fin-

[9] The figures are compiled from Woodcroft's *Titles of Patents of Invention*, I. See also Price, *English Patents of Monopoly*, chs. 1, 5, and *passim*.

[10] Compiled from Woodcroft's *Subject-matter Index of Patents of Invention*, I.

[11] *Abridgements of the Specifications Relating to Marine Propulsion*, 13. London, 1857.

[12] Woodcroft, *Titles of Patents of Invention*, I, 57.

ished inventions but for mere ideas and suggestions, for vaguely defined processes or devices, in some instances not far removed from the occult arts of the middle ages. Worthless or unfinished inventions were patented after 1760 as well as before; but in the later period the tendency to patent mere mechanical dreams is less and less observable. The contrast may be explained in part, no doubt, by the general increase in scientific and technical knowledge. Fanciful claims like those of earlier times, based upon misconceptions of natural laws, were less apt to be made, and when made were more readily discerned and repudiated. This increase of knowledge was accompanied by more rigorous rules for the submission of definite specifications, drawings, and models in order to secure valid patent rights. Nor should one fail to observe, on the basis of the evidence of the patent records, that the later patents, in contrast with those issued before the middle of the eighteenth century, put the emphasis on the invention of new machines rather than on the introduction of new industries; and that in the later period a smaller proportion of the patentees were foreigners. These facts afford significant and cumulative evidence of the sudden outburst of inventive activity in the later decades of the eighteenth century.[13]

Having examined the statistical and prosaic evidence of public documents concerning patents, we may now for a moment attend to the more picturesque but none the less valid testimony of contemporary journalists and other writers, concerning unpatented as well as patented inventions, and concerning the mechanical interests of the people generally.

The student of the past occasionally finds it possible to be honestly grateful even to the appallingly dull pseudo-classic muse of the eighteenth century. Dull, indeed, as poetry, is *The Patent*, published in 1776; but

[13] Concerning patent law and practice, see below, pp. 25-30.

as a facetious expression of the inventive spirit of the time it has lively interest and real significance. "Hail to the Patent!" exclaims the author; and after enumerating by way of illustration some of the varied performances attributable to patented inventions, he asks:

> What man would scruple to resign his breath,
> Provided he could die a patent death?

At length he grows prophetic:

> The time may come when nothing will succeed
> But what a previous Patent hath decreed;
> And we must open on some future day
> The door of nature with a patent key.

It will be observed that the rimester spoke of *patented* inventions; and the public records mentioned above were concerned solely with patents. But the securing of a patent was itself an expensive proceeding, and yet it was merely the initial step in the protection of the rights of the inventor. There developed during this period, especially in the north of England, in connection with textile inventions, an organized and effective opposition to patents as a method of rewarding inventors, and various other methods were devised or suggested. Because of these facts, and also because of the generosity of many inventors and societies in giving inventions to the public, there was an immense inventive activity unrecorded in the patent office. A survey of the various types of literature current at the time reveals innumerable unpatented devices and processes, some of them very successful; and it reveals, also, a widespread public interest in mechanical improvement.

In 1764 a new periodical, the *Wonderful Magazine,* was founded with the purpose of recording things "out of the common road." In 1779 the editors of the

Gentleman's Magazine emphasized as an important part of their policy the announcement of "the discovery of every new invention and the improvements in every useful art." A correspondent of the same magazine suggested that readers exchange through its columns their knowledge of the progress of invention.[14] The *Annual Register* had a department regularly devoted to "Useful Projects." The *Museum Rusticum et Commerciale,* begun in 1764 under patronage of members of the Society of Arts, and devoted to the recording of new and valuable discoveries, was of such interest, according to the editors, that "there was scarcely a newspaper or magazine in the kingdom" that had not reprinted portions of its contents.[15] The publications of the Society of Arts, to which further reference will presently be made, were so popular as to call repeatedly for reprinting.

This was the period, too, of the rise and rapid development of encyclopedias, dictionaries of arts and sciences, and similar semi-technical compilations. Their popularity, evidenced by their numbers and their frequent editions, is an obvious indication of widespread interest in technical progress.

The literature of the time describes so vast a number and variety of inventions that to venture upon the briefest analysis would take this essay far beyond its proper limits. Suffice it to say that there was a lively interest not only in the well-known and successful inventions of the time, such as spinning machines and the steam engine, but as well in various lines of mechanical achievement commonly associated with much later periods.

So great was the interest in ballooning that in 1786 was published a book entitled *Airopaidia,* claiming to be "an introduction to the science of aerial navigation."

[14] *Gentleman's Magazine,* XLIX, 439, LV, Pt. II, 684.
[15] *Museum Rusticum et Commerciale,* I, Preface, II, Advertisement.

Popular journals introduced departments dealing with "aerostatic experiments." A play produced at Covent Garden in 1784 was entitled *Aerostation,* and the plot centered around "the passion of a lady of fortune for balloons." According to a rimester of the time, "admirals forsake the swelling tide," and "surgeons leave their patients to their fate," in order "high on the wings of mighty winds to ride." The "celebrated aeronauts" of the time were "sumptuously entertained." The exploits of a balloonist in 1785 were said to have been witnessed by more than 40,000 persons. Not content with the amusement thus afforded, those of prophetic inclinations foresaw the time when "the inquisitive turn of mind which distinguishes the present era will improve . . . the art of ascending and exploring the upper regions . . . [so as to apply it] to many useful purposes of which at present we have no conception." [16]

Two other inventions not successfully developed till much later times—the submarine and the "horseless carriage"—also exercised over ingenious minds a fascination which seems to have been little abated by the not infrequent fatality of the hazards of experiment.[17]

Not the least important of the varied manifestations of mechanical interest was connected with popular amusements. Readers of Edmund Cartwright's account of the origin of the power loom will recall how he refuted the arguments of the Manchester manufacturers against the possibility of a power loom "by remarking that there had lately been exhibited in London an au-

[16] Some typical passages on "aerial navigation": *New London Magazine,* I (1785), 93, 301; *European Magazine,* VI, 394; *Gazetteer,* April 2, 1785; *Gentleman's Magazine,* LV, 522, 1002; *Annual Register,* 1784-5, 223 (Chron.), 323 (Chron.). An interesting flight of imagination in connection with aerial navigation is in Darwin's *Botanic Garden.*

[17] *Annual Register,* 1774, 245-248 (1st part), 1783, 206 (Chron.); *Universal Magazine,* LV (1774), 352; *Gentleman's Magazine,* LVI, Pt. II, 664; *Manchester Mercury,* July 3, 1787; *European Magazine,* XXI, 411-413.

tomaton figure which played at chess. Now you will not assert, gentlemen, said I [he continues], that it is more difficult to construct a machine that shall weave, than one which shall make all the variety of moves which are required in that complicated game." [18] The outcome of this unique idea, he asserted, was his power loom. During the rise of inventive activity, there seems to have been a veritable vogue of exhibits such as that referred to by Cartwright. In periodicals and in booklets and circulars, varied and elaborate mechanical shows were extensively advertised. In one of these booklets, *A Descriptive Catalogue of the Several Superb and Magnificent Pieces of Mechanism and Jewelry Exhibited at Mr. Cox's Museum* (London, 1772), twenty-two exhibits are described. The following is an illustrative quotation from this curious document:—"Piece the Fifteenth" is a chronoscope in the form of an obelisk under a great and magnificent canopy, with profuse ornaments and with "a prodigious variety of motions. It stands in the center of a rich gallery, upon a table, . . . upon which an elephant . . . moves round the obelisk; upon his back is a castle of gold; . . . within the castle is a curious clock, with three dials; above the clock, on the top of the castle, . . . are automaton figures, playing various tunes on twelve bells; over the music gallery is a figure that strikes the hours and quarters; above that, a pyramid of moving stars, which terminate with four dolphins, in the middle of which is an animated dragon, dropping pearls into one of the dolphin's mouths, moving his wings at the same time. The pedestal consists of four bulls, in contrary directions, . . . upon a ground . . . upon which dragons, storks, lizards, and various ornaments are placed."

It is probable that the prevailing ideas and interests

---

[18] Quoted in Baines, *History of the Cotton Manufacture*, 229, 230. Dr. W. Hooper's popular *Rational Recreations* was based largely on mathematical and mechanical knowledge.

of a given period, especially those that are of relatively recent and sudden development, find spontaneous and therefore significant expression in the popular amusements of the period. An ingenious student might profitably try to test the validity of such a generalization in wider fields. In any case, the extensive patronage given to these "museums" and traveling shows seems to have been an unconscious reflection, during the period of the present study, of popular mechanical interest.

The prevailing spirit of technical progress, while more or less active throughout the country, found most intensive and successful expression in the regions of Birmingham and Manchester.

A rimester of Birmingham, writing as early as 1751, described "beneath a fable's thin disguise the virtues its inhabitants display"; these virtues were the "spirit of industry" and "bright inventive genius." [19]

The "inventive genius," particularly of the north of England, found expression in the work of a large number of men interested in a wide variety of projects—men whose obscurity is due in part, no doubt, to the fact that they were in most cases members of the so-called lower classes. "It is generally allowed," wrote Richard Townley of Manchester in 1784, "that more ingenious improvements and useful inventions in machinery have taken their rise in these northern parts . . . than in all others throughout the kingdom; . . . [and] that most of these inventions and improvements have been struck out by such as are usually denominated the inferior ranks of mankind." [20] To recount briefly the work of two or three north-of-England mechanics of this obscure type will perhaps not be without significance as illustrating an

---

[19] "Industry and Genius; or, the Origin of Birmingham," in *Birmingham Gazette*, January 28, 1751. (Reprinted in Langford, *Century of Birmingham Life*, I, 38-40.)

[20] In *Manchester Mercury*, January 6, 1784.

important phase of popular interest in problems of technical advance.

One of these was a tenant farmer of Belford, Cuthbert Clarke, whose work was recorded by Arthur Young in his *Northern Tour.* This man, wrote Young, "is very famous in the north for his knowledge of mechanics." Among his inventions were a machine for draining swamps, for which he received an award from the Society of Arts; a mechanical turnip slicer (important on account of the prevalent feeding of turnips to live stock); and "the grand machine on which he builds his reputation, . . . one for the threshing of corn." To his various activities in connection with mechanics he added another, —experimentation with electricity for stimulating the growth of plants; and Young declared that his experiments afforded "strong proof that the electric fire had a remarkable power in promoting and quickening the vegetation." The mechanical and experimental interests of Farmer Clarke are not without interest in themselves; but they are mentioned here because they illustrate the "great spirit of improvement" and experimentation which Young and others found to be characteristic of the region.[21]

Young's tour of the north, when the observations just mentioned were recorded, was made before Arkwright's cotton factories were built. The mechanical interests of the people in the newly developing northern industrial regions before the introduction of machinery are illustrated even more significantly by the career of another self-taught mechanic of that part of the country, Adam Walker. At his home on the border between Westmoreland and Lancaster counties, he was set to work at a very early age, but while a boy he found time to acquire (according to a contemporary) a remarkable mechanical ability by making devices for his own amusement. "He

[21] Young, *Northern Tour,* III, 44-52, 194.

copied corn mills, paper mills, fulling mills, etc., and had them all going in model in the brook near his father's dwelling, to the great terror of strangers who passed them in the night." Though deprived by his father's poverty of schooling (so we are told), he nevertheless by his own efforts prepared himself by the age of fifteen to begin his career as a teacher; and at the age of eighteen, "was elected writing master and accomptant to the free school of Macclesfield in Cheshire." This was about 1750. Later he located at Manchester and "conceived a system of education more adapted to a town of trade than the monkish system still continued in our public schools (at least thought so by many)," and he put his ideas into effect in the form of a course of lectures which met with popular approbation. He continued his studies along mechanical and scientific lines, and at length embodied his knowledge in a series of public lectures which he gave in the regions of Manchester, Liverpool, Halifax, Leeds and Birmingham, his fame in the provinces preparing him at length, by 1778, for a successful career in the metropolis. So popular were his lectures in the north of England that in some of the smaller towns rooms large enough to accommodate his audiences could not be secured. By 1792, eight editions of his published lectures on mechanics had been issued. Nor was he merely a theorist and lecturer; his knowledge of mechanics he applied in the field of invention. Contemporaneous records attribute to him more than a score of inventions, some of them extremely elaborate, only two of which are said to have been patented.[22]

The high esteem enjoyed by Clarke and Walker was shared quite generally by men of their type. On many occasions and in varied ways the country was urged "to record and publish inventions . . . and to take care that

[22] *European Magazine*, XXI, 411-413; Langford, *Century of Birmingham Life*, I, 252.

the fame of singular ingenuity do not expire with the possessor," both "for the honor of the discoverers," and for insuring "a rich harvest of future discoveries." [23] It is true that on certain occasions, as in 1779 during the period of unemployment and suffering accompanying the war against the American colonies, the workers held inventors of labor-saving machines partly responsible for their misfortunes. But the workers had no opportunity for education in self-restraint and foresight, no control over the machines, and no share in the profits save their meager wage, which was cut off entirely in times of depression and unemployment; and in view of these circumstances, their occasional hostility toward inventors was natural and inevitable.

The statement that inventors generally were held in high esteem should be qualified in another way. That is, a distinction should be made between public esteem and financial reward. It is unquestionably true that some of the inventors were not adequately rewarded financially, but the injustice has been exaggerated. John Kay, the inventor of the flying shuttle, is frequently cited as an instance of unrewarded genius. His career was in a somewhat earlier period, however, the flying shuttle having been patented as early as 1733, and his ill treatment he himself attributed to the attitude prevailing about 1740. Kay's misfortunes, and those of other inventors, mostly of earlier times, were utilized in exaggerated form by writers who were trying to counteract the occasional hostility of the workers to machines. When Arkwright was trying to maintain his monopoly of his patented machines for spinning, he resorted to the same device, seeking sympathy by comparing his own case with the exaggerated misfortunes of other inventors, and particularly of Hargreaves. The tradition that Hargreaves died in a workhouse has been traced directly to the statements

---

[23] T., *Letters on Employing Machines to Shorten Labor*, 21.

by Arkwright. Hargreaves was perhaps rewarded inadequately for the invention of the spinning jenny (though the obscurity of the records makes judgment difficult), but in any case, instead of being forced to pass his last days in a workhouse, he was able to spend them in comfort. His estate at the time of his death amounted to several thousand pounds. Nor does the case of Samuel Crompton, inventor of the spinning "mule," afford unqualified evidence of ill treatment of inventors. An attempt to patent it would probably have involved him in difficulties with Arkwright, because of the use of rollers, common to the "mule" and to Arkwright's patented "water frame." In any case a patent would have been expensive, and difficult to utilize. The importance of the invention seems not to have been fully recognized at first, either by Crompton or by his contemporaries; and indeed the machine, as it came from Crompton's hands, was crude and far from satisfactory. Crompton's personal idiosyncrasies also had something to do with his failure to profit fully from his invention. Finally, it should be remembered that he received a small subscription as early as 1780; that Robert Peel offered him a partnership; and that ultimately he and his family received, in the form of subscriptions and grants, aside from business profits, several thousand pounds in recognition of his services.[24]

The unjust treatment of inventors has been exaggerated, and yet there was injustice. Inventors as well as people generally, unless possessed of wealth and position, had precarious legal rights (as witness the laws against

[24] T., *Letters on Employing Machines to Shorten Labor*, 18-21; *Case of Mr. Richard Arkwright and Co.*, in *Trial of a Cause to Repeal a Patent Granted to Mr. Richard Arkwright* (King's Bench, June 25, 1785), 97-103; Baines, *History of the Cotton Manufacture*, 161-163; Chambers' *Encyclopedia*, IV (1783), Art. *Spinning;* Abram, *History of Blackburn*, 209; Daniels, *Early English Cotton Industry*, 116-124, 149, 197.

debtors, the game laws, and the Draconian penal code for the protection of property) ; and they commonly experienced great difficulty, unless patronized by some one of position, in maintaining such legal rights as they possessed. This condition seems to be an inevitable accompaniment of a differentiation of social classes such as existed in eighteenth-century England. The inventors belonged for the most part to the unprivileged classes; and in securing the enactment of laws as well as in taking advantage of legal rights, they encountered the difficulties inseparable from rigorous class rule in society and government. Furthermore, many inventors were working at the same time on similar problems, and justice was often complicated by rival claims.

3. The reward of invention

It is true that too often inventors had to solace themselves with the thought that genius, like virtue, is its own reward. But it is equally true that there was an unprecedented interest in the question of rewards—an interest which found expression in varied and curious forms. This widespread interest is significant for a number of reasons. It is an indication of the prevailing spirit of invention; it tended to stimulate further inventive activity; and it is evidence of the essentially social character of the mechanical revolution.

Among the curious manifestations of interest in the question of rewarding inventors might be placed the views of Edward Goodwin of Sheffield in his discussion of the question, "Whether a patent, or a public premium, is the more eligible mode of encouraging useful inventions." In emphasizing the importance of the subject, he remarked that in ancient times "mortals who had signalized themselves by their beneficial inventions" were so honored by posterity as to be "often exalted into

deities." Classical allusions were reinterpreted in the
light of mechanical interests, as when aviation was described as a lost art well known of old to Daedalus and
Hanno.[25]
Contemporary interest of a more tangible nature found
expression in another somewhat curious form—a booklet
published as early as 1774 entitled *An Address to the
Artists and Manufacturers of Great Britain Respecting
an Application to Parliament for the Farther Encouragement of New Discoveries and Inventions in the Useful
Arts.* The author, W. Kenrick, ridicules the idea, which
he says has been all too prevalent, that devotees of literature and other "polite arts" are more honorable than
those who seek out "new inventions and discoveries."
His own vigorously expressed views as to the relative
importance of "polite art" and "useful invention" were
reinforced by quotations from the expressive if inelegant
verses of a contemporary rimester:

> 'Tis great, 'tis wonderful, sublime,
> No doubt, to build the lofty rime!
> But, deaf to what the poet sings,
> Tho' charm his muse the ear of kings,
> The *patriot* sees more wit and good in
> Th' invention of a marrow pudding.

But the main purpose of the writer who quoted these
lines was to advocate a reform of patent law and procedure to the end that inventors might be more adequately rewarded. It was generally agreed that the inventor should be compensated in some way other than
by the privilege of allowing him to sell his invention or
to apply it himself to its intended use, but belief in the

[25] *Gentleman's Magazine,* LVI, Pt. I, 25, 26; *European Magazine,*
VII, 84-88; *Annals of Agriculture,* IV, 205-210, VIII, 161, 162. See
also a booklet by J. Peacock, *Proposals for a Magnificent and Interesting Establishment,* which, while savoring less of antiquity, presents
a singular plan for encouraging and rewarding invention.

desirability of monopolistic patents was by no means unanimous. Some argued for the supplanting, others for the supplementing, of patents by special rewards and compensations to be granted by the government. Many were opposed to the monopolistic feature of patents, and were at the same time fearful of corruption and favoritism in special governmental grants; and persons of this type were the principal advocates of a third method of rewarding inventors, namely, by means of private aid, usually in the form of premiums and medals by societies. These three methods, in their development and application during the latter part of the eighteenth century, are characteristic of the age of invention.

The patent system as first devised and long applied by the Crown had very slight connection with inventions in the modern sense, but dealt with the granting of monopolies and special privileges. Letters patent concerning economic interests involved "the sole buying, selling, making, working or using" of a wide variety of things. The abuses and disadvantages connected with monopolies led to the limiting of the patent system by the famous Statute of Monopolies of 1624. It has been said that the principle therein set forth "still forms the basis of the whole of the English patent law, and . . . of the patent laws of the world." [26]

The law, after uttering a sweeping condemnation of monopolies, makes an important exception by allowing letters patent to be issued granting a fourteen-year monopoly for "the sole working or making of any manner of new manufactures . . . to the true and first inventor and inventors of such manufactures, . . . so . . . they be not contrary to law nor mischievous to the state, by raising prices of commodities at home, or hurt of trade, or generally inconvenient." But "inventor" meant not

[26] Moulton, *Present Law and Practice Relating to Letters Patent for Inventions,* 2.

necessarily, nor even generally, a person who devised some new instrument or process, but rather a person who first brought into use some industry or machine, as when Thomas Lombe introduced the silk industry by means of Italian machines.

With the exception of this very important change in the meaning of the term inventor, the principle of the law remained essentially the same; but the procedure for granting patents became more elaborate. The interminable red tape furnished a paradise for lawyers and clerks, but it was the despair of the too often indigent inventor. A person seeking a patent was directed first to file a petition with his affidavit at the Home Secretary's office. A few days later, the petitioner was referred to the Solicitor General or the Attorney General for report on the petition, and the report, when received, was to be taken to the Home Secretary's office for the king's warrant. The warrant was to be taken to the Attorney General or the Solicitor General for the bill of the letter patent. The bill was to be taken to the Home Secretary's office for the king's sign manual, and when thus approved was to go to the clerk of the signet office for a warrant to the clerk of the Lord Keeper of the Privy Seal, and the clerk of the Privy Seal might then make his warrant to the Lord Chancellor. The Lord Chancellor's office then prepared the patent. The specifications, there prepared, were acknowledged, and lodged at the Enrollment office for a week or a fortnight. In a specimen bill for a patent, thus secured, forty-four separate items are listed, and the total cost for securing a patent valid in England and the colonies is given as £143 0s. 7d.—and for Scotland and Ireland separate and distinct patents were necessary.[27]

Along with this needless and burdensome increase of red tape, there was a wholesome tendency toward greater

[27] Hands, *Law and Practice of Patents for Invention*, 12-15, 50-54.

exactness in the specifications. It was the vagueness of the specifications of Arkwright's patent of 1775 which led in 1785 to its being annulled.

The elaboration of procedure, which was undesirable, and the tendency toward greater definiteness in the specifications, which was desirable, had in one respect the same result, an increasing difficulty in securing patents. It is to be observed that it was in spite of these obstacles encountered by inventors that there occurred after 1760 the remarkable increase in number and variety of patents.[28]

As a result of such conditions, the patent system was criticized by many champions of inventors. Efforts were made to modify the law and practice in favor of inventors,[29] but without success. For at the same time that some were trying to smooth the patentee's rough pathway, others sought to bar the way completely. This opposition to patents was the result of varied motives, including a desire to promote the interests of inventors. It was observed then, as in later times, that the greatest of inventors, when subjected to the ruthless conditions of the business world, are apt to prove incompetent in the arts of self-seeking. The users of inventions too often exploit not only the inventions but their creators as well. The expenses and legal intricacies of the patent system subject the inventor to men inferior to him in all save wealth or cunning. The system was unjust because it failed to

[28] 21 Jas. I, c. 3; Davies, *Collection of the Most Important Cases Respecting Patents of Invention;* Kenrick, *Address to the Artists and Manufacturers of Great Britain; Trial of a Cause to Repeal a Patent Granted to Mr. Richard Arkwright* (King's Bench, June 25, 1785); Hulme, "Early History of the English Patent System," in *Select Essays in Anglo-American Legal History,* III, 117-147; Hulme, articles in *Law Quarterly Review,* XII, 141-154, XIII, 313-318, XVI, 44-56, XVIII, 280-288; Price, *English Patents of Monopoly.*

[29] Among the men who advocated such changes was James Watt. See Boulton and Watt MSS., *Letter Book (Office),* 1786-1788, 162 (Watt to Garbett, March 25, 1787).

provide proper protection for creative genius. Others put the case with a certain brutal frankness, which was more effective, probably, than the logic of abstract justice. That is, appeal was made to the dominant acquisitive motives by the argument that the creative genius of the inventor, if unrewarded, will cease to function, or will seek rewards in foreign lands.[30] The patent system imposes upon the inventor a financial burden which relatively few can bear; and it attributes to him an acquisitiveness and business acumen not characteristic of the creative temperament. Therefore it is a matter of prudence for those who would profit by the work of inventors to devise some better method of nourishing the tender plant of inventive genius.

Patents were opposed by others because they created monopolies. It is to be remembered that this was the original ground of opposition to letters patent in the time of Elizabeth and of James I. Monopolies created by patents of invention were disliked by many manufacturers because they were thereby deprived of the use of the new inventions. This was the meaning of the phrase "the pernicious effects of patents" as used by the Manchester Commercial Committee, organized in 1774; this was the motive of the cotton manufacturers in their ultimately successful war against the patents held by Arkwright; and this was the explanation of their attempts to devise other means of rewarding inventors. Naturally the manufacturers phrased their hostility to patents not so much in terms of watch and ward over their own fortunes as in terms of concern for the general welfare. The attempt, often unconscious, to identify narrow group interests with the interests of society in general seems to spring from a deep-seated trait of human nature; and to scrutinize historical records with alert critical faculties in

---

[30] Such views found expression, for instance, in T., *Letters on Employing Machines to Shorten Labor.*

order to separate group interests from general interests is a vitally important and often neglected duty of the student of human affairs. Particularly is this true of the records of groups that are in positions of privilege and power. Groups less influential, in order to gain prestige and fighting strength, are likely to champion, in formal terms at least, those interests that are of a more general character. This seems to have been the position of the manufacturers who opposed the monopolies created by patents in favor of Arkwright and his partners in the cotton spinning industry. By basing their case on opposition to monopolies in general, they allied themselves with, and ultimately directed in their own interests, the rapidly developing forces of economic freedom which at first gave promise of social rather than mere group advantage.[31]

In spite of the various attacks on the patent system, it was retained; for it was generally believed that in spite of its defects it did on the whole tend to stimulate invention. But opposition to the system produced, nevertheless, important results. It led to the revocation of certain patents; it secured more exact requirements as to specifications; and it aided, mainly by judicial decisions, in limiting the use of the term inventor to the modern sense of the person who devises rather than merely introduces some new instrument or process. Furthermore, the general recognition of the inadequacy of the patent system was responsible for the introduction of other methods which in some degree took the place of letters patent.

Recognition of the importance of rewarding inventors, both as a matter of justice and as a means of promoting

---

[31] *Trial of a Cause to Repeal a Patent Granted to Mr. Richard Arkwright; Owen MSS.*, LXXX, 3, 4; Wheeler, *Manchester*, 521; Commons *Journals*, XXXVIII, 687, 865, XXXIX, 147, 263-313; *Parliamentary Register*, IV, 358-370, 378-382, 392, 396; *Parl. Hist.*, XXXVIII, 311, 467-472, 538.

improvement, found expression in an increased resort to special grants by the government. This method, though infrequently used, was not unknown in earlier times. An important precedent was established in 1731 by a parliamentary grant to Sir Thomas Lombe as a reward for the introduction of machines for the manufacture of silk. He was not the inventor, as the term was later used, nor, to be exact, did he introduce the machinery. It was he who established the silk industry by means of the machines brought to England by his brother. According to the somewhat romantic accounts of the time, it appears that knowledge of the machinery was stolen from the Italians by John Lombe, who was later pursued to England and poisoned in revenge by an agent of the Italian manufacturers. But whatever may have been the fate of the adventurous John, his brother, Sir Thomas, profited by the bold theft of the Italian machines, for in 1718 he secured a patent for "his new invencion of three sorts of engines, one to wind the finest raw silk, another to spin, & ye other to twist ye finest Italian raw silk into organzine in great perfection." In 1731, when the patent was about to expire, he applied to parliament for an extension, on the ground that his establishment at Derby was not in operation till several years after the patent had been granted. The petition was at first favorably received, but before final action, the House of Commons was deluged with hostile petitions from Derbyshire and from industrial centers in the adjacent counties. As a result, the patent was not extended, but instead a grant of £14,000 was voted in recognition of his services in the establishment of the silk industry in England on the basis of machines which had given superiority to Italians.[32]

[32] Commons *Journals,* XXI, 782, 795, 798, 840-842, 855; Lords *Journals,* XXIV, 73, 77, 79; Woodcroft, *Titles of Patents of Invention,* I, 76; Mantoux, *La Révolution Industrielle,* 184-187.

The generosity of parliament to Sir Thomas was exceptional and was probably due to his influential position. In any case he was not an inventor in the later sense of the word, though the case seems to have been regarded as a precedent for later action in behalf of inventors. Before 1760, special grants were rarely made, in contrast with the period following, when they became numerous. The king on several occasions showed interest in new inventions and even bestowed personal rewards. Many of the ministers also were interested in promoting experiments and in providing compensations. But the most important cases of special rewards were those made by parliament.

To avoid wearying the reader with a multitude of instances, and at the same time to set forth the significance of public patronage of invention, reference will be made only to the grant of £20,000 to John Harrison for his device for determining the longitude at sea. As early as 1713 a reward was offered for a practical method of finding the longitude, but in 1753 it was still unassigned, and another law was passed "to render more effectual" the act of 1713. During the years 1761 to 1780, the interest of the government in the problem led to the enactment of no less than nine laws, to the making of numerous experiments, and to the expenditure of large sums of money. John Harrison, the successful competitor, was of humble parentage, and he had only a meager, self-acquired education. After spending several years in trying to solve the problem defined by parliament, his efforts culminated in 1772 in the perfecting of a "marine watch" which met the requirements of the most rigorous tests. During various stages in the progress of his work, he had been paid a total of £11,250, and in 1773 an act was passed appropriating the remainder of the £20,000 which had been offered as an inducement.

This instance of special rewards by the government

has been chosen for a number of reasons. It was more than a mere grant of money to reward an inventor; it was an illustration of the desire of those in authority to foster inventive activity, the reward being offered in advance and paid by installments as the device was developed and perfected. Furthermore, by conducting costly experiments and tests to aid the inventor and to verify his claims, the government became an active partner in the work of invention. The case is an illustration of the social and cumulative character of the great mechanical transformation, which has been erroneously described as the work of a few persecuted and unrewarded individuals.[33]

The important part played by the government in promoting technical improvement is shown also by laws for the development of transportation, for the protection of machines, and for the maintenance of British monopoly in the use of inventions.

The government's policy of making special grants was

[33] Sources dealing with the problem of determining the longitude at sea: 12 Anne, St. 2, c. 15; 26 Geo. II, c. 25; 2 Geo. III, c. 18; 3 Geo. III, c. 14; 5 Geo. III, cc. 11, 20; 10 Geo. III, c. 34; 13 Geo. III, c. 77, sec. 29; 14 Geo. III, c. 66; 17 Geo. III, c. 48; 20 Geo. III, c. 61; *Annual Register,* 1765, 113-133 (2d part), 1777, 24-26 (2d part); *European Magazine,* XVI, 235, 236; *Principles of Mr. Harrison's Timekeeper with Plates of the Same.* For some other cases of the interest shown by the government in new inventions and improvements, see *Annual Register,* 1772, 98 (Chron.), 1773, 111 (Chron.); *European Magazine,* XI, 211; *Gentleman's Magazine,* LVI, Pt. II, 26; *Universal Magazine,* XLIX, 52; Kenrick, *Address to Artists and Manufacturers,* 22-27; Anderson, *Historical Origin of Commerce,* IV, 71; *Reports from Committees* (House of Commons, 1715-1802), IX, 3-23; Commons *Journals,* XXXII, 15, 160, 194, 240, XXXIII, 534, 600, 661-664, 745, XXXIV, 104, 371, 372, 382, 740, 746-748, 756, XXXVI, 30-33, 238, XXXVII, 367, 368, 392, 393, 422, XXXVIII, 311, 467-472, 538; *Parliamentary Register,* IV, 358-370, 378-382, 392, 396. The last reference records debates in 1781 in the House of Lords, in which considerable hostility to special grants found expression. This opposition was apparently successful, though at a later date important awards were made, as to Cartwright and Crompton in connection with their power loom and spinning mule.

subjected to severe criticism, but the objections were based not on the principle involved or the end in view, but rather on the belief that the method was inadequate or inequitable, or subject to abuses. It was apparent, indeed, that the rewards were unequally distributed, and were apt to be the result not of merit but of influence. Favored inventors with slight claims might secure recognition, while others, more deserving, but lacking position or connection with parliamentary and ministerial forces, were likely to be neglected. Minor improvements or devices and discoveries of dubious merit were at times discussed at length and even liberally patronized, while many of the most important inventions were entirely unnoticed.[34]

The disadvantages inseparable on the one hand from special grants and on the other hand from monopolistic patents were generally recognized, and had it not been for resort to non-governmental agencies of reward, it is possible that the government's relation to inventive activity would have been more vitally affected by constructive criticism. One interesting and comprehensive plan was formulated, but was not put into effect. This plan had the merit of eliminating many of the defects of both patents and special grants, and of putting the whole problem of promoting and rewarding technical improvement on a broad international basis.

This far-reaching proposal was put forward by Sir John Sinclair, President of the Board of Agriculture, under the title, "Plan of an Agreement, among the Powers of Europe and the United States of America, for the purpose of rewarding discoveries of general benefit to society." The plan was not published till 1795, but in

[34] For contemporaneous criticisms, see *Parl. Hist.*, XXXVIII, 311, 467-472, 538; *Parliamentary Register*, IV, 358-370, 378-382, 392, 396; *Gentleman's Magazine*, LVI, Pt. II, 26; Kenrick, *Address to Artists and Manufacturers*, 24-27.

connection with the extensive interests, foreign travel, and correspondence of Sinclair, and probably also of Arthur Young, Secretary of the Board, it had been gradually taking shape for more than a decade. "Discoveries of general benefit to society" included, according to the plan, improvements in rural economy and in medicine as well as inventions in "the useful arts." The international agreement was to provide adequate rewards for "any new invention" of a useful character, but it was to go much further and see that "every means be taken to have the same rapidly extended and brought to its ultimate state of perfection." The portion of expense paid by each country, though not burdensome to any, would provide in the aggregate such rewards as would lead, it was hoped, to unprecedented progress. The plan was to be carried out by a system of boards and secretaries acting in concert in the various countries—a definite international organization with comprehensive aims and powers, and with the purpose of spreading knowledge of new inventions and discoveries throughout the world for the free use of all, in opposition to private and national monopoly of the means of progress.

Sinclair associated with his plan a most ambitious prospect of worldwide concord and prosperity. Such a system of international cooperation for the promotion of general economic progress and common peaceful interests would tend to swallow up the prevailing intrigue and discord in a régime of goodwill and happiness. "If the measures . . . hinted at were adopted, a new scene in politics might be the happy consequence, and the rulers of nations might in future boast, not of their numerous fleets,—not of their gallant armies,—not of extended commerce . . . or luxurious arts or acquisitions by intrigue or conquest,—but of *this,* that within their respective dominions a greater number of human beings enjoyed all the blessings of political society in greater perfection than ever they had been able to attain in any former period of human history." [35]

It is hardly necessary to say that the attempts of the Board of Agriculture to carry out such a far-sighted and ideal policy—and serious attempts were made—were ineffective. It is probable that the plan would have failed because its proponents too far transcended in statesman-like vision the many diplomats afflicted at that period with myopia as in later times. But the age was not auspicious. The governments of Europe, soon to drag after them the United States of America, were already slipping one after another into the whirlpool of war which long swallowed up their kindlier and more rational conceptions of peaceful progress.

The solution of the problem with which Sir John Sinclair wrestled unsuccessfully remains one of the major tasks of modern industrial society. To prevent machinery and applied science from being used to exploit men in peace and to destroy them in war,—to make technical improvements minister to the happiness of all men the world over,—this would surely be a statesman-like achievement of incomparable beneficence. But statesmen we are prone to praise unduly, or unjustly to reproach. A statesman may hasten or retard the solution of deep-lying problems, but their solution is beyond his power. Such a problem is the control of machinery and of the technique of economic life. It is bound up with a vast complex of historical and social forces which collectively are the master and not the servant of statesmen. And yet this complex of forces may be reduced to relatively simple terms. The extent to which men are exploited approximates the extent to which they are lack-

[35] The text of the plan was published in Sinclair's *Account of the Origin of the Board of Agriculture*, App. O, 74-76; and in *European Magazine*, XXVIII, 76-78. The extensive foreign travels and correspondence of both Sinclair and Young are well known.

ing in self-consciousness. The natural self-interest of the few whose good fortune it has been to rise to conscious intelligence operates exploitively within the vicious circle of social ignorance and unconsciousness. The supreme function of statesmanship is to work in harmony with the forces making for awareness. The genius of a society which devised the well-nigh omnipotent technical instruments is surely capable of devising a happier and more successful method of utilizing them. He who would not impede men but set them forward in that direction can do no more and must do no less than add his own strength to the forces which are substituting the power of intelligent self-consciousness for the servility of ignorance.

But according to the conception of class relationships prevailing in the eighteenth century, the existence of an ignorant multitude living at a subsistence level was natural and even desirable. This conception involved as a corollary a definition of public welfare which assumed that the happiness of the "lower orders" of society depended upon the virtues of industry and docility in degree not far removed from the state of domestic animals; their superior intelligence must be confined to their immediate tasks, and must be kept subservient to those who gave them opportunity to earn their subsistence.[36]

If we keep clearly in mind this definition of public welfare, we may properly say that the aim of the government, during the era of invention when the instruments of power in modern industrial life were being forged, was to control and utilize these instruments in the interest of the public. The modification of the patent system by the courts to require more definite specifications was for the purpose of enabling the public to utilize the invention at the end of the fourteen-year period of the patent. The rewarding of inventors by special grants was for the purpose of eliminating monopoly entirely by giving the

[36] See below, pp. 224, ff., 262, 263.

invention to the public at once. Those who favored private instead of governmental agencies for rewarding inventors believed that that method was best fitted to promote the public welfare. They desired to eliminate monopoly by giving inventions to the public as soon as devised, and to aid public progress by stimulating inventive activity.

Those who favored private as opposed to governmental rewards depended mainly on societies for patronizing experiment and granting premiums and medals. Such methods were used on a small scale by local commercial committees. The Manchester Commercial Committee was organized in 1774 partly for the purpose of opposing patents and of devising "some other mode of reward for ingenuity, so as to prevent the pernicious effects of patents." Grants were made from time to time by this committee to various inventors; and committees in other places displayed similar interest. But "to prevent the pernicious effects of patents," there seems to have been an increasing dependence on the work of societies organized for the specific purpose of promoting scientific and technical progress.[37]

By far the most important of these was the Society Instituted at London for the Encouragement of Arts, Manufactures, and Commerce, founded in 1754, and commonly known as the Society of Arts.[38] The early history of the Society of Arts coincided with the beginning of the mechanical revolution, and the relation of the society thereto was so important that a writer of the time attributed the technical progress being made largely to the founding of the society. Its organization, he said,

[37] *Owen MSS.,* LXXX, 3, 4; *Reports from Committees* (House of Commons, 1715-1802), X, 733; Daniels, *Early English Cotton Industry,* 94, 95, 103, 120; Axon, *Annals of Manchester,* 100; Baines, *History of the Cotton Manufacture,* 144; James, *History of the Worsted Manufacture,* 299.

[38] In 1909 it became the Royal Society of Arts.

inaugurated "one of the most remarkable epochs in the history of the arts." [39] This was no doubt an exaggeration; but the work of the society, even when subjected to a view more rigorously critical, deserves a much more prominent place in the history of the time than has commonly been given it.

The founders of the London Society of Arts were not without precedent, for the Dublin Society, the pioneer in the field of the "useful arts," dated from 1731. The Dublin organization was a semi-official body: it served as a board for the promotion of trade, manufactures, and agriculture; and though at first supported by private subscriptions, it soon secured parliamentary aid, the usual subsidy being £10,000. Its relation to invention was slight; only in its general purpose of promoting the arts of economic life did it serve as a precedent for the society founded at London in 1754.[40]

It appears that the plan of the London society was formulated in 1753 by William Shipley, who is variously described as an artist and as "an ingenious mechanic . . . deriving no advantages from learning." In any case he was recognized as the society's principal organizer, and was chosen as its first secretary. There is little of value to be derived from the details of organization; the significant facts are those concerned with the purposes and activities of the society. It will suffice, therefore, to say that the plan adoped was comprehensive and thorough, and that it was put into operation with vigor and success. Many of the more prominent men of the time became members. The names of inventors and manufacturers occur side by side with the names of lords, gentry, and high officials. Richard Arkwright, Matthew Boulton, and Josiah Wedgwood and his sons were mem-

[39] *Encyclopædia Britannica*, 3d ed., XVII, 586, 587.
[40] Young, *Tour in Ireland*, II, 131-133; Sheffield, *Observations on Ireland*, 204, 260; *Annual Register*, 1765, 157 (2d part).

bers, and Edmund Cartwright was at one time a candidate for the position of secretary.[41]

"Whereas, the riches, honor, strength and prosperity of a nation [runs the preamble of the original *Plan*] depend in a great measure on knowledge and improvement of useful arts, manufactures, etc., several of the nobility and gentry of this kingdom, being fully sensible that due encouragements and rewards are greatly conducive to excite a spirit of emulation and industry, have resolved to form themselves into a society. . . . The intent and purpose of this society is to encourage ingenuity and industry by bestowing of premiums." It is to be seen that the society was by no means confined to the encouragement of invention. The extensive nature of its activities is shown by the names of its committees. The organization was slightly modified from time to time, but according to the *Rules* of 1760, the work of the society, aside from such formal details as those connected with accounts and correspondence, was in the hands of six groups, each group concerned with rewards in a particular field. One group had charge of rewards in the field of "polite and liberal arts"; another, agriculture; another, manufactures; a fourth, mechanics; a fifth, chemistry, dyeing and mineralogy; and a final group had oversight of rewards for improvements of various kinds in connection with colonies and trade.

But mechanical interests were not confined to the committee on mechanics; the terms applied to the committees were arbitrary. Machinery for use in agriculture,

---

[41] *Plan of the Society* (a circular, February 19, 1755, in Br. Mus., 1801.d.1(59)); *Rules and Orders* (frequently republished with alterations); *Transactions*, I, Introduction, and pp. 276-281, and lists of members in the various volumes, III, 124-128, IV, Frontispiece (Shipley's portrait), LV, Preface; Dossie, *Memoirs of Agriculture*, I, 28; *Encyclopædia Britannica*, 3d ed., XVII, 586, 587; Anderson, *Historical Origin of Commerce*, II, 407 (ed. 1764); [Strickland], *Memoir of Edmund Cartwright*, 162; Wood, *History of the Royal Society of Arts*, 1.

for instance, was under the jurisdiction of the committee on agriculture; and the other committees promoted the invention of improved implements and processes in their appropriate fields. Before the founding in 1768 of the Royal Academy of Arts, the Society of Arts paid much attention to the "polite and liberal arts"; but its interests even in this field were largely technical and practical. Designing, for instance, was recognized by the society as in need of improvement to enable English manufacturers to compete with the French, whose superiority in the arts on the border between the "fine" and the "useful" was generally acknowledged. The society was interested in improvements of various kinds, but it is to be distinguished from other institutions and given a position of unique historical importance primarily because of its work in promoting inventive activity. The scope and variety and far-reaching significance of its interests in this field of activity are revealed impressively by the long lists of the premiums and medals awarded, by the much longer lists of rewards offered, and by the numerous accounts of experiments inspired by it and printed in contemporaneous periodicals and in the society's own publications. Its policy was based upon the belief that "on the improvement of mechanical engines the advancement of the manufactures, and ultimately the arts and commerce of the kingdom, must in a very material manner depend." The "noble enthusiasm" of the inventor was therefore stimulated and rewarded by the society, which prided itself upon being a "bank of generosity" which could be drawn upon for "the reward of merit as well as a mark of honor." [42]

Nor was the claim an idle boast. The operations of

[42] *Plan* (1755); *Rules and Orders* (1760), 18; *Transactions*, I, 27, 28 and *passim*, XIII, Preface, xv; Dossie, *Memoirs of Agriculture*, I, 32-36 and *passim;* Bailey, *Advancement of Arts, Manufactures and Commerce.*

the "bank of generosity" during the years from 1754 to 1782 include an outlay for premiums and medals alone of £28,212 11s. 4d. Furthermore, the cost of the rewards bestowed is not an accurate measure of the influence of the society. It initiated and supervised experiments as well as offered premiums and medals. Many of its rewards were honorary; and in some cases premiums paid in money were returned. The society's purpose was achieved if its suggestions as to needed improvements were acted upon, even if the resulting invention or formula never came into its possession. The proportion of premiums awarded to the premiums offered was small. In 1784, a typical instance, premiums were offered for 167 items, while in the following year, when the awards offered in 1784 were to be made, the number of awards was only twenty-one. The original intention, not always rigorously adhered to, seems to have been to encourage invention as far as possible by the stimulus of public spirit, and to reward with premiums only "the most deserving." [43]

The underlying aim of the society as repeatedly stated in one form or another by its officials and its admirers was to find means for "employing and applying inventive genius to national benefit." It sought to encourage with its rewards those inventors who were in need of financial assistance; and by means of rewards, public honors and emphasis on the national welfare it sought to increase the number of those who were willing to allow public use of their inventions, thus foregoing private recompense legally permissible in the form of the monopolistic patent. Rewards were never granted for patented inventions; and all machines and models for which premiums or medals were awarded, as well as others donated to the society, became the property of the society, and through it, of the public. For its aim was not merely the pro-

[43] *Transactions,* I, 62, II, 271-346, IV, 231-239.

moting of "inventions, discoveries and improvements," but "the laying open any such to the public." Since material progress depends "on the improvement of mechanical engines," it was stated that "the society have from their institution invariably endeavored, by every means in their power, to bring forward to public use and notice, all such machines as have a tendency to promote that end." The models and machines in their repositories have been "open to the free and uninterrupted examination of all persons," and from these exhibits, "it is well known great advantages have arisen." Appeals for financial support were made on the basis of the public benefits resulting from the work of the society. It was claimed by the secretary in 1789 that no nation had ever received "more real advantage from any public body whatever than has been derived to this country from the rewards bestowed by this society." [44]

These professions of public spirit were accepted by the people of the time as genuine. Commendations of its work were numerous and in tone superlative, as when Arthur Young declared that for every guinea spent by "this most laudable society" the country had been benefitted to the extent of a thousand pounds. "The public spirit of this age," asserted another writer, "is nowhere more remarkably shown than in the flourishing condition of this valuable society." In 1765 the city of Liverpool gave the society £100, and in the same year London contributed £500. The popularity of its *Transactions* was so great that many of the volumes were repeatedly reprinted. The epoch-making importance which was attributed to the society in the history of the arts was due, however, it was believed, not alone to its own work but to the influence of its example in the establishment of

[44] *Rules and Orders* (1760), 21; *Transactions,* I, 27, 28, 40, 41, 269, 270, 309-322, XIII, Preface, xv, XX, Preface, iv-vi; *Gentleman's Magazine,* LIX, Pt. I, 478.

similar associations throughout the country "for promoting useful knowledge and solid improvement." [45]

This, indeed, was a claim made by the society's own officials. A "great and general effect" of its work had been not only to produce inventions "every year increasing," but to "excite and diffuse a spirit of improvement," supplanting the "old vulgar prejudices." Robert Dossie, closely connected with the society, and an early chronicler of its work, writing fourteen years after it was founded, stated that its aim, which he said was "to cherish invention and propagate intelligence in matters of this sort," was being emulated not only by individuals but by "many country societies." [46]

Even the Royal Academy of Arts, founded in 1768, was influenced by the utilitarian spirit of the Society of Arts. The former was indeed in a sense an offshoot of the latter. To the work of the two organizations has been attributed the success of Englishmen in overcoming their deficiency in taste and skill in various industries requiring artistic workmanship, notably in the making of drawings, designs and patterns for textiles, in which they had been surpassed by Continental craftsmen.[47]

There were other organizations which, like the Royal Academy of Arts, were in name devoted exclusively to cultural aims, but which allowed themselves to be diverted therefrom by the universal interest in technical

[45] Young in *Annals of Agriculture,* I, 64; *Dictionary of Arts and Sciences,* IV, 2992; *Annual Register,* 1765, 111, 136 (Chron.); *Encyclopœdia Britannica,* 3d ed., XVII, 586, 587. In the mass of contemporaneous references to the society, only a few of which are here cited, there is a remarkable unanimity in praising the public spirit of its work in promoting the national welfare.

[46] *Transactions,* I, 40, 41; Dossie, *Memoirs of Agriculture,* I, Preface, x.

[47] *Transactions,* I, 46-49; Dossie, *Memoirs of Agriculture,* I, 32-36; Wendeborn, *View of England towards the Close of the Eighteenth Century,* I, 230. Wendeborn also mentions (II, 194) the organization in 1773 at Liverpool of a Society for the Encouragement of Designing, Drawing, and Painting.

progress. Two of these were the Manchester Literary and Philosophical Society and the Literary and Philosophical Society of Newcastle-on-Tyne. The latter organization took as its model the former, and its history need not detain us. But to the Manchester society there attaches in the history of invention no inconsiderable importance. The part played in its origin by the Society of Arts, as well as the union of cultural and technical aims in the minds of its founders, is shown by the fact that the Society of Arts and the Royal Society of 1662 were both regarded as models. It was organized because it was believed that the work of both of these societies should be "more widely extended by the forming of societies with similar views in the principal towns." Its informal beginnings are obscure, but a definite organization was effected in 1781.

Its aims from the first included an application of science to mechanical improvement, but its relation to technical progress is more evident in the organizing under its auspices in 1783 of a "mechanic school," called the Manchester College of Arts and Sciences. The founders of the school hoped to make it "a kind of oracle, which those might consult who were engaged in mechanical improvements, and who might here, at once, gain that information which it might cost them months and years to obtain by their own unassisted efforts." The influence of the Society of Arts appeared in a plan for a repository for the exhibiting of machines and models of all sorts, particularly in textile manufacturing. But the plan was in fact more ambitious and far-reaching than that of the London Society. There was to be not merely an exhibit but a laboratory and a superintendent to give lectures, advice and assistance. Furthermore, instead of having merely an exhibit in one place only, a "mechanic school" with the exhibit as its center "should be established in every large town, and particularly in the center of every important manufacture." The plan was proposed, for Manchester, in 1782, and in the following year the College of Arts and Sciences was founded, with the officers of the Literary and Philosophical Society serving as governors.

As was perhaps to have been expected, this unique and radical proposal to unite cultural with utilitarian aims was not entirely approved by the more conservative members of the society, and certain members withdrew in protest. It appears that their action adversely influenced the carrying out of the plan. Although the more technical features of the plan of 1782 were either dropped or modified, yet the underlying aim of the college as organized was the investigation of the physical and chemical sciences and their application in the improvement of industrial methods.[48]

The example set by the national Society of Arts in its public-spirited promotion of material progress was imitated more literally by various other local organizations than by the Manchester Literary and Philosophical Society. It is probably true that the general impulse toward activities of this kind was inherent in the spirit of the times; but the particular form of expression assumed by the general impulse so clearly corresponded to the pattern of the Society of Arts that its immediate influence is obvious. Thus the year 1777 witnessed the origin of the Society Instituted at Bath for the Encouragement of Agriculture, Arts, Manufactures and Commerce, even the name being virtually a copy of the

[48] Manchester Literary and Philosophical Society's *Memoirs*, I, Preface, and pp. 80-89, II, 16-29, 42-46; *College of Arts and Sciences Instituted at Manchester, June 6, 1783* (a circular dated July 9, 1783); *Manchester Miscellaneous Papers, 1784-1791* (MSS.), No. 106. Comments and official announcements in regard to the College of Arts and Sciences appeared in the *Manchester Mercury*. Concerning the Newcastle society, see *Plan of the Literary and Philosophical Society of Newcastle upon Tyne*.

London society's name. It offered premiums, mostly for experiments in agriculture and for the invention and improvement of implements; and it published a series of *Letters and Papers* resembling the *Transactions* of the national society. A society was organized in 1767 for Salford Hundred, and was later extended to include the region thirty miles or so around Manchester. Its object was to promote improvements, particularly in agriculture, by encouraging experiments and offering premiums. It was in connection with the work of this organization that Arthur Young, during his tour in the north, made soon after it was founded, observed "a great spirit of improvement" in the agriculture of Lancashire. An organization at Odiham in Hampshire promoted improvements by offering premiums, and by the interesting method of purchasing improved implements as well as seeds and reselling them at cost to non-members as well as to members, "in order to make the use of them more common." Organizations of the same general nature, with varying degrees of resemblance to the London society, were instituted in various other localities, including the East Riding and the West Riding of Yorkshire, Leicester, Kent, Durham, Melford and South Devon.[49]

In their relation to the general problem of material progress, these various organizations resembled the Society of Arts, but in their slighter emphasis upon the particular problem of stimulating and rewarding invention, most of them deviated somewhat from its example. The unique relation of the Society of Arts to the mechani-

[49] Concerning the society at Bath: *Rules and Orders* (1783); *Letters and Papers* (1783 and later); *Annual Register*, 1789, 72 (2d part). Manchester: *Manchester Mercury*, July 18, 1769, and *passim;* Holland, *General View of the Agriculture of Cheshire*, 339-341; Young, *Northern Tour*, III, 194, ff. Odiham: *Annals of Agriculture*, III, 231-239, 304, 481-490, IV, 195, 321, V, 286 and *passim*. Other localities: *Annual Register*, 1780, 207 (Chron.), 1781, 104 (2d part), 1792, 51 (Chron.); *Gentleman's Magazine*, L, 243; Young, *Eastern Tour*, I, 356, ff.; *Annals of Agriculture*, XIX, 541-551, XX, 404-410, XXII, 69-72.

cal revolution is its principal claim to historical importance. Its methods and influence in promoting inventive activity have now been sufficiently discussed, and details concerning particular inventions and improvements resulting from its work need not detain us. But there remains one pertinent question. In view of the outstanding importance of the mechanical revolution in the textile industries, what was the relation of the society to the invention of the epoch-making machines for spinning and weaving? The question is important not only because of the exceptional significance of the textile inventions, but as well because the work of the society in connection with them has usually been either ignored or misunderstood.

Hargreaves invented the spinning jenny about 1764, and the water frame was patented by Arkwright in 1769. As early as 1760, that is, four years before the invention of the spinning jenny, the Society of Arts offered premiums for "the best invention of a machine that will spin six threads of wool, flax, cotton, or silk, at one time, and that will require but one person to work it and to attend it." The premiums offered in that year were £40 for the best machine and £20 for the second best. In 1761 the premiums offered were increased to £50 and £25; and in 1763, to £100 and £50. It has been suggested that these offers of premiums were not for "the construction of a spinning machine—the idea did not enter the minds of its members—but only an improvement of the wheel." [50] But such a supposition is contrary to the plain terms of the society's offers of premiums; and it is contradicted as well by contemporaneous interpretation. Robert Dossie,

[50] Mantoux, *La Révolution Industrielle*, 208. Mantoux's comprehensive and thorough work is here in error. Baines' *History of the Cotton Manufacture*, and Wood's *History of the Royal Society of Arts*, similarly fail to note the vital distinction between a new machine and a mere improvement in the wheel made by the society in its offers of premiums.

who was well informed concerning the early history of the society, and acquainted with many of its members, tells us that their interest in the problem was aroused by knowledge of the unsuccessful spinning machine patented by Lewis Paul in 1738. They were fearful that mechanical resources had been exhausted in the expensive attempt, involving an outlay of more than £60,000, to perfect this machine for practical use. And yet they ventured to "carry their speculation further" than a mere improvement of the wheel, by the thrice repeated offer, beginning in 1760, of a premium for "the best invention of a machine that would spin six threads." Dossie himself, in view of the failure of Paul's device, was doubtful of success, and he intimates that this was the determining factor in the discontinuance of the offer in 1764. And yet the fact remains that in three successive years preceding the invention of the spinning jenny, and with increasing rewards, the society published broadcast its proposals calling the attention of those interested throughout the country to the nature and urgency of the problem.[51]

The obscurity surrounding the invention of the spinning jenny and the water frame is so great that it is impossible to say whether or not the society's offer was a source of inspiration. But it is known that the offer aroused much interest, as is evidenced by the fact that during the years 1761 to 1764 premiums were paid for several devices with which more than one thread at a time could be spun. Thus in 1763 George Buckley presented an invention which, in accordance with the society's proposals, could spin six threads at once. The committee which examined the machine declared it to be

[51] *Premiums Offered by the Society of Arts* (lists published annually by the society); *Transactions*, I, 33; Dossie, *Memoirs of Agriculture*, I, 96-98; Bailey, *Advancement of Arts, Manufactures and Commerce*, 194, 195.

constructed imperfectly, but believed it to be capable of improvement, and therefore awarded the inventor a prize "as an encouragement to his ingenuity." [52]

The attempt of the Society of Arts to solve the problem of mechanical spinning was but one of many measures it undertook for the improvement of textile manufacturing. The catalog of machines and models on exhibit in 1783 includes a variety of inventions—a combing machine, three winding machines, four looms, and other devices. Two of the looms were for the weaving of hosiery, known as stocking frames. The inventors of these improved stocking frames were awarded £100 each, and one of them received in addition a subscription raised by manufacturers. Before the introduction of these improved stocking frames, important advances had been made in the weaving of hosiery, and also of small-wares (tapes, laces, etc.), but in the weaving of ordinary cloth, progress was confined mainly to the use of Kay's flying shuttle. With the introduction of mechanical spinning, the increased output of yarn shifted the problem of technical progress in the textile industries from spinning to weaving. This change was early recognized by the Society of Arts. In 1783, two years before Cartwright's first power-loom patent, the society offered premiums for the solution of the problem of mechanical weaving, and the offer was continued in effect during the next two years.[53]

The influence of the society in bringing about the transition to mechanical production in the textile industries cannot be estimated with accuracy. It was the

[52] Bailey, *Advancement of Arts, Manufactures and Commerce,* 200 (an account of Buckley's invention). For various other awards and contemporaneous accounts, see *Ibid.,* 195-202; Dossie, *Memoirs of Agriculture,* I, 16-18; *Annual Register,* 1764, 66, 67 (Chron.); *Museum Rusticum et Commerciale,* IV, 72, 73.

[53] *Transactions,* I, 26, 200, 217, 218, II, 338, III, 292; Dossie, *Memoirs of Agriculture,* I, 136, 137, 180-184.

belief of the editor of the *Transactions* (1783) that "the great improvements in spinning, which have taken place within twenty years in these kingdoms, . . . are to be assigned to the premiums paid by this society." [54] To one who studies the entire period in due perspective, the society occupies indeed a unique position; but a more acceptable view is that its work was but one of many manifestations of a very general interest in the improvement of all instruments of production.

4. *Causes of the revolution in technique*

This remarkable and widely diffused outburst of inventive activity constitutes one of the major phenomena of history. From this judgment few students of history would be inclined to dissent. As to its causes, there is less uniformity of judgment. Many, indeed, have ventured no explanation, contenting themselves rather with a study of the attendant facts. But this attitude in its extreme form leads to an undue emphasis upon details. Mastery of details is not in itself the worthiest of ends but may be made the means of formulating generalizations. Ignorant men seek vainly and oftentimes claim pretentiously to pierce the veil of truth; while men of learning, having climbed to the vantage-ground of facts, where alone the truth is discernible, oftentimes needlessly deny themselves the vision thereof. Students have too often bowed down to the facts of history as to idols, forgetting the supreme reverence due to the truth of history.

In the study of the spirit of invention suddenly arising in England in the second half of the eighteenth century, it is less difficult, to be sure, to describe its manifestations than to explain its causes or evaluate its importance. Its causes are indeed so obscure, and the results of inquiry are so uncertain, as to lend color of justification, in this

[54] Vol. I, pp. 32, 33.

case, to those students who would content themselves with a statement of details. In order to simplify the problem if possible, we may approach the subject from the point of view of the people of the time, and see how they explained the remarkable changes going on in their midst. This inquiry, aside from being worth while in itself, ought to put us on a vantage ground for an independent view.

There is apparently no carefully thought out, rational explanation of the mechanical revolution that is contemporaneous with the event in its earlier stages, but as might naturally be expected, the nearest approach to such an explanation is to be found in the *Wealth of Nations*. Adam Smith in one of his most noted passages tells us that "the invention of all those machines by which labor is so much facilitated and abridged seems to have been originally owing to the division of labor." This, he explains, is a result of the whole attention of each worker being directed "towards some one very simple object. It is naturally to be expected, therefore, that some one or other of those who are employed in each particular branch of labor should soon find out easier and readier methods of performing their own particular work." The same principle of division of labor is made to account for those machines invented by others than the workmen who use the machines, for the making of machines becomes in time, by division of labor, a business in which specialization leads to ingenuity. Furthermore, in the progress of society there arise "philosophers, or men of speculation, whose trade is not to do anything, but to observe everything"; and at length this trade, like others, "is subdivided into a great number of different branches, each of which affords occupation to a peculiar tribe or class of philosophers; and this subdivision of employment in philosophy, as well as in every other business, improves dexterity," and often leads to a rational inventiveness in contrast with the empirical and spontaneous ingenuity of the workman.

Adam Smith's interesting interpretation leaves many questions unanswered. Is it a fact of history, the critic may inquire, that the division of labor had increased so greatly and so suddenly as to be the source of the veritable deluge of inventions during and soon after the writing of the *Wealth of Nations?* And if so, how may one account for the increased division of labor?

What was in the minds of Smith's contemporaries an explanation of the era of invention? One of the favorite methods of accounting for the invention of particular devices was by resort to chance, as the flying shuttle attributed to Kay's lame back; the automatic valve, to the string tied by a boy to a valve handle; and the spinning jenny, to the accidental overturning of a spinning wheel by Jenny Hargreaves. But even when chance was believed to have been the immediate cause, an underlying human motive was recognized, as when the Society of Arts offered premiums in 1760 for a spinning machine because it had been informed that "manufacturers of woollen, linen, and cotton find it extremely difficult, in the summer season, when the spinners are at harvest work, to procure a sufficient number of hands." [55]

A more comprehensive explanation is found in the curious suggestion that "the spirit of invention" was an outgrowth of the maritime experiences of Englishmen. "Mariners are, in general, not only the boldest and most enterprising, but also the most inventive of men: the frequent difficulties to which they are reduced in the course of the many adventures they go through, sharpen their wits; . . . hence they are fertile in contrivances." [56]

[55] Bailey, *Advancement of Arts, Manufactures and Commerce,* 194, 195. See also *Annals of Agriculture,* XIX, 189; *Annual Register,* 1781, 97-99 (2d part); *Historical and Political Remarks upon the Tariff of the Commercial Treaty* (1786), 160, 161.

[56] *European Magazine,* VI, 19.

Others offered an explanation connected with maritime activities but in another way: inventive activity was attributed to commercial competition. "In manufacturing and commercial countries, when demands from abroad slacken, and foreign competitors working cheaper endanger the loss of a manufactory, then necessity sharpens the human intellect; men's geniuses awake and are animated; and discoveries are made that astonish the world." [57]

It is probable, as will be observed later, that invention resulted from expansion rather than from contraction of foreign markets. And yet the earlier steps in England's mechanical progress were taken in imitation of foreigners, during periods when English manufacturers and merchants were at the mercy of superior Continental craftsmanship. There were Englishmen who were not deterred by national pride from some acknowledgment of the debt owed to foreigners, as when Arkwright's inventions were attributed to his study of the silk mills at Derby, which in turn had been erected from models introduced from Italy.[58]

Although imitation of foreigners can hardly account for the surpassing of foreigners so apparent in the latter part of the eighteenth century, yet the indebtedness of Englishmen to the peoples of the Continent for technical skill is greater than Englishmen of that period realized or perhaps cared to admit. The skill and ingenuity of

[57] T., *Letters on Employing Machines to Shorten Labor*, 9. See also Chambers' *Encyclopædia*, IV (1783), Art. "Spinning."

[58] *Gentleman's Magazine*, LXII, Pt. II, 863; *Memoirs*, Manchester Literary and Philosophical Society, I, 78; *Worsted Small-ware Weavers' Apology*, 3, 4; [Ogden], *Description of Manchester*, 82. Those who may wish to pursue the interesting subject of the foreign origin of English crafts and industries will find suggestions in Salzmann's *English Industries of the Middle Ages*, Cunningham's *Alien Immigrants to England*, Hulme's articles on the patent system in *Law Quarterly Review*, XII, XIII, XVI, and XVIII, and Price's *English Patents of Monopoly*.

foreigners was utilized by England in two ways: by means of the direct importation of machines and new industries, and by means of foreign immigration into England. This immigration was in large part the result of age-long disturbances on the Continent. The Protestant Reformation, religious persecution, and the long-continued wars, strangely mixed and varied in their motives but uniform in their dismal, devastating results,—from all these disturbances England was relatively free, and by the middle of the eighteenth century, innumerable peace-loving and enterprising craftsmen had brought to England the long-accumulated skill and ingenuity of the Continent.

These immigrants naturally found greater freedom and opportunity for plying their trades in the unincorporated towns than in those where corporate and gild restrictions tended to maintain monopoly and prevent change; and enterprising but unprivileged natives also naturally sought out the towns relatively free from the network of regulations and monopolies connected with corporations and gilds. The government of the towns of England had in earlier times been regulated largely by charters which were precious instruments of municipal liberty. They checked the aggressions of feudal barons and of despotic kings. But by degrees the charters of liberty were themselves transformed in many cases into instruments of oppression. The powers of government came to be exercised by small, self-perpetuating groups; and the forms of government came to be increasingly out of harmony with the needs engendered by the growth of towns and the changing conditions of town life. Similar in some respects to the history of the chartered and incorporated town governments was that of the industrial gilds and the commercial companies. These organizations, especially the gilds, maintained in earlier times what was in many respects an admirable economic system. Their members enjoyed monopolies of the local markets as against both "foreigners" and non-member townsmen. At the same time, the abuses of monopoly were largely avoided by public regulation of prices and wages; by public control of standards of workmanship; by the cultivation of pride of workmanship; and by the ideal of an income sufficient simply for comfort as opposed to the unrestrained accumulation of riches. Producers were protected from the ruthless forces of competition, and they were at the same time restrained from the unscrupulous gratification of the acquisitive instinct. In comparison with modern society's riotous and disastrous orgy of competition and wealth-accumulation, the earlier organization of urban economic life undoubtedly possessed many excellencies. But it had also a serious defect. It was too static. It lacked adaptability. It developed elaborate regulations which, while affording protection, fettered initiative and barred the way of progress.

Town life and industrial activities in the north of England developed when the vogue of charters and gilds was declining. Urban growth in the north was in fact stimulated by the shifting to that region of elements of the population which were hostile to the restrictive and monopolistic regulations of corporations and gilds. The relative freedom of northern counties in these respects was early recognized and confirmed by national statutes.[59] "Towns where manufactures are most flourishing," wrote Thomas Walker, one of Manchester's great early manufacturers, "are seldom bodies corporate, commerce requiring universal encouragement instead of exclusive privileges to the natives and freemen of a particular district. Those who first introduced the cotton manufacture

[59] 2 and 3 Phil. and Mary, c. 11 and 5 Eliz. c. 4. These laws and various related sources are quoted in Bland, Brown and Tawney, *English Economic History: Select Documents*.

into Lancashire were Protestant refugees, who probably found small encouragement for themselves and their industry amongst the corporate towns of England." It was this condition of municipal and industrial freedom which, in the view of many contemporaries, gave rise to the unparalleled ingenuity and enterprise of the north of England. Manchester is described by an enthusiastic visitor as a place of such note "that to name it is sufficient," and its position is attributed to its freedom:— "Such is the force of industry unfettered by any restrictions! Such the vigor of ingenuity unrestrained by fine-spun regulations!" The sentiments thus voiced were echoed and reechoed; the belief found expression in many forms that the mechanical and industrial progress of the country was due to the opportunity of ingenious aliens and enterprising natives to escape from the monopolies and fettering regulations of gilds and corporations.[60]

Obviously a negation—the absence of corporate and gild restrictions and monopolies—could not of itself create a spirit of invention; it was merely a condition favorable for ingenuity and novel enterprise. Nor did the people of the time fail to observe that there were various other favorable conditions which had been lacking in earlier periods. It seems to have been taken for granted that many men are naturally ingenious, but that in past ages ingenuity had remained latent or unappreciated, and was active and successful in that generation because the prevailing state of mind and social tendencies were auspicious.

It was indeed an age of social change and innovation.

[60] Walker, *Review of Some of the Political Events which have Occurred in Manchester during the Last Five Years*, 23, 24; Campbell, *Political Survey of Britain*, I, 322; [Ogden], *Description of Manchester*, 93, 94; Wright, *Address to Parliament on the Late Tax Laid on Fustian and Other Cotton Goods*, 26, 27; *Companion to the Leasowes, to Which is Prefixed the Present State of Birmingham*, 15, 16; Gisborne, *Enquiry into the Duties of Men*, 551.

Styles and manners remained formal and urbane, and as yet the smooth surface of society was little disturbed. But in the depths there were ferments varied and active. Agitation for political changes, especially for reform of parliament, was extremely wide-spread and intellectually stimulating. The evangelical movement centering around Whitefield and the Wesleys, though ultra-conservative in its reverence for the existing social régime, was powerful nevertheless in stirring the too often languid sensibilities and in rousing masses of men out of their accustomed lethargy of mind. There was vigorous and promising agitation for prison reform, for the relief of debtors, for the abolition of the slave trade, for the amendment of the poor law, for the education of the masses, and for the amelioration of the state of Roman Catholics and of Dissenters. Especially in the north there was observable a breaking away from religious traditions and social conventions which, whatever may have been their historical importance, were nevertheless barriers in the way of change and therefore of progress.[61]

It was a period when men were in a measure freeing themselves from the age-long grip of supernaturalism; a period when thought and action were being directed more generally by reason; and this tendency created a favorable, even a necessary condition for a spirit of invention. In order to appreciate its importance, one needs only to call to mind the experiences of Roger Bacon, Bruno, and Galileo, as well as a host of lesser innovators, in ages when supernaturalism prevailed over rationalism as a test of social sanction. It is true that not only supernaturalism but custom, tradition, and social privilege

[61] A few passages particularly pertinent to this large topic are Traill, *Social England*, V, ch. 18 ("An Era of New Departures, 1742-1784"); Chalmers, *Estimate*, ed. 1794, Dedication, xxiv, xxv; *Annals of Agriculture*, XX, 132 (on religious liberalism in the north); Harland, *Collectanea Relating to Manchester*, II, 144-173 (an illustration of the breaking away in the north from social convention).

are in many cases inconsistent with rationalism. But the adherents of these are less likely to make war on rational changes than are the proponents of supernaturalism, because, on the one hand, they are not committed to the defense of any principle of absolute truth likely to be endangered by innovation; and on the other hand, they more readily find it possible to utilize changes engendered by reason for the maintenance of irrational privileges or conditions.

Supernaturalism has its origin in a primitive reaction to the unknown: thunder is the voice of the sky-god, the lightning his weapon. Rationalism is an outgrowth of experience and knowledge, as when Franklin, utilizing the accumulated store of information, made tests of his own, and explained the phenomena of the clouds on natural grounds; and even thought out an invention for protection against what had been deemed in earlier ages the invincible agency of a supernatural power. There had been promise of the substitution of rationalism for supernaturalism centuries earlier; for during the age of the recovery of ancient culture and of the discovery of the New World, knowledge expanded almost incredibly, and experience became diversified as never before. But there intervened, perhaps inevitably, the long struggle between rival camps of supernaturalists. The primitive dogmas and taboos of the middle ages, crowded into the background by the expanding knowledge and experience of the age of the Renaissance and of exploration, were again marshaled in the forefront by the unreasoning passions of the age of religious conflict. Much of the bitterness of the conflict resulted from old customs disrupted and the uprooting of long-flourishing privileges; but men were deeply disturbed by what to them was a grave question of life and destiny. The problem they wrestled with for two centuries was the problem of the source of authority for determining the proper form of super-

naturalism. At length men began to realize the alterna-
tives before them: they must go back to the medieval
system of an all-inclusive ecclesiastical authority, or else
they must go forward to the authority of individual
reason. With the acceptance of the latter alternative,
involving the principle of religious freedom, men's
thoughts began to run once more, as during the Renaissance, in rational channels; the old fear of innovation as
the enemy of absolute truth was no longer strong enough
to keep in check the spirit of change and readjustment;
and theological speculation and controversy were more
and more trenched upon by experimental and applied
science.

Dr. Priestley's lament over the destruction of his laboratory and manuscripts by a "church and king" mob in
1791 brought to him at least a pathetic realization of
the fact that rationalism is a tender plant cultivated in
the midst of the jungle of elemental passions and super-
stitions which press relentlessly on all sides to regain
complete sway over the human mind. But it was with
profound satisfaction that sympathetic observers before
the French Revolution noted the growth of rationalism
from Newton's age to the time of Priestley. This com-
paratively unhindered growth culminated in an unprecedented curiosity of mind, a rationalizing of all phenomena, a habit of experimentation, a desire for readjustment when sanctioned by reason. Theories were decried
as "little more than ingenious amusements; a series of
well-made experiments can alone establish matters of
fact"; it is by this method that "new discoveries ought to
be attempted." Men rejoiced that "theory" no longer
prevailed, but that "experiment [had] regained its true
honors"; and that new discoveries were in consequence
being made "such as the human mind had hitherto no
conception of." The tendencies of the age found characteristic expression in Arthur Young's boast that he had

no fixed principle except "the principle of change" based on experience—"the only principle worthy of an experimenter." [62]

It is to be supposed, on first thought, that tendencies so prominent would find expression in the education of the period. But the theological origin and the ancient endowments of the leading schools combined to make them (so Adam Smith tells us) "sanctuaries in which exploded systems and obsolete prejudices found shelter and protection, after they had been hunted out of every other corner of the world." To the same effect was Arthur Young's criticism: "The universities are curious to teach whatever is perfectly useless," while useful knowledge is avoided with extreme care. Shall educational establishments be exempt from change, he asks, "because they are ancient? Shall considerable revenues remain thus misapplied without at least turning a small part into a channel that may disperse its streams to the general fructification of the kingdom?" Not content with negative criticism, he desired that experimental and applied science be introduced; and that "practical agriculture" be taught in each institution by a professor acquainted with practical and experimental farming, in association with professors of the sciences able to explain the connections between agriculture and such subjects as chemistry, botany, mineralogy, and mechanics.[63]

Many other writers emphasized the dependence of the "useful arts" on the sciences, and desired equally far-reaching changes in the system of education. The government was urged to establish institutions "open to all of every rank, religion, or nation," in which "the study of the useful arts and sciences and of modern languages

[62] Harte, *Essays on Husbandry*, 34; *Museum Rusticum et Commerciale*, III, 121, 122; *Gentleman's Magazine*, LV, 789; Young, *The Example of France a Warning to Britain*, 3, 4.

[63] Smith, *Wealth of Nations*, sections on education; *Annals of Agriculture*, I, 78-82, X, 240, XI, 368.

should certainly be preferred . . . to the study of the languages and the works of taste of *decayed* nations; especially as both the histories and the moral writings of these nations, when thought of any peculiar utility, may easily be translated for the general advantage." [64] There were proposals also for the establishment of agricultural schools with experiment farms and courses in the sciences under the auspices of the societies interested in agriculture and the arts. These were to be attended by "smart boys selected by each society," and these, returning to their several communities with knowledge of new and improved methods, would become centers of community education. "Like smaller rivulets, branching from the main stream, they would water and fertilize those lands where a large river cannot . . . expand." [65] Nor was industrial education for the children of the poor without its advocates, as Jonas Hanway, an early humanitarian. He believed in "the lowest of mankind" being taught not only to read but to work properly. He favored the establishment of "schools wherein children should turn their hands to every useful work," by the utilization of the natural inclination of the young toward the manipulation of material objects.[66]   These and many similar criticisms and suggestions had no great effect on the work of the schools and universities, except perhaps at Manchester, where, as has been seen, the College of Arts and Sciences was organized.[67] Its purpose was not merely to promote mechanical improvements, but in general to supply the practical educational needs of a "town of trade." But even here conservatism obstructed the way.

Tradition, in spite of vigorous criticisms, maintained

[64] *New and Old Principles of Trade Compared,* 44, 45.

[65] *Letters and Papers,* Bath Society of Arts, I, 269-318; *Annual Register,* 1781, 104-112 (2d part).

[66] Jonas Hanway, *Letters,* quoted in *Lloyd's Evening Post and British Chronicle,* XX, 563.

[67] See above, pp. 45, 46.

its control of educational institutions, but throughout the range of economic activities, a spirit of experimental change and rational readjustment prevailed. In Young's *Tours*, in periodicals, in various books on agriculture and related subjects, and in the publications of societies many thousands of agricultural experiments and improvements were recorded; and yet Young complained that "the present imperfection of agriculture does not arise from a want of experiments, but from the backwardness of gentlemen taking any care to make known those which are every day tried." [68] "New undertakings" or "projects" were said to be "more frequent in this than in any other country in the world." Many of these enterprises, being connected with roads, bridges, canals, harbors, paving and other parochial and municipal developments, were authorized by parliament; and the laws connected with such undertakings increased immensely in numbers after the middle of the century. [69]

Of these various undertakings, the most important was canal construction of a new type, beginning with Brindley's epochal canal opened in 1761. Canals were immediately significant in the revolutionizing of transportation, but they also had an indirect result of incalculable importance—the stimulation of interest in material improvements of all kinds. For the canals were then most marvelous feats of engineering skill. It was said at the time that most of the nobility and gentry of the entire country visited Lancashire in order to see the early canals; and indeed they commanded "the attention and admiration of all Europe." "Such wonders are abroad," wrote Arthur Young concerning his anticipated visit to the Bridgewater canal, that "if only half are true I shall

---

[68] *Annals of Agriculture*, I, 133.

[69] Impressive evidence is found compiled in Chalmers' *Estimate*, various editions. See also *Increase of Manufactures, Commerce and Finance*, 107.

be not a little entertained." Nor was he disappointed with the view: he and other travellers who described their sensations seem to have exhausted their store of superlatives. A man with Brindley's "inventive genius . . . moves in a sphere that is to the rest of the world imaginary, or at best a *terra incognita*." As for Bridgewater, his canal will "convey his name with peculiar brilliancy to the latest posterity." The work is "amazing," but it is after all in keeping with the spirit of the time: "By such noble undertakings is the present age peculiarly distinguished." Intelligent and self-disciplined observers were smitten with amazement; the sensations of the common people we can only imagine. We read, for example, that on June 4, 1777, "the grand canal from Leeds to Liverpool was opened into the River Aire, at the former place, amidst such a concourse of people as was never seen in that town before; some computed them at 20,000, others at 30,000." How keen must have been the interest; how rudely shocked must have been faith in the old, unchanging ways of doing things, when vessels in the canals were

> Seen and acknowledged by astonished crowds
> From underground emerging to the clouds.

Since it was generally believed that one of Brindley's new engineering devices had "eased the expense" of his employer, the Duke of Bridgewater, "at least 5,000%" and that another "was better than £20,000 in the Duke's pocket": since he was beheld doing such profitable as well as marvelous things, it is not at all surprising that vast numbers of people were stimulated to follow the great engineer's example by seeking new and better ways of doing things.[70]

[70] [Ogden], *Description of Manchester*, 3, 4, 49; Young, *Northern Tour*, III, 187, ff.; *Annual Register*, 1777, 185 (Chron.). Concerning the effects of the canals on the people: At least the good Duke's

Many circumstances thus combined to create a condition favorable for mechanical improvements. The incoming of independent-minded and skilled artisans from the Continent; the escape, especially in the north, from the monopolistic restrictions of corporations and gilds; the social ferments tending to dissolve the traditions opposed to change; the rise of rationalism and experimental and applied sciences; the application of experimental change and rational readjustment to a wide variety of "useful projects," especially important in the case of canal construction because of the accompanying nation-wide stimulation of mechanical ingenuity: these are some of the elements in a complex of forces which had long been gathering momentum and which made inevitable a great increase of inventiveness.

But there is one other factor more positive, more decisive probably, in its influence than any that have been mentioned. The circumstances already described undoubtedly stimulated interest in technical progress, but the determining factor was the opportunity for the profitable use of mechanical inventions. Naturally, the profitable use of new and improved instruments of production depended largely on the demand for the output. It was in respect to the demand for English goods that the eighteenth century differed most radically from earlier periods. Pressure for goods was felt alike by the manufacturer, the trader, and the farmer. It was the pressure of excess of goods demanded over goods available by existing methods of production that made profitable the exercise of inventive ingenuity which otherwise would have remained in a measure dormant. Englishmen were at first not clearly conscious of the operation of this

workmen must have been duly impressed, for we learn that during the construction of one of his canals, "upwards of 600 of his Grace's workmen were entertained upon the lock banks, with an ox roasted whole and plenty of liquor." (*Annual Register,* 1773, 66 (Chron.)).

force; but they were not long in assigning to the machine its proper place in the control of the world's markets. With clear-sighted adaptation of means to ends, invention was then consciously and publicly promoted, and the mechanical transition became a matter of national policy.

An important element in the situation was the very great increase of wealth and consequent expansion of demand for consumption goods at home. "That our riches are in fact amazingly increased within a few years," declared an Englishman in 1767, "no one who is in the least acquainted with this country can entertain a doubt; whoever will cast his eyes on our public works, our roads, our bridges, our pavements, and our hospitals, the prodigious extension of our capital, and in some proportion that of every considerable town in Great Britain; whoever will look into the possessions and expenses of individuals, their houses, furniture, tables, equipages, parks, gardens, cloths, plate, and jewels, will find everywhere round him sufficient marks to testify to the truth of this proposition." The merchant, acquiring a fortune far more rapidly than ever before, "vies all the while with the first of our nobility in his houses, table, furniture, and equipage." Wealth and luxury have even infected the "lower orders." "The shopkeeper who used to be well contented with one dish of meat, one fire, and one maid, has now two or three times as many of each: his wife has her tea, her card parties, and her dressing room; and his apprentice has climbed from the kitchen fire to the front boxes at the play houses."

How may this increase of wealth and expansion of demand at home for consumption goods be accounted for? The same observer attributes it in part to the funding of the debt following the Seven Years' War. The "enormous sums" then expended are now "annually returning into the pockets of the merchants, contractors, brokers, and stockjobbers," and these "lend it again to the public on

a new mortgage the following year." But more dependable sources of prosperity are described. If one calls to
mind "the immense riches daily flowing in since . . .
[the Seven Years' War] from our commerce extended
over every quarter of the globe, from the new channels
of trade opened with America, and the amazing sums
imported from the East Indies, it will not be difficult to
account for the opulence of the present time." [71]

The increase of wealth, diffusion of prosperity, and
widening of contacts led to an expansion of wants and
to the introduction of new tastes. In consequence, the
increase in purchasing power was accompanied by an
even greater increase in demand for goods.

To the pressure of increasing demand in the home
markets was added the unparalleled expansion of English
control over foreign markets. France, the great imperial
rival of England, was defeated and crippled. Her territories and commercial monopolies in America and the
Far East were taken over by Englishmen. Shipping
facilities had been enlarged and made more efficient.[72]
There had been rapid progress in the making of the great
imperial network of fortifications in strategic locations
controlling the maritime trade routes. England's advantages were the greater because of her relative freedom
from invasion and internal disturbance while her Continental rivals were exhausting themselves by wars.
England, to be sure, had just emerged from the Seven
Years' War, but her direct participation was relatively so
slight as to give color of justification to the statement
that the imperial French dominions were won from
France in Germany, by means of English subsidies to the

[71] This keen analysis of conditions following the Seven Years' War is
by an anonymous writer in the *Annual Register,* 1767, 165-172 (2d
part), in an essay entitled "Thoughts on the Causes and Consequences
of the Present High Price of Provisions."

[72] Concerning maritime improvements, see Traill, *Social England,* V,
209-212.

Prussian enemies of France. There were Englishmen, indeed, who were dubious of war as an instrument of commercial expansion, and who deplored "the amazing and unnatural height to which the commerce of this country was carried by the war—being literally erected on the ruins of that of half our neighbors." [73]

So large was the demand at home, and so extensive were the overseas markets controlled by Englishmen, that without new methods of production, "no exertions of the manufacturers could have answered the demands of trade." Therefore, "the animating influence of large demand," bringing liberal rewards to the producers of goods, is observable "in a variety of inventions . . . and in works of ingenuity and taste." [74]

The mechanical revolution, set in its proper historical background, is seen to assume the form of a natural, inevitable result of gradually developing forces; it becomes an integral, rationally explicable part of the age. Men had long been stirred by a strong, yet rational, sense of change and readjustment, which at length penetrated to the material foundations of society. This was the first phase of the mechanical revolution—the desire to bring about a more effective utilization of the material environment. To that end, as the second phase, new instruments and processes were devised. The final phase was the application of these inventions to productive processes.

In none of its aspects was this revolution the work of a few unappreciated individuals. It was rather the creation of social forces finding expression, to be sure, in the

[73] Young, *Political Arithmetic*, 87. See also his article in *Annals of Agriculture*, III, 170, 171; similar views of Samuel Eaton in *Ibid.*, X, 45; and Dean Josiah Tucker's denunciation of England's "strange phrenzy which has infected the whole English nation" for making England "sole mistress and sovereign of the seas" (in *Reflections on the Present Matters in Dispute between Great Britain and Ireland*, 2, 3).

[74] [Ogden], *Description of Manchester*, 87; *Historical and Political Remarks upon the Tariff of the Commercial Treaty* (1786), 164.

work of individuals, but far more significantly in governmental patronage and in organized, cooperative activities intended primarily to promote not the fortunes of individuals but the welfare of the nation. The men who seized upon the new machines and by means of them attained wealth and power in a newly rising industrial society—the great industrialists—appropriated instruments which in their origins were distinctly social.

CHAPTER II

THE TRIUMPH OF THE MACHINE

1. *Contemporaneous views*

THE machines brought into being during the era of invention were applied to economic processes with revolutionary effects because of their productive and competitive power. A statement so obvious may seem to need no elaboration. To the people of the time the fact, however obvious, was by no means commonplace, nor was it deemed unworthy of comment in superlative terms.

It has been asserted that the writers of the time were unconscious of the great economic transformation, and that the revolutionary power of the new machinery was practically without contemporaneous recognition. It is true that writers of the conventional forms of literature of that period, perhaps more generally than in more recent times, were inclined to look with disdain upon economic processes either new or old as common or vulgar. Doctor Johnson attributed the lack of attention paid to Dyer's poetic description of the woollen industry, *The Fleece,* to "the meanness naturally adhering, and the irreverence habitually annexed, to trade and manufactures." [1] The subjective judgment of the learned doctor was not inapplicable to the general state of literary opinion. The catholic spirit of recent writers comprehends all manner of men and their commonest pursuits. But in the literary world of the eighteenth century, a book like Arnold Bennett's *Clayhanger* would have been

[1] Johnson's *Lives of the Poets,* cited by Wood, *Industrial England in the Middle of the Eighteenth Century,* 44, n. 1.

70

as much an innovation as was the invention of the spinning jenny in the world of industry.

And yet there was a large and rapidly increasing number of writers outside the field of pure literature who were frankly and keenly interested in the forces and phenomena of economic society. By putting oneself in the place of a contemporary observer, and by remembering, too, that the eighteenth-century mind was exceptionally rational and restrained, we may the more readily perceive the significance of the superlatives applied to the new inventions. They are described as "great and extraordinary"; "most wonderful"; "astonishing"; "amazing"; "almost miraculous"; "unexampled"; "unparalleled in the annals of the world." Their effect is beyond description, but is likened to a sudden explosion, and is called by many writers a "revolution." They have reached an "incredible" perfection, with productive value "beyond the powers of calculation." They give a facility to labor "scarcely conceivable." They have laid "the foundations of a very extended commerce," and their effect on industry has been progress "rapid beyond example." They have enabled industry to make "a gigantic stride," to attain an "enormous height," and to achieve a "progressive and astonishing increase." They have caused Manchester goods in particular "to spread in ten thousand forms and colors, not only in these kingdoms, but over all Europe, and even into distant continents." They are expected to produce "great changes . . . in the appearance of the civilized world," and the magnitude of their benefits "can scarcely be estimated." The "discoveries and improvements" of the age "diffuse a glory over this country unattainable by conquest or dominion," and promise to "stamp a luster" on his Majesty's reign "to the latest generations." [2]

[2] *Annals of Agriculture*, IX, 286, 502, X, 253, 281, 579, XII, 513; *European Magazine*, XI, 364, 367, XX, 216; *Gentleman's Magazine*,

Such are some of the terms of unmeasured praise recurring in the writings of the time in recognition of the productive value of the new machines. Most writers contented themselves with indefinite exclamations, but some ventured exact estimates. This was particularly true of cotton manufacturing, where the change was most remarkable, and also most readily measurable. While contemporaries in general recognized the futility of attempting to ascertain the exact increase of productive power resulting from machines, they were vitally interested in tangible manifestations of creative power.

This creative power was evident in the first instance in the transition from hand methods to mechanical processes in various industries and regions. This transition involved a second readily observable phenomenon, namely, a concentration and increase of capital, energy and population in those industries and regions where the technical improvements were being adopted. Thirdly, the inevitable consequence of the adoption of improved methods and of the concentration of economic resources was the irresistible competitive advance of the industries thus armed, alike at home and in foreign markets. These are the three stages or aspects of the triumph of the machine which seemed most remarkable to contemporary observers, and which we may now most profitably consider. For it was out of these vital changes brought about by machinery that a new industrial society emerged.

LVII, Pt. I, 465; *Transactions,* Society of Arts, I, 34, 35; Owen, *Life,* I, 22; Aikin, *Description of the Country Round Manchester,* 172; T., *Letters on Employing Machines to Shorten Labor,* 4, 9; *New and Old Principles of Trade Compared,* 32, 33; Gisborne, *Enquiry into the Duties of Men,* 551; [Ogden], *Description of Manchester,* 90; *Important Crisis in the Calico and Muslin Manufactory of Great Britain Explained,* 1, 2; Anderson, *Historical Origin of Commerce,* IV, 705, 706 (ed. 1789); *Encyclopædia Britannica,* 3d ed., V, 488, 489, X, Art. "Manchester"; *Chambers' Encyclopædia,* I, Dedication, i, ii (dated 1786).

2. The adoption of new technique

The first of these great changes—the transition from hand methods to mechanical processes—was of course the immediate outcome of the spirit of invention prevalent since about the middle of the century. In a general view of human progress, it becomes apparent that the use of tools and machines to supplement or to supplant hand methods is a continuous process, practically coincident with man's advance from the brute stage, when, like animals of today, he supplied his wants by the use of unassisted muscular power. "Read the history of mankind," exhorted an advocate of the new cotton-spinning machines in 1779, "consider the gradual steps of civilization from barbarism to refinement, and you will not fail to discover that the progress of society from its lowest and worst to its highest and most perfect state has been uniformly accompanied and chiefly promoted by the happy exertions of man in the character of a mechanic or engineer. Let all machines be destroyed, and we are reduced in a moment to the condition of savages; and in that state men may indeed exist a long time without the aid of curious and complex machines; though without them they can never rise above it." [3]   The transition is indeed a process which reaches back to the beginnings of human life, and which will go on as long as man survives with rational powers. The process in its gradual, age-long aspect had wrought incalculable changes; the relatively swift and sudden transition that resulted from the era of invention was appropriately termed a revolution.

The beginning of the transition was marked by the use not of machines to supplant, but of tools to supplement, the operations of the hand. Spinning by distaff and even by wheel is in essence dependent upon the supple and

[3] T., *Letters on Employing Machines to Shorten Labor*, 2, 3.

dexterous use of the hand. The substitution of jenny, water-frame and mule for distaff and wheel meant the supplanting of the hand in the immediate process of drawing out and twisting the thread. Vast changes resulted in early times, no doubt, from the use of the simplest of tools—the club, the ax, the hammer, the spade, the distaff, the lever. But so limited were the possibilities of improvement by the use of mere tools that eighteenth-century industrial processes were not radically different from those prevailing at the dawn of history. In contrast, the mechanical revolution of the eighteenth century involved potentiality of change practically without limit. For in place of tools for merely supplementing and perhaps strengthening the hand, mechanisms were introduced which did what only the hand had formerly done, and the number of hands was in effect multiplied indefinitely by the use of new motive forces for operating the new mechanisms.[4]

The early stages of the accelerated transition of the eighteenth century are commonly associated with the textile inventions of Kay, Hargreaves, Arkwright and Crompton, but there were important forerunners. The harnessing of water and wind had long given evidence of the docility of nature's forces in bearing heavy burdens otherwise borne by the muscle of man or beast. Furnaces gigantic in size and complex in operation in contrast with the primitive hand forge had been devised for the more effective utilization of natural products. But the most important forerunners of mechanical revolution were in the textile industries.

The making of hosiery by machinery goes back to the time of Elizabeth, when the stocking frame was invented by William Lee, about whom many interesting anecdotes

[4] The differences between devices for aiding the hand and those for supplanting the hand are discussed by Mantoux in *La Révolution Industrielle*, 179, 180.

have been told. His machine was extensively introduced in the seventeenth century, and by the middle of the eighteenth century, framework knitting was carried on not only in Nottinghamshire, its original home, but in various neighboring counties, and in Middlesex. The stocking frames, though not commonly owned by the workers, being loaned to them at a rental, were nevertheless generally operated by them in their homes rather than in a plant set aside for manufacturing. The industry was intermediate between the older forms of organization and the factory system.[5]

In a curious old pamphlet published at Manchester in 1756 there is an account of another industry, of minor importance in itself, but significant in setting an early example of transition to mechanical methods. This was the small-ware industry—the weaving of such articles as ribbons, tapes, braids, filleting, and certain kinds of laces. "Timothy Shuttle" in his *Worsted Small-ware Weavers' Apology* tells us quaintly that the small-ware business "was formerly carried on in what we call the single loom; and about thirty years ago [*i.e.*, about 1725], was begun to be took out of that, and put in the engine, or Dutch loom. . . . As in the single loom they can but work one piece at a time, and in the Dutch loom twelve or fourteen; and there being in Manchester at this time more than three times the quantity of Dutch looms than ever there were single looms, it follows that where there was one gross of goods made this way thirty years ago, there is now made upwards of thirty." [6]

But probably the most important pioneering in mechanical manufacturing was in the silk industry. As

[5] Fox Bourne, *Romance of Trade*, 203-207; Mantoux, *La Révolution Industrielle*, 182-184; *Parliamentary Register*, XXIII, 540; Commons *Journals*, XXXVI, 635, 638, 740-742.

[6] The *Apology*, 3, 4. See also [Ogden], *Description of Manchester*, 82; Daniels, *Early English Cotton Industry*, 40, 72; Chapman, *Lancashire Cotton Industry*, 19-22.

in the small-ware industry, the machinery used was of foreign origin. Unlike both the small-ware and the hosiery machines, those used in the manufacture of silk were so large, so intricate, and so costly as to involve in their use the essential features of the modern factory system. The elaborate Italian machinery for preparing silk for the loom, introduced into England by John Lombe and his brother, Sir Thomas,[7] was described by contemporaries as marvelous alike in appearance and in productive power. The factory—for such it was in nature if not in name—which was erected by Sir Thomas near Derby on the River Derwent was described as containing a "stupendous" mechanism, an "amazingly grand machine." The mechanism, it was said, "contains 26,586 wheels and 97,746 movements, which work 73,726 yards of organzine silk thread every time the water wheel goes round, being thrice in one minute, and 318,504,960 yards in one day and night. One water wheel gives motion to all the other movements, of which any one may be stopped separately, without obstructing the rest. One fire engine conveys warm air to every individual part of this vast machine, containing, in all its buildings, half a quarter of a mile in length." At Sheffield there was erected "a copy of the famous one at Derby," and Arthur Young states that the Sheffield plant cost about £7,000 and employed 152 hands. The "copy" seems to have been a miniature, however, for the Derby plant is said to have employed at least 300 hands, and to have cost about £30,000. Various other mills were established, and the silk industry, though relatively of minor importance, had the distinction of leading the way toward industrial organization as well as mechanical methods characteristic of the factory system.[8]

[7] See above, p. 31.

[8] Anderson, *Historical Origin of Commerce*, III, 91; Young, *Northern Tour*, I, 134, 135; *Historical and Political Remarks upon the Tariff of the Commercial Treaty* (1786), 160, 161; Axon, *Lancashire Glean-*

The epochal transition in the spinning of cotton occurred within the brief compass of a quarter of a century, beginning with the earliest use of Hargreaves' spinning jenny, about 1765, and culminating in the application of steam power in spinning factories. The jenny, relatively small and inexpensive, and operated by hand, was less revolutionary in its effects than was Arkwright's water-frame. The former, like the wheel, was at first extensively used in the home; the latter, run by water power and later by steam, wrought an immediate revolution in the organization as well as in the technique of the spinning industry. The jenny was adapted for the making of the finer threads, and the water-frame for the coarser warp yarns. In consequence, there was a fairly distinct field for each machine. But the introduction of Crompton's mule in 1779 and its rapid improvement and general adoption for the spinning of the finer threads soon resulted in the eclipse of the jenny in the cotton industry. The mule, like the jenny, was at first generally operated by hand in the home, instead of by water power in special plants. It was soon improved, however; the number of spindles was increased; and by 1790 mule spinning was being successfully carried on by power in factories.

The success of the factories established by Arkwright and his partners, beginning about 1770, led to the putting up of similar establishments with great rapidity. To trace the course of the transition in detail is impossible. The most definite and extensive information available is for the year 1788. In March of that year, Messrs. Smith, Colquhoun, Whittaker, and Dunlop, claiming to be "delegates from the manufacturers of calicoes and muslins in England and Scotland," presented to the Board of Trade a paper entitled "An Important Crisis in the Cotton Manufactory of Great Britain Explained."

ings, 289; Fox Bourne, *Romance of Trade,* 52; Smiles, *Men of Invention and Industry,* 113-118.

In the following month, under date of April 9, 1788, this paper in slightly altered form was published anonymously under the title "An Important Crisis in the Calico and Muslin Manufactory of Great Britain Explained." [9] In this document of the manufacturers it is stated that in 1788 there were 143 water-power factories of the Arkwright type for spinning warp thread, 550 mules having as many as 90 spindles each, and 20,070 hand jennies. The distribution of the water-power factories is stated to have been as follows:

Lancashire	41	Gloucestershire	1
Derbyshire	22	Cumberland	1
Nottinghamshire	17	Lanarkshire	4
Yorkshire	11	Renfrewshire	4
Cheshire	8	Perthshire	3
Staffordshire	7	Midlothian	2
Westmoreland	5	Ayrshire	1
Flintshire	3	Galloway	1
Berkshire	1	Annandale	1
Surrey	1	Bute	1
Hertfordshire	1	Aberdeenshire	1
Leicestershire	1	Fifeshire	1
Worcestershire	1	Isle of Man	1
Pembrokeshire	1		

The purpose of the manufacturers in publishing this information was to emphasize the importance of the industry and gain support in their appeal to the government for protection against the alleged dumping by the East India Company of cotton goods made in the Far East, the charge being made that the company was using its monopolistic privileges and power in an attempt to ruin the newly developing English cotton industry. The information presented by the manufacturers was therefore not without bias. Their estimate of the number of jennies was obviously no more than a guess. Robert Peel, when asked in 1785 "whether the skill of making Mr. Arkwright's machine is now fully possessed by other

[9] *Board of Trade Papers*, 6/140, Docs. 24-26, 41.

people," replied, "By every joiner in the country." [10] Knowledge of the relatively simple mechanism of the jenny must have been accessible to all ordinary mechanics; and the small and inexpensive nature of the device unquestionably led to its construction and use in the homes of large numbers of people independently of any factory or any definite arrangement for employment. This fact would indicate a probable under-estimate of the number of jennies in use. There seems, moreover, to be no sufficient reason for believing that the number of mules and water-frames was exaggerated. Evidence of a somewhat later date for particular regions indicates a much larger number of factories. Thus the number of mills assigned to Nottinghamshire in 1788 was only seventeen, whereas a report to the Board of Agriculture in 1794 stated that there were thirty-one in the county, and two others under construction. The number assigned to the entire county of Chester was only eight, whereas Aikin's famous *Description of the Country from Thirty to Forty Miles Round Manchester,* published in 1795 after prolonged labor of compilation, stated that at Stockport alone there were "twenty-three large cotton factories, four of them worked by steam engines," besides a large number of smaller cotton-spinning "shops." About the same time it was reported that there were thirty-nine cotton mills operated by water power in Scotland, as compared with nineteen in the statement for 1788.[11]

The transition to power machines in the spinning of cotton warp was more rapid than in the spinning of weft, but it is certain that before the end of the century

[10] *Minutes of the Evidence taken before a Committee of the House of Commons,* 1785 (on Irish Resolutions), 18.

[11] Lowe, *General View of the Agriculture of the County of Nottingham,* 126; Aikin, *Description of the Country Round Manchester,* 445, 446; McPherson, *Annals of Commerce,* IV, 528, 529; Dumbell, "Early Liverpool Cotton Imports," in *Econ. Jour.,* XXXIII, 372.

the jennies and hand-operated mules had given place, even in the spinning of weft, very largely to power spinning. Mules too large to be worked by hand like ordinary jennies were operated by streams or by horses, and in one instance frankly avowed, by "the thews and sinews of a stalwart Irishman." [12] It was well after the end of the century that the steam engine gained the ascendancy as the motive power in the spinning industry, but its experimental use in spinning is said to have begun as early as 1783.[13]

The wide field for the application of mechanical methods in the cotton industry is shown by the variety of processes in addition to spinning. Lord Sheffield in 1785 enumerated twenty-three operations in the manufacture of dyed cotton velverets, and stated that each operation was usually performed in Lancashire by a craftsman of a distinct class. Perhaps this is a uselessly elaborate classification. Robert Peel was asked by a committee of the House of Commons in the same year (1785) as to the different stages in the manufacture of cotton, and he replied that there were four—spinning, weaving, bleaching, and printing. When asked in which of these processes machinery was employed, he replied, "In the process of spinning." [14] Peel obviously meant to include under spinning the preparatory processes such as carding, which had undergone a considerable degree of mechanization.

[12] *A Century of Fine Cotton Spinning*, 8, 9.

[13] Radcliffe, *Origin of Power-loom Weaving*, 61-65; *Annals of Agriculture*, X, 579, 580; Pilkington, *View of the Present State of Derbyshire*, II, 50-53; Dumas, *Étude sur le Traité de Commerce* (1786), 153; Aikin, *Description of the Country Round Manchester*, 458; *Factories Inquiry Commission, Suppl. Rep.* (1834), Pt. I, 168; *Journal and Corresp. of Auckland*, I, 517; Daniels, *Early English Cotton Industry*, 81; Unwin, "Transition to the Factory System," in *Eng. Hist. Rev.*, XXXVII, 206-218, 383-397; Dumbell, "Early Liverpool Cotton Imports," in *Econ. Jour.*, XXXIII, 372.

[14] Sheffield, *Observations on Ireland*, 202, 203; *Min. of the Evidence, Com. of H. of C.*, 1785 (on Irish Resolutions), 18.

As for the second stage mentioned by Peel, namely, weaving, it will be remembered that it was Kay's flying shuttle which in 1733 began to disturb the balance between the output of the spinners and that of the weavers. Later devices, the drop-box and the draw-boy, made the looms used in weaving figured and intricate patterns too expensive for ordinary weavers, and the looms in consequence were "mounted for them at great expense, which the employers advanced." [15] The stocking frame for knitting and the Dutch loom for the weaving of narrow goods met with continued improvement and extended application to the making of cotton goods.[16] The use of Cartwright's power loom had a negligible influence on output and industrial organization before the nineteenth century. But under the influence of the general concentration of capital and labor, there was a tendency for weaving factories to be established even before the introduction of the power loom.[17]

Radical changes in the bleaching of cottons were due to chemical discoveries more than to the invention of machines, but the distinction is unimportant: technical improvements of various kinds were manifestations of the same general spirit of progress; and the results of such improvements were similar. The old process of bleaching was unbelievably crude, expensive, and prolonged. It consisted of alternate "bucking" and "crofting"—soaking in lye and other liquids and exposing, after being washed, to the light and air in bleaching fields. The process sometimes required a period of eight months.

[15] [Ogden], *Description of Manchester,* 77 (cited by Chapman, *Lancashire Cotton Industry,* 22).

[16] See above, pp. 74, 75.

[17] McLean (ed.), *Local Industries of Glasgow and the West of Scotland,* 142, 143; *Annual Register,* 1792, 47 (Chron.); Heaton, *Yorkshire Woollen and Worsted Industries,* 296, 353-356; Dumbell, "Early Liverpool Cotton Imports," in *Econ. Jour.,* XXXIII, 371, n. 5, 372; Unwin, Hulme, and Taylor, *Samuel Oldknow and the Arkwrights,* 98, 110, 200.

Scheele's discovery of chlorine in 1774, and Berthollet's announcement in 1785 of its adaptability for bleaching vegetable fibers, led to the experimental introduction of chemical bleaching in Britain in 1786 by James Watt, and its scientific development by Thomas Henry of Manchester as a part of his work in the College of Arts and Sciences. In consequence the crofters' fields of cotton and linen, whose principal virtue was their picturesqueness, were rapidly displaced by bleaching factories, reducing the time required from months to days and even hours.[18]

Printing, the final stage in cotton manufacturing, was carried on in 1785 by means of the primitive block and plate designs applied by hand. But soon thereafter there was a transition in printing rivaling in suddenness and in the increase of productive power the earlier transition in spinning. Although there had been no essential change in the method of printing before 1785, the organization of the calico printing industry had early begun to assume the characteristics of the factory system.[19] There had been established a number of large printing enterprises which employed men not in their homes but in central plants. Such was in part at least the nature of Robert Peel's business. Joseph Smith, another Lancashire manufacturer, told a committee of the House of Commons in 1785 that he employed from seven hundred to a thousand printers; and that while "the weavers employed in the manufacture (many of them) frequently work for more than one house, those in the printing are constantly employed by one house." When the simple block and plate designs were superseded by the elaborate and expensive cylindrical method, a full-fledged form of

[18] Baines, *History of the Cotton Manufacture*, 245-253; Mantoux, *La Révolution Industrielle*, 241.

[19] Several instances of early printing factories using the older technique are mentioned by P. J. Thomas in an article in *Eng. Hist. Rev.*, XXXIX, 206-216.

the factory system in the printing industry was the immediate result.   In 1784, Thomas Bell, "the elder, of Walton-in-the-Dale [near Preston] in the County Palatine of Lancaster, copper plate printer," secured a patent for his "new, peculiar and improved art or method of printing 1, 2, 3, 4, 5 or more colors, all at one and the same time, upon linens, cottons, . . . or any other species of goods capable of being printed, by a much cheaper method than any hitherto found out." Bell's cylindrical method, with improvements made by Adam Parkinson and others, rapidly encroached, in the north, on the older devices, and furnished the mechanical basis for some of the largest and most highly organized factories of the time.   The same mechanical principle was utilized later in the development of the modern printing press.[20]

The cotton industry was confined to limited areas and to relatively few forms.   The manufacture of wool, in contrast, was carried on to some extent, and in one form or another, in nearly every part of the country.   Difficult as it is to trace the course of the transition in the manufacture of cotton, it is much more difficult to do so in connection with the woollen industry.   But there is at least one fact which stands out in clear relief:—the transition in the manufacture of woollens was neither so rapid nor so uniform as in the cotton industry.   From Yorkshire came reports as early as 1786 of "those curious models of Arkwright's machines" being "worked to such an advantage on their woollens in Yorkshire."   Four years later a writer in Anglesea described the survival of primitive methods there.   "Almost every farmer combs, cards, and spins his own wool, and sends it to the

[20] *Min. of the Evidence, Com. of H. of C.*, 1785 (on Irish Resolutions), 44; Woodcroft, *Titles of Patents of Inventions*, I, 265; Aikin, *Description of the Country Round Manchester*, 268; *Calico Printer's Assistant*, Retrospect, n. 10 (not paged); Baines, *History of the Cotton Manufacture*, 262-266.

weaver. . . . I believe that no improvement has been made in the machines used here for wool since the days of Adam." Such are the contrasts and inconsistencies constantly encountered in the study of the transition in the woollen industry.[21]

But it is not necessary to go to an out-of-the-way place such as Anglesea for evidence of conservatism in respect to either the instruments or the organization of the industry. A characteristic incident occurred in a committee of the House of Lords in 1785, when a woollen manufacturer of Hampshire was being questioned in connection with Irish affairs. He stated that Irish yarn was cheaper than English yarn, yet insisted that Hampshire manufacturers used only English yarn. Being pressed for reasons, he was at length forced to explain that "it never was used by our forefathers." As late as 1782, it was declared that "not a single weaver in the Norwich trade understands the use of the fly shuttle." From the last decade of the century came numerous reports of the uninterrupted use of the spinning wheel, of premiums offered for improvements in the wheel, and of spinning schools for training in operating it.[22]

The inert and torpid nature of the woollen industry was repeatedly described and criticized by Arthur Young with characteristic vigor. "Examine the trade and you

[21] *Board of Trade Papers,* 6/111, Doc. 39; *Annals of Agriculture,* XIV, 408. For brief studies of the transition in the woollen industry, see Mantoux, *La Révoiution Industrielle,* 259-269; Cunningham, *Growth of English Industry and Commerce,* II, Pt. II, 642-668. Heaton, *Yorkshire Woollen and Worsted Industries,* though mainly concerned with earlier history, contains information on early phases of the transition.

[22] *Min. of the Evidence, Com. H. of L.,* 1785 (on Irish Resolutions), 287, 288; *Memoirs,* Manchester Lit. and Phil. Soc., I, 84; *Annals of Agriculture,* XX, 179, 182, 411; *Letter to Sir T. C. Bunbury,* 16; Marshall, *Review of Reports from the Eastern Department,* 615, 616; Marshall, *Review of Reports from the Midland Department,* 244, 407, 408; *Transactions,* Society of Arts, XI, 152, XIII, 233; *Reports,* Society for Bettering the Condition of the Poor, I, 213-225.

will look in vain for that ardor of enterprise, that activity of pursuit, that spirit of invention, which have so nobly distinguished the efforts of British industry when exerted on iron, cotton, porcelain, glass, etc. All is sluggish, inactive, dead." But in his general criticism there was a notable exception—the industry as carried on in Yorkshire. With his view of Yorkshire various other observers concurred.[23]

A carding machine capable of saving 75% of labor costs came into general use in Yorkshire as well as in certain other regions; and Yorkshire seems to have led the way in the adoption of machines in other preliminary processes.[24] The spinning jenny made its way in the Yorkshire woollen industry less rapidly to be sure than in cotton manufacturing, but much more rapidly than in most of the other woollen centers. By the time the more conservative woollen manufacturers were being forced by competition to consider the adoption of the jenny, the Yorkshire industry was entering upon the much more significant transition from wheel and jenny spinning in cottages to power spinning in factories involving administrative and social reorganization as well as technical change.

As early as 1786, Yorkshire woollens were being spun with great advantage by means of Arkwright's machinery. Two years later the innovation was reported by Arthur Young as so promising that "it is also in contemplation to weave by machinery." In 1789 Boulton and Watt reported that they were erecting "two pretty large engines" for spinning wool at Leeds. In 1791 a great many spinning mills were reported in the *Annals of Agriculture* as having been established, and "no less

[23] *Annals of Agriculture*, VII, 162-164, IX, 360-364, 369, 502, 503; Wansey, *Wool Encouraged without Exportation*, 49, 69; *Observations on a Bill Relating to Wool*, Preface (by Sir Joseph Banks), v.

[24] Cunningham, *Growth of English Industry and Commerce*, II, Pt. II, 650.

than seventy additional machines are now setting up in the neighborhood of Leeds, Bradford, and Huddersfield." A report from Somerset to the Board of Agriculture in 1794, deploring the backwardness of the woollen industry in that region, stated that Yorkshire and "north country" manufacturers "are beforehand . . . particularly in the application of water, the best *primum mobile* of all machinery." From Yorkshire itself came a report to the Board in the same year of a new type of industrial organization as well as of technical method—of establishments where "the whole progress is carried on, from buying the wool to finishing the goods." We are not able to measure accurately the progress of the new system, but it was seriously encroaching upon the old. In 1794, for instance, West Riding petty manufacturers petitioned parliament to put a stop to its advance. They said that the manufacturing of cloth had long been carried on "with a very trifling capital, and by the unremitting labor of themselves, their wives and children, united under one roof." This system, which "has so happily long prevailed in Yorkshire, is now in danger of being broken up and destroyed" by a system "supported by great capitals" and carried on in "large factories." Complaint is made that many have already established such plants, particularly in Leeds and Halifax, and that others propose to follow their example.[25]

But the separation of Yorkshire from neighboring shires in studying the transition means an exaggerated emphasis upon county boundaries. The woollen manufacturers of the "north country" generally had the same

[25] *Board of Trade Papers*, 6/111, Doc. 39; *Annals of Agriculture*, IX, 370, XVI, 422; Boulton and Watt MSS., *Letter Book (Office)*, 1788-1790, 98, 99; Billingsley, *General View of the Agriculture of Somerset*, 57, 91; Rennie, Broun, and Sheriff, *General View of the Agriculture of the West Riding of Yorkshire*, 120; Commons *Journals*, XLIX, 276, 277, 431, 432.

incentives for progress—the example set by the neighboring cotton manufacturers and the stimulus of competition with machine-made fabrics. Various men of influence advocated the general extension of mechanical methods to the woollen industry as a "subject of the first magnitude." [26] Lancashire woollen manufacturers, as might naturally be expected, early turned their attention to the new methods; and it was soon reported that "a great number of factories are erected . . . for carding and spinning both cotton and sheep's wool." One of these was "a large factory six stories high and a steam engine, with dye houses, and other extensive buildings, for the woollen business." [27] An opponent of innovation in Leicestershire complained as early as 1788 that "spinning mills are now setting up all around us" for spinning wool "after the model of the cotton mills." It was stated that mills put up for spinning cotton were being turned into woollen mills, and "new ones are daily erecting" for the woollen business.[28] Within five miles of Darlington in the county of Durham there were in 1789 three water mills for spinning hemp and flax as well as wool, and several similar mills were said to be in operation in that region.[29] In 1792 a factory near Mansfield in Nottinghamshire was destroyed by fire with a loss of £18,000. During the early years of the last decade of the century, several woollen mills were in operation in that county. Indeed, as early as 1788, Arthur Young described a Nottinghamshire "mill for spinning wool, . . . not jennies, but a machinery in the nature of the cotton mills,"

[26] See for instance Wedgwood's reference to conference between Arkwright and Sir Joseph Banks in 1785: *Corresp. of Josiah Wedgwood,* 35.

[27] Aikin, *Description of the Country Round Manchester,* 267, 299, 300. See also Taylor, *Modern Factory System,* 72.

[28] *Humble Petition of the Poor Spinners.* (See below, bibliography, p. 322.)

[29] Anderson, *Historical Origin of Commerce,* IV, 709 (ed. 1789).

and added that "a revolution is making" in the woollen industry.[30]

While Yorkshire and some of the neighboring counties were introducing power machinery and going through the early stages of the factory system in the woollen industry, many other regions were adopting the spinning jenny. The contemporaneous accounts that have come down to us fail in some cases to distinguish the jenny from the mule and even from the water frame.[31] In some places, as we have seen, the spinning wheel maintained undisputed sway. But in the principal woollen centers outside of the Yorkshire region, the early years of the last decade of the century were marked by the rapid introduction of the hand jenny. The situation is described by a rimester in 1791, who put his views into the mouth of a "spinster"— a girl who had been accustomed to augment the family income by wheel spinning, and who was made to complain that "now the jennies take all work away."[32] The old system of domestic industry by which the wife and the children of farm workers were expected to supplement the wages derived from farm labor was supported by landlords and farmers as a means of reducing their labor costs. The new methods of manufacturing vitally affected, therefore, the prevailing rural economy. It is because of this fact that much valuable information concerning the transition is to be found in the *Annals of Agriculture*,[33] and in the reports from the various

[30] *Annual Register*, 1792, 47 (Chron.); Lowe, *General View of the Agriculture of the County of Nottingham*, 126; Anderson, *Historical Origin of Commerce*, IV, 709 (ed. 1789); *Annals of Agriculture*, X, 281.

[31] For instance, there is a confusion of terms, not always so obvious, however, when Fullarton in his *General View of the Agriculture of Ayr* (79, 80) writes of "spinning jennies" being "moved by horses where water could not be procured."

[32] *The Discarded Spinster*, 20.

[33] The question had become a serious one with employers of farm labor by 1788, as indicated by a series of inquiries sent out by the editor (Arthur Young) in that year, and by the replies thereto.

counties to the Board of Agriculture, immediately after its organization in 1793.

We are not entirely without evidence of the beginnings of factory organization due to machinery in some of the more conservative centers. One Richard March testified in 1785 before a committee of the House of Lords that he and his partners had spent £26,000 on an establishment for spinning wool near Barnstaple in Devonshire. A clothier "opened a spinning house" in 1788 at Pucklechurch in Gloucestershire. In Wiltshire in 1794 the landlords were said to be suffering from the loss of spinning to supplement the wages of their employees because of the use of "machines to supply the place of manual labor whereby all those parts of the manufactory that have hitherto been done in the country villages will be done at the immediate residence of the manufacturers." A mill for carding and spinning was put up in North Wales in 1794, and in the same year a similar establishment was erected by means of local subscriptions in northwestern Scotland.[34]

In woollen manufacturing, household industry was exceptionally important. It is necessary to keep clearly in mind the difference between manufacturing carried on in the home for family needs and for exchange among neighbors on the one hand, and so-called "public" manufacturing to supply general market demands on the other hand. The former is described by a Scottish correspondent of the *Annals of Agriculture* in 1788: "There is no public manufacture in this part of the country for wool, but a considerable domestic one, as all over Scotland; every housewife and family spins; has the yarn wove, dyed, etc., at her own expense; having clothed her fam-

[34] *Min. of the Evidence, Com. of H. of L.*, 1785 (on Irish Resolutions), 85; *Annals of Agriculture*, IX, 298, 299, XV, 497; Davis, *General View of the Agriculture of Wilts*, 158, 159; Kay, *General View of the Agriculture of North Wales* (Montgomeryshire), 22; Robson, *General View of the Agriculture of Argyll*, 23.

ily, she sells the overplus." [35]   In many places this system, involving the use of the wheel, long outlived the century.   It is true, also, that wheel spinning continued beyond the turn of the century to furnish a small portion of the supply of yarn used by the professional clothiers in the regular markets.   But the available information, though inadequate, indicates that even as early as 1793, when war-time conditions inaugurated a new period, the principal supplies of woollen goods on the market were being made by the use of power-spun and jenny-spun yarns, the former mainly in the Yorkshire region, the latter more largely in the older centers.

There had been only a slight application of steam power to the textile industries by 1793, but the characteristic aspects of modern industrial organization resulted from the use of water power no less than of steam power. The utility of the steam engine, it is true, was rapidly being demonstrated, and the development of industrial plants away from water-power sites was already under way.   Steam engines were in such common use at Manchester as early as 1786 as to cause Dr. Percival, a prominent physician of Manchester, to correspond with James Watt concerning methods of abating the smoke nuisance.[36]   Its adaptability to an "almost incredible" variety of uses was soon recognized, and prophecy was made as early as 1787 that it would change "the appearance of the civilized world." [37]   But during the epochal eighteenth-century transformation of the textile industries, its effect on industrial reorganization was slight.

During the transition in the textile industries there was

[35] Vol. X, p. 559.

[36] Boulton and Watt MSS., *Letter Book* (*Office*), 1786-1788, 109, 110.

[37] *European Magazine*, XI, 364, 367; *Companion to the Leasowes, to Which is Prefixed the Present State of Birmingham*, 14, 15; Aikin, *Description of the Country Round Manchester*, 176, 177; *Memoirs*, Manchester Lit. and Phil. Soc., I, 79.

going on in coal mining and metal manufacturing a series
of changes analogous to those in the making of cloth.
Textile manufacturing, especially the carding, spinning
and printing of cotton, assumed the essential features of
the nineteenth-century factory system long before the
revolution in coal and iron had brought about the general
use of steam power and the more extensive use of metals
in the manufacture of machinery. The transformation
in coal mining and iron manufacturing brought about a
vast expansion of these industries in the eighteenth century, but their significance in relation to other branches
of economic life was not so vital as in the nineteenth
century, when not only the textile industries but practically all other manufactures, and transportation as well,
became vitally dependent upon steam power and upon
new methods of smelting and molding iron and making machinery. In considering the eighteenth-century
changes in the iron industry, one should remember, too,
that the accompanying reorganization of economic
groups was slighter than in the textile industries, for the
relatively large iron works had for a long time more
nearly resembled the factory system than had the small-
shop and household organization of textile manufacturing. And yet, in comparison with earlier changes, the
transformation even in the iron industry was rapid, even
revolutionary, in its social effects as well as in its technique. The adoption of the new methods and devices
(coke-burning furnaces, power blast, Huntsman's steel-
casting process, rolling and puddling) enabled the British
iron industry, which had long been declining, to revive
and rise rapidly to a position of independence and
superiority. These changes, together with the devising
of machine tools such as the lathe, made possible the
rapid nineteenth-century advances in mechanical methods throughout the machine-using world of industry and
transportation; and they contributed significantly, dur-

ing the closing decades of the eighteenth century, to the reorganization of economic society.[38]

Unlike the changes in iron and coal, the contemporaneous transformation of pottery making had no vital connection with other industries. Its main distinctive contribution was in developing the artistic side of manufacturing; and its esthetic influence on other industries was negligible. But pottery making was of great importance in itself: by means of improved processes and formulas it developed into a leading branch of English industry; and its rise involved a reorganization of economic society characteristic of modern large-scale enterprises. In technical progress, in volume of business, in concentration of capital and labor, and in the newly acquired wealth and influence of its leading representatives, it became one of the three principal modern-type manufacturing industries which emerged immediately out of the era of invention. Though intrinsically less important than either of the other two,—the cotton and the iron and ironwares industries,—pottery making, on account largely of the active genius of Josiah Wedgwood, acquired at times an equal and even a superior influence.

In each of these groups of industries,—cottons, iron and ironwares, pottery,—the new technique and organization gained ascendancy by the time of the wars with the French revolutionists; and by virtue of their new methods, these industries by that time acquired a dominating, decisive influence in the industrial life of the country. The superiority of the new system was so obvious, and the position of these transformed industries was so commanding, that the rapid transition from the old to the new in other branches of industry was assured. The decisive period, therefore, in the revolutionizing of industry, was the generation preceding the French wars.

[38] See below, pp. 98-100.

3. The creative powers of the new technique

In seeking the causes of interest in mechanical improvements, we found that new methods of production were needed because old methods were failing to produce enough goods to meet increasing demands. The new instruments of production, when devised, became the means not only of increasing the supply of consumption goods but of controlling the fluid wealth of the country, of attracting it through various channels into the regions and industries where improved methods were in vogue, and of converting it in large part into industrial capital. As the end of the century drew near, the triumph of the machine became more and more apparent in the shifting of capital and also of energy and population into the newer industrial centers. Among these centers the most prominent were Birmingham, the Staffordshire potteries, and Manchester with its satellite towns. But there should also be included the forges and foundries particularly of Shropshire, the more progressive woollen manufacturing towns of Yorkshire, the cotton industries of Glasgow and Paisley, the port of Liverpool, and midland and north-country collieries.

There was a certain tendency, it is true, for capital to flow into these regions, particularly the cloth-making centers of Lancashire and the West Riding of Yorkshire, long before the era of invention. There was also in the north a readier flow of capital from industry to industry than in the country generally. This was due in part to the relative freedom of these regions from monopolistic restrictions such as were generally imposed by the chartered towns, the gilds, and the commercial companies.[39] By the time of the transition from primitive to modern

---

[39] This point of view is emphasized by Professor Unwin in his Introduction to Daniels' *Early English Cotton Industry.* See also above, pp. 55-57.

methods of production in the midlands and the north, the removal of restrictions on the flow of capital had become more general throughout the country, and conditions therefore were favorable for the unprecedented mobility of capital when subjected to the attractive forces of the technical innovations in those regions.

Manufactures "are leaving the southern counties and traveling to the north," wrote Joseph Townsend in 1786; and his observation was confirmed by many of his contemporaries, but by none more vividly than by Arthur Young, who stated in 1793 that "all the activity and industry in this kingdom is fast concentrating" in the northern industrial regions, and that the whole kingdom is seeking "as immediate a connection with coals and manufactures, by means of inland navigation, as possible." [40]

The wealth and energy already in those regions, but previously devoted largely to agriculture, were now, by "the prospect of a quicker return and greater gain," diverted in considerable part into industrial enterprises. It was asserted in 1792 that in the Lancashire region "the whole stock of hands, money, and intellectual abilities (in all of which powers this part of the country does greatly abound) are employed in working up iron, flax, hemp, and cotton, and in the matters immediately connected with them; and only the dregs and inefficient scraps are employed on the lands." Even more emphatic was the testimony of the Board of Agriculture reporter who collected data for Lancashire in 1793. He complained that "capital, labor, ingenuity, and attention are in this country diverted from agriculture. . . . Never inquire about the cultivation of land or its produce within

[40] Townsend, *Dissertation on the Poor Laws*, 31; *Annals of Agriculture*, XVI, 552. See also the statement by Lord Sheffield, 1791, in *Parl. Hist.*, XXVIII, 1380; Hutton, *Considerations on Coal and Culm*, 33; *Annals of Agriculture*, IX, 524, 525; Baines, *History of the Cotton Manufacture*, 262.

ten or twelve miles of Manchester; the people know nothing about it: speak of spinning jennies, and mules, and carding machines, they will talk for days with you." Similar observations were made by various men in respect to the neighboring counties, the industrial regions of the midlands, and the valley of the Clyde.[41]

Technical improvements in the newly developing industries of these regions served as magnets to attract not only capital but population as well. In the controversies preceding the first census of 1801 concerning the question as to whether population was increasing or declining, there seems to have been common agreement that there had been a rapid increase in the population of the northern industrial centers. Even Dr. Price in his famous *Essay on the Population of England,* in which he tried to prove that population was decreasing, conceded that there had been "a great increase of people as well as of houses" in the industrial centers, the increase having been "derived from the population of country parishes and villages." It is "allowed on all hands," wrote one of Dr. Price's critics, "that the principal manufacturing and trading towns have increased, and some of them, as Manchester, Leeds, Birmingham, Sheffield, Liverpool, and Bristol, most amazingly." Another of Dr. Price's critics wrote concerning "the north, that most growing and populous part of our community," as having had a recent increase in numbers so rapid as to be "altogether astonishing," "amazing," "unparalleled." [42]

Aside from the increase by excess of births over deaths,

[41] J. H. Campbell, in *Annals of Agriculture,* XX, 123; Holt, *General View of the Agriculture of the County of Lancaster,* 12 (ed. 1794), 210, 211 (ed. 1795); Brown, *General View,* Derbyshire, 13; Wedge, *General View,* Cheshire, 71, 72; Naismith, *General View,* Clydesdale, 79; Martin, *General View,* Renfrewshire, 20; *Annals of Agriculture,* VII, 463, 464.

[42] Price, *Essay on the Population of England,* 27; Wales, *Inquiry into the Present State of Population,* 5; Howlett, *Examination of Dr. Price's Essay,* 129, 132, 151, 153.

there were several important sources from which the northern industrial centers drew their population. Large numbers were attracted from the surrounding agricultural regions. Workers in the cotton industries were disdainfully described as "herds of Lancashire boors" who had come from neighboring farms. There was very general complaint by farmers and landlords that farm laborers, especially those of the more efficient types, were being drawn into industrial pursuits.[43]

But large numbers came from regions more remote from the factories, the foundries, and the mines, and their coming was often due to expulsive forces in their old homes as well as to the attractive forces of the new industrialism. In the south of England, two economic phenomena,—agricultural enclosures and declining industries,—while radically different in nature, were nevertheless producing the same result, namely, a decrease of economic opportunity for the workers. The consequent natural northward trend of population was stimulated by handbills and advertisements calling attention in southern counties to northern opportunities. But in general there seems to have been little occasion for such methods of promoting the shifting of workers. Officials in the growing industrial centers often became alarmed, in fact, by the rapid influx of laborers, and because of their fear of increasing poor rates they even made attempts, especially by means of the settlement acts, to check the flow from the vast reservoirs of unemployed in other regions.[44]

North of the industrial regions, particularly in Scotland, conditions were the reverse of those in the south of

[43] *Calico Printer's Assistant,* Retrospect, n. 11 (not paged); Wedge, *General View,* Cheshire, 26. See also below, p. 253. ff.

[44] Davis, *General View of the Agriculture of Wilts,* 87, 88; *Historical and Political Remarks upon the Tariff of the Commercial Treaty* (1786), 167, 168; [Mackenzie], *Woollen Draper's Letter,* 27, 28; *Annals of Agriculture,* IX, 660, X, 280, 281. See also below, ch. IV, pp. 240, 259 and *passim.*

England, in important respects, and yet similar in promoting emigration. Relatively unacquainted with the arts long cultivated in the south, and knowing little save the harshest of labor for the most frugal subsistence, the people of the Highlands and the far north saw to the south of them undreamed-of opportunities suddenly springing into being. Therefore, "multitudes left the country, the abode of poverty, and fled to the town, the fountain of riches." More highly favored by nature but cursed by centuries of feuds with alien intruders, Ireland had long been increasing in numbers while declining in prosperity. Destitute of everything save the barest subsistence, thousands of Irishmen were eager then as in other ages to escape from the misfortunes of their native land. Many went to the south of England for casual labor there, often drifting north as vagrants. But most of the immigrants seem to have reached the larger island by way of Galloway, conveniently located between the industrial regions of northern England and southern Scotland. It is said that an advertisement would "bring over hundreds of them in a few days" to the adjacent Galloway coast for distribution wherever workers were in demand, particularly to replace native Scotch and English farm laborers who had been drawn into industrial life. Discharged from casual farm work for which they had been brought over, or lured by prospects of better opportunities in manufactures or mining, thousands of migratory Irish laborers passed to and fro through the industrial regions. Many of them were herded together by the magistrates and shipped in overloaded vessels back to Ireland. But large numbers, making places for themselves, fused at length with the other varied elements of the population.[45]

[45] Roger, *General View*, Angus or Farfar, 23, 24; Webster, *General View*, Galloway, 15, 16; *Report of the Committee of the Magistrates of the Counties of Chester and Lancaster on Vagrants in the Said Counties.* See also below, p. 256.

The movement of population, energy, and productive wealth into the new industrial centers was an impressive phenomenon when observed in general outline. But the nature and significance of the movement can best be appreciated when studied in relation to particular industries and regions. External capital and energy and man power, rapidly flowing in and combining with local resources for the utilization of the unprecedented technical improvements—these forces united to create new wealth with marvelous rapidity. The new wealth in turn gave added stimulus to the original creative impulses. And thus industries expanded, waste places became towns, villages grew into cities, wealth begot power, and the deceptive calm of the surface strata concealed an epochal social upheaval. It is this movement, small in its beginnings, and confined at first to a few centers in the British Isles, which has rapidly enlarged the area of its operations and the momentum of its progress till it has divided the world into industrialized and unindustrialized regions and put the latter into bondage of tribute to the former.

The latent power of industrialism was not without its heralds and interpreters in the beginning of the movement. Englishmen were told, by a poet, as early as 1765, that since they possessed iron and the arts necessary for its utilization, they need not envy Golconda's sparkling mines, nor the splendid barbarity of Montezuma's palaces, though roofed with gold.

> Thankful ply
> Your iron arts, and all the world is yours.[46]

The poetic prophecy found early fulfillment, for England's "iron arts" soon played a vital rôle in the acquisition and maintenance of world power. The principal

[46] Richard Jago, *Edge-Hill: a Poem*, published in part in *Annual Register*, 1767, 2d part, 232-238. The entire poem, in revised form, is in R. Anderson's *British Poets*, XI, 679-702.

center of the iron industry was the "Black Country" extending northwest from Birmingham. This region as it was being rapidly developed in 1787 was then described as "a figure of 200 square miles . . . having the town of Dudley near its center"; and its industrial population and activities had been so rapidly increasing, due to a "great era of improvement," that not more than one-sixth of its population was being supported by agriculture.[47] Not far from Dudley were some of the forges of John Wilkinson, the "iron-mad" prophet and innovator, who even ordered an iron coffin for his burial. It was in this region that most of the coke-burning, power-blast furnaces were located. To the west, along the River Severn, were the famous forges of Coalbrookdale, where coke-burning furnaces were first successfully constructed.[48]

Birmingham, on the southeastern border of the "Black Country," was believed in 1790 to have built 8,000 of its 12,000 houses during the preceding thirty years, and the vestry clerk of the city reported that most of the occupiers of new houses were "poor persons with large families who came into town from other parishes." The city was described in 1783 as a "seat of invention" which was undergoing an "astonishing increase" because of the prevalent ingenuity and skill. "The traveller who visits her once in six months supposes himself well acquainted with her; but he may chance to find a street of houses in the autumn where he saw his horse at grass in the spring." [49] "I have trained up many," said Matthew Boulton as early as 1770, "and am training up more plain country lads into good workmen." Most of these "plain country lads" probably came from neighboring regions; but one at least,—whose history we know because of the

[47] *Annals of Agriculture*, VII, 463.

[48] Important comparative figures of the extent and distribution of the iron industry at different periods are conveniently available in Scrivenor's *History of the Iron Trade*, 86-88 (ed. 1854).

[49] Langford, *Century of Birmingham Life*, I, 297, 444, ff.

name he made for himself in association with Boulton and Watt,—one at least came from far-away Scotland, William Murdoch, whose story Samuel Smiles has recorded with characteristic *naïveté*.[50] The energy and activity concentrated at Birmingham gave rise under the direction of Boulton and Watt to the world-famed Soho plant.[51] It was described by a writer in 1789 as "one of the most extensive manufactories in the kingdom. It consists of four squares with connecting ranges, or rather streets of shopping, warehouses, etc., capable of employing above a thousand workmen. . . . Here the artist avails himself of every aid of mechanism . . . to accelerate his various works." It was here that the mind of Watt and the wealth of Boulton added their united contribution to the development of probably the most important single mechanism in history—the steam engine.[52]

Not many miles north of the "Black Country" was the group of towns known as the Potteries, in the region about Newcastle-under-Lyme. The manufacture of pottery in this region had extended back to early times, but the methods had been primitive and the extent of the industry small. Burslem, the "mother of the potteries," was until past mid-century an insignificant village; Etruria was "a desert waste." It was the work of Josiah Wedgwood and his contemporaries, during the period of expansion in iron and textile industries, to convert "a rude and inconsiderable manufacture into an elegant art and an important part of national commerce." [53]

[50] Fox Bourne, *Romance of Trade*, 238; Smiles, *Men of Invention and Industry*, ch. 5.

[51] The original site was about two miles from the city of that time, being located in Handsworth Parish, Staffordshire.

[52] *Companion to the Leasowes, to Which is Prefixed the Present State of Birmingham*, 14; Langford, *Century of Birmingham Life*, II, 145-157.

[53] From memorial tablet to Wedgwood in St. Peter's church, Stoke-upon-Trent, quoted by Jewitt, *The Wedgwoods*, 360.

The potters, led by Wedgwood, early recognized the fact that as long as pack horses, or even horse-drawn vehicles, remained the principal mode of transportation, the weight of the raw materials and the bulk and fragile character of the products of the industry would interpose a peculiar obstacle to its expansion. But this obstacle was in large measure removed by the construction of the Grand Trunk Canal, 1766-1777, between the navigable waters of the Mersey and the Trent, connecting the potteries with the rapidly developing network of canals in the north and the midlands. Wedgwood estimated that one horse could draw as many tons on the canal as forty could draw on land; and naturally, in the case of such a commodity as pottery, there was less danger of damage *en route*.[54]

But the canal itself was not the primary cause of expansion; it was the result of industrial growth and ambition, and it merely meant an opportunity for the more extensive exploitation of the natural resources of the region, and a more adequate utilization of the innumerable technical improvements that were being made in the various processes of pottery making. At the time of Wedgwood's death in 1795 it was said of him that "his inventions have prodigiously increased the number of persons employed in the potteries, and in the traffic and transport of their materials from distant parts of the kingdom: and this class of manufacturers is also indebted to him for much mechanical contrivance and arrangement in their operations; his private manufactory having had, for thirty years and upwards, all the efficacy of a public work of experiment." This unusual praise was in a measure justified by the fact that among his numerous inventions and improvements, one only was patented, and it was of minor importance. The transformation of

[54] Jewitt, *The Wedgwoods*, 167-176, 298; Aikin, *Description of the Country Round Manchester*, 117-123.

the region by the attracting of people, energy, and capital,—a process with which he was connected more prominently than any other individual,—was once pictured by Wedgwood himself. He recalled the time when the "houses were miserable huts; the lands poorly cultivated, and yielded little of value for the food of man or beast; and these disadvantages, with roads almost impassable, might be said to have cut off our part of the country from the rest of the word, besides rendering it not very comfortable to ourselves." He then in contrast showed how the present state of the country bore "evident marks of the most pleasing and rapid improvements,"—wages doubled; houses new and comfortable; lands, roads, and the entire face of the country transformed, by industry, till the region attracts the "notice and admiration of countries which had scarcely heard of us before." Wedgwood in this connection was trying to allay the discontent of the workers in the potteries in 1783, resulting from scarcity and high prices attending the American Revolution. Men as admirable and as veracious as the great potter have been known to give exaggerated evidence in order to win their point, but in this case the evidence of remarkable industrial expansion, if not of social betterment, is incontestable.[55]

The Staffordshire potteries, the iron centers, and the city of Birmingham thus became important nuclei of economic life and growth. But as compared with the cotton manufacturing centers, they were of slow development, and their expansion depended on the abundance of iron, limestone, coal, and potter's clay, as well as on mechanical improvements. As for the woollen manufacturers, even those of Yorkshire who were progressive

[55] Jewitt, *The Wedgwoods*, 358-362, and *passim* (quoting contemporaneous records); Wedgwood, *Address to the Young Inhabitants of the Potteries.* See also the lives of Wedgwood by Meteyard and Julia Wedgwood, and the account of the potteries in Aikin's *Description of the Country Round Manchester*, 516-537.

enough to copy the machines used in cotton manufacturing depended on monopoly of raw materials and of home markets, as well as on machines, for their advancement. Liverpool was merely a commercial metropolis, growing or declining with the industry of the hinterland. The cotton manufacturing centers, on the other hand, were in a different position. The cotton industry was in the first place dependent on commodities produced abroad. It not only attracted capital and energy and population from various parts of the British Isles, but from the first it put distant regions under tribute for its raw materials. Furthermore, the adoption of machinery was more rapid and complete than elsewhere. In a sense which differentiates it from other branches of commerce and manufacturing, the cotton industry was very largely the creation of machines.

This contrast was magnanimously drawn by Josiah Wedgwood the potter. In reply to a letter of inquiry from Lord Auckland in 1792, he estimated that the pottery industry had increased in value twenty-five fold in eighty years. As for ironwares, the idea of making an estimate "makes my head giddy," he wrote. "I feel it just as impossible . . . as to number the sands on the seashore. The difficulties are nearly equal with respect to the cotton trade; with this difference, indeed, that one must here shoot flying, for this darts forward with such an amazing rate as to leave all the others far behind. This business is supposed to have increased with ten times the celerity of any other; owing chiefly to the machinery invented by that truly great man, Sir Richard Arkwright." [56]

It was the cotton industry—the rapidity of its expansion, its extent, and its mechanical basis—that called forth most of the superlative expressions used in connection with the transition. It is generally believed, stated

[56] *Corresp. of Josiah Wedgwood,* 188-194.

the widely quoted author of the pamphlet entitled *An Important Crisis in the Calico and Muslin Manufactory of Great Britain Explained,* that cotton manufacturing has become very extensive and is of great value, but "the national advantages derived from such a combination of human labor with ingenious machinery can scarce be supposed to have made an impression equal to the importance of the object; because the progress has been rapid beyond example. It has burst forth, as it were, upon the country in a moment, giving a spring at the same time to the industry of the people unexampled in the annals of the world." The elaborate statistics which the author gives as to the extent of growth in the cotton industry are obviously inaccurate. Accuracy as to these details was probably then, and is certainly now, impossible. But the main outlines of development were clearly observable: the substitution of "mechanical for human power," by improving production, "has expanded the villages of Lancashire [observed another writer of the time] into towns next to the metropolis." [57]

The significance of the inventions in the transformation of Manchester and the surrounding region was not at first apparent, but became a subject of frequent comment and marvel. Typical of the change is the contrast between the accounts in the second edition of the *Encyclopædia Britannica* and those in the third edition. The article on Lancashire in the second edition, published as late as 1780, mentioned in detail the streams of the county, saying that the region was thoroughly watered, but aside from this the only significance assigned to the

[57] *Annals of Agriculture,* IX, 534, 535. Concerning the pamphlet quoted, see above, pp. 77, 78, and below, bibliography. The statistics contained in this booklet were quoted, usually without reference to the source, by a large number of writers. See *Encyclopædia Britannica,* 3d ed., V, Art. "Cotton"; *Annals of Agriculture,* XII, 513-520; and Aikin, *Description of the Country Round Manchester,* 178-181 (where reference is made to the source).

streams was that one of them was "noted for producing the fattest eels in England." The article on Manchester made no mention of inventions, and merely stated that the town was prosperous and had several curious manufactures known at London by the name of "Manchester goods." The similar articles in the third edition were written about ten years later. In the article on Lancashire in the third edition, there was a description of the industrial processes going on along the rivers and canals of the region. The article on Manchester gave a detailed picture of the growth of the city in wealth, industry, and population. The writer estimated that the city's population had trebled in fifty years, the immediately preceding years in particular having witnessed the building of innumerable houses, in spite of which there was serious congestion. The city had been remodeled, and the new streets were described as "spacious and airy"; two thousand streets lamps had been installed, and nearly two hundred watchmen were employed by the city. Among its total estimated population of 68,580, about twenty thousand were supposed to be employed in the factories connected with the cotton industry. The remarkable growth of the city is specifically credited to "the happy concurrence of ingenuity and industry" and "the astonishing improvements daily making in its numerous manufactures."

The city had been prosperous for some time, but the phenomenal growth attended the introduction of the new technique of industry. "Cart and boatloads of people of both sexes and all ages" are described as pouring into the city. "The town extended on every side," wrote one of Manchester's intellectual leaders, Thomas Henry, "and such was the influx of inhabitants that though great numbers of new houses were built, they were occupied even before they were finished." It is said that among the floods of immigrants, five thousand Irishmen had settled at Manchester by 1787, the number rapidly increasing thereafter.[58]

The rapidity of growth is evidenced by records of christenings, marriages, and burials. The average number of christenings recorded during the years 1765 to 1767 was 900, as compared with an average of 1,838 during the years 1783 to 1785. For the same sets of years, the number of marriages recorded diverged even more—367 was the average during the earlier period in contrast with 807 during the later period. Burial records, though not so divergent, confirm the conclusion to be drawn from christenings and marriages: the average for the earlier period was 811, and for the later, 1,468.[59] Significant evidence is to be found, also, in the city directories published during the period of transition. The number of names of "principal inhabitants" (such alone being included) was in 1773, 1,530; in 1781, 1,920; in 1788, 2,580; and in 1794, 5,544. The increases are significant, despite probable variations in the proportion of "principal inhabitants" to the total population. The expansion of the city in wealth and enterprise no less than in population is portrayed by the increase of thoroughfares. The number included in the directory of 1773 was 167; of 1781, 197; of 1788, 260; and of 1794, about 600. The number given for 1794 followed an extensive remodeling of the city, and the statement is made that sixty-one of the streets had been "laid out but not built upon." [60]

Such evidence seems to justify the description of Manchester in 1791 as a city "doubled in its size the last

[58] Dr. Percival in *Philosophical Transactions*, LXVI, 167; Thomas Henry, in *Memoirs*, Manchester Lit. and Phil. Soc., III, 160; Holt, *General View of the Agriculture of the County of Lancaster*, 213 (ed. 1795).

[59] *Memoirs*, Manchester Lit. and Phil. Soc., III, 163-167 (vital statistics compiled by Thomas Henry, F.R.S.).

[60] Raffald's *Directory*, 1773, 1781; Holme's *Directory*, 1788; Schole's *Directory*, 1794. See also Harland, *Collectanea Relating to Manchester*, I, 119-154.

thirty years—more than doubled in the number of its inhabitants—and enriched by the cotton manufactory beyond the powers of calculation." This prosperity found expression in "handsome country houses on every hill [about the city], elegantly furnished, and surrounded by as elegant pleasure grounds—and a great part of the old town pulled down to make room for spacious and ornamental mansions. These"—continued the writer with waxing enthusiasm—"these are thy blessings, O Commerce! these are thy rewards, O Industry!" The writer was a tourist, and his enthusiasm is pardonable. It is apparent that he essayed no revolution in the time-honored habits of tourists. If he had escaped from the show-places of the city long enough to explore the attics and cellars of the crowded hovels as they were being flooded by the incoming tides of workers, perhaps he would have modified his judgment concerning the blessings and rewards of industry and commerce. The organized cotton spinners, in their printed rules of 1792, viewed the further influx of workers with less optimism, and in self-defense were even in favor of measures for limiting immigration.[61]

Meager as was the portion of prosperity enjoyed by the recently arrived workers at Manchester, their condition was probably better than before they reached the city.[62] But in any case, the effect of mechanical power in the enlargement and enrichment of the northern industrial metropolis was justly viewed by the people of the time as most remarkable. But it was not merely a city that was transformed: it was an extensive region. "The center we have chosen [for description]," wrote Dr. Aikin, "is that of the cotton manufacture"; and in carrying out his purpose he fittingly chose as the title

---

[61] *European Magazine*, XX, 216; *Articles of Agreement of the Friendly Associated Cotton Spinners* (Manchester, 1792), 2, 9.

[62] The subject here suggested is discussed below (ch. IV).

of his invaluable work published in 1795, *A Description of the Country from Thirty to Forty Miles Round Manchester.* Bolton, Blackburn, Wigan, Stockport, Ashton, and various other encircling towns were described as sub-centers or satellites of Manchester; and the entire country intervening between these various towns was described as taking "its character from its relation to them." Many of these towns had long carried on no inconsiderable manufacturing of the older type, but Aikin's attention was focused upon them not because of the age of their industry but because of its recent "rapid and prodigious increase," which he believed was "unparalleled in the annals of trading nations." Again, the diffusion of the industry throughout the region, and its recent extraordinary development, were described by means of the analogy of a tree. "Manchester is the stock of that vast tree which has lately grown with such wonderful rapidity, and spread its branches through so large an extent of country, the cotton manufacture." So impressive was the sudden outburst of industry to a traveler in 1791 that he feared it could be but temporary, for, said he, "there is scarcely a stream that will turn a wheel through the north of England that has not a cotton mill upon it." [63]

At Bolton, long noted for its manufactures, the introduction of the new system of industry led to phenomenal prosperity and to the increase of population in sixteen years from about 5,000 to nearly 16,000.[64] Preston's first cotton factory was established in 1777; and thereafter "the sudden and great call and temptation for hands from the country, of this county, and many distant parts," doubled the population in less than two decades.[65] A

[63] Aikin's work, pp. 3, 4; a review of the work in the *Analytical Review,* November, 1795; *European Magazine,* XX, 140.

[64] Aikin, *Description,* 261, 262.

[65] *Annals of Agriculture,* XV, 564; Fishwick, *History of the Parish of Preston.*

census of Ashton in 1775 showed the town to have 553 houses and 2,859 inhabitants. Within eighteen years its houses and population had trebled; and "the other towns and villages in this neighborhood," ran a report in 1793, "have increased in nearly the same proportion as Ashton." [66] Concerning Middleton, near Manchester, it was said that "little more than twenty years since, there were scarcely more than twenty houses in the village; there are now between four and five hundred, which contain more than two thousand inhabitants. Business is increasing daily." [67] Further to multiply instances would be a work of supererogation.

The country parishes where domestic manufacturing had been carried on, no less than the towns, were touched as by a magic wand. This was due in part to the building of mills along the streams, and in part to the introduction into cottages of jennies and hand mules and the increase in the number of looms in the country districts. In these regions the cottage weavers and spinners were naturally more tardy than in the towns in giving up their contact with the land and their domestic arrangements in favor of the concentration of labor observable in the towns and in the stream-side mills of the country.

Contemporaneous records of the transition in these country parishes have all but disappeared, but the student is fortunate in having the reminiscences of a man who, in one of the townships involved, had an active part in the remarkable series of changes that remolded the economic and social structure of the community. This man was William Radcliffe, born about 1760, in the parish of Mellor, about fifteen miles southeast of Manchester. His oft-quoted account of the transformation of Mellor parish is found in his book, published in 1828,

[66] Aikin, *Description,* 227-229.
[67] *Ibid.,* 243-245.

with the title *Origin of the New System of Manufacture Commonly Called Power-loom Weaving*. His father, a weaver, had married a "spinster"; and "my mother", he tells us, "taught me (while too young to weave) to earn my bread by carding and spinning cotton, [and] winding linen or cotton weft for my father and elder brothers at the loom, until I became of sufficient age and strength for my father to put me into a loom." His father, he informs us, belonged to the class described as cottagers, who paid cottage rents to the farmers of the township, of whom there were fifty or sixty, the cottage thus rented including a "convenient loomshop and garden attached."

Assuming that Radcliffe began to spin at the age of seven, which he mentions as customary, he had had two or three years' experience before the transition which began about 1770. Within a few years, the spinning wheels, with the exception of those in one "establishment" owned by some elderly women, sisters, who refused to yield to innovation, found refuge in lumber rooms; and spinning was carried on by means of carding engines and spinning jennies.

But the period of jenny spinning in the cottages ended about 1788, and it was after that date that the phenomenal changes in the life of the community began to occur, "when all hands went to work on machine yarns." Weaving rather than spinning came to predominate in Mellor township—*cottage* weaving of *factory-made* yarns. Machine spinning coming into vogue about that time, "with an increasing demand for every fabric the loom could produce, put all hands in request, of every age and description. The fabrics made from wool or linen vanished, while the old loom-shops being insufficient, every lumber-room, even old barns, cart-houses, and outbuildings of any description were repaired, windows broke through the old blank walls, and all fitted up for loom-shops. This source of making room being at length exhausted, new weavers' cottages with loom-shops rose up in every direction; all immediately filled, and when in full work the weekly circulation of money, as the price of labor only, rose to five times the amount ever before experienced in this subdivision, every family bringing home weekly 40, 60, 80, 100, or even 120 shillings per week!!!" Other members of the community, as well as the cottagers, felt the "agreeable effects of the sudden increase in the circulating medium," for the money "in its peregrinations left something in the pockets of every stone-mason, carpenter, slater, plasterer, glazier, joiner, etc., as well as the corn-dealer, cheese-monger, butcher, and shopkeepers of every description." Farmers, also, by the enlarged demands for farm produce, and the rise in prices, profited greatly; and the landlords also were enriched marvelously by unearned increments, "the rents of their farms being doubled, and in many instances trebled."

But one, at least, of the cottagers,—William Radcliffe himself,—instead of allowing his surplus income to "peregrinate" into the pockets of artisans, dealers, farmers, and landlords, retained it in his own pockets till he was able to set himself up as a manufacturer. In 1785, "with my little savings," he relates, "and a practical knowledge of every process from the cotton bag to the piece of cloth, . . . I was ready to commence business for myself; and by the year 1789, I was well established, and employed many hands both in spinning and weaving, as a master manufacturer." Later he formed a partnership, and the firm in 1801 removed to Stockport. "We had at that time," his narrative continues, "a large concern in Mellor, that with its various branches for putting out work employing upwards of 1,000 weavers, [was] widely spread over the borders of three counties, in a vast variety of plain and fancy goods, all of which had been raised (like a gathering snowball) from a single spindle, or single loom by myself." [68]

The case of William Radcliffe and Mellor township is an illustration of the blending of old and new. Radcliffe took advantage of the new machines, and in part of the new factory organization of industry. But it seems that even in his spinning enterprises he continued to make some use of the "putting-out" system, which had long been used and had in fact been the basis of such large-scale organization of manufacturing as existed before the coming of the factory system. Unfortunately his account is not as clear as to the transition in his own business and in the township generally from the "putting-out" system to the factory system of organization as it is in respect to the transition in technique. But it is apparent that in the remoter areas where domestic manufacturing had prevailed, and especially where water power was not readily available, the jenny and the hand-operated mule would survive in the cottages of working folk longer than where conditions were more favorable for the concentration of workers in factories. But in either case, the introduction of machines meant in the first instance for many, a new life, an increase of wealth and opportunity; and for all, a stirring of the community to its depths.

It would be far from the truth to say that the effects of the change from the old system of hand labor to the new one of machinery were everywhere so stirring as in Radcliffe's township, but on the other hand, the transition was in many rural communities even more complete. Particularly is it true that Mellor appears from Radcliffe's narrative to have been more tenacious of the old

[68] Radcliffe's narrative as here recounted is in the earlier portion of his work, particularly pp. 9-16, 58-65. His purpose in writing the book was to advocate laws prohibiting the export of yarn, and this accounts for the exaggerated emphasis on weaving, and on the prosperity of the weavers.

cottage industry and "putting-out" system than were many other places, where factory conditions closely resembling those of modern industry were being more rapidly introduced.

Radcliffe's account of the transformation of Mellor township is supplemented by documents of rare interest discovered since Radcliffe's day in the ruins of a cotton mill the foundation of which dates from 1790, some of the records antedating the founding of the mill. This mill, the property of the great muslin manufacturer, Samuel Oldknow, advanced the industrialization of the community definitely beyond the stage described by Radcliffe, by the introduction of the factory system.[69]

The change at Manchester and in the surrounding towns and country parishes was being duplicated, on a smaller scale to be sure, in other regions. Radcliffe named three centers in addition to Manchester where "the machine yarns were immediately adopted for the fabrication of every description of clothing, from the strong fustian to the finest book muslins,"—namely, Nottingham and neighboring towns (where many of Arkwright's factories were located), Carlisle in the extreme northwest of England, and Glasgow, with subcenters as at Manchester thirty to forty miles around the city.[70]   In addition to these, the neighborhood of Dublin, beginning about 1780, witnessed a rapid development of cotton factories. It is not improbable that further study of the immediate consequences of the industrializing process in each of these districts would reveal developments of more than local interest, but the early history of the movement in the region of Glasgow is particularly significant.   The textile industries in that district seri-

---

[69] Extensive quotations from the account books, business letters, and other intimate records of Oldknow's activities are given in Unwin. Hulme, and Taylor, *Samuel Oldknow and the Arkwrights.*

[70] Radcliffe, *Origin of Power-loom Weaving,* 58, 59.

ously declined after the financial troubles of 1857, but the original introduction of mechanical methods effected an economic and social revolution second only in ultimate importance to the transformation of the Manchester country.

The "machine yarns" used in these centers were to be sure not necessarily spun there: Glasgow muslin weavers, for instance, were indebted for some of their yarns to Radcliffe's Mellor township spindles.[71] But when Arkwright's patent rights lapsed in 1785, and when, about the same time, Crompton's mule began to prove its fitness for spinning both warp and weft, local spinning facilities were rapidly developed. A few spinning mills had already been in operation in Scotland for several years; and it was at about that time that Arkwright himself, in association with David Dale, became interested in the extensive development of cotton spinning in North Britain. Within a few years the Scotch, dependent though they were upon inventions from beyond the Tweed and the Cheviot Hills, developed, by means of those inventions, a virtually self-sufficing spinning industry.[72]

Paisley and other towns, and particularly Glasgow, had been developing manufacturing industries by the traditional methods long before the introduction of machinery gave pre-eminence to cotton. The Act of Union of 1707, by admitting Scotchmen to a greater share of colonial trade, had vigorously stimulated the commercial activities of the Clyde. "The opulence of Glasgow," runs a report to the Board of Agriculture in 1793, "first arose from its trade in tobacco, sugar, and other goods, the produce of America and the West Indies. These gave rise to a great demand for articles manufactured in this

[71] Radcliffe, *Origin of Power-loom Weaving*, 10.
[72] Marwick, "The Cotton Industry and the Industrial Revolution in Scotland," in *Scot. Hist. Rev.,* XXI, 207-218.

country, with which the cargoes imported from the colonies were chiefly purchased. Thus the foreign trade of Glasgow called forth a multitude of manufactures, which overspread Renfrewshire and part of Ayrshire. When the separation of America from England put an end to the great profits . . . [arising in particular from the tobacco trade], the merchants withdrew from a concern no longer profitable, and the habits of manufacture formerly established in the country enabled them to apply their capitals to the various branches of iron, glass, inkle, linen, woollen, gauze, and particularly cotton." [73]

This account from Ayrshire was confirmed by a similar report in 1794 from Clydesdale to the Board of Agriculture; and the latter report, even more clearly than the former, pointed out the significance of the new inventions in giving employment to the idle commercial capital. "The war," we are told, "which for some years had checked the progress of trade, was no sooner ended than the capitals, acquired by a long course of successful industry, were sent in quest of new employment. That wonderful exertion of human genius, the machinery for spinning cotton, had now been invented and brought to such a height as to prepare the material for the loom in much greater perfection and at a much cheaper rate than heretofore. The manufactures of Lancashire . . . enflamed the emulation of Glasgow." [74]

Under these conditions, a rapid concentration of capital, energy, and population, such as accompanied the introduction of new methods in northern England, was inevitable also in Scotland. As early as 1785, Viscount Stormont, addressing his peers, "desired their lordships to look at the state of Paisley. Thirty years ago there was not a loom in the place; now there were upwards of 6,000 in that remote and obscure corner." The noble

[73] Fullarton, *General View*, Ayrshire, 76, 79.
[74] Naismith, *General View*, Clydesdale, 74-76.

lord was protesting against allowing industries to leave
the kingdom, and his argumentative fervor no doubt
betrayed him into making his unkind remark about the
remoteness of Paisley, located as it was near the mouth
of the Clyde, only seven miles from Glasgow, but it must
be remembered that this world-famed region was then,
as indeed the Viscount's statement indicates, in the in-
fancy of its industrial growth. The rapid expansion of
the village was described by a manufacturer, who told
a committee of the House of Lords that the new industries and rising wages were attracting large numbers of
young people from the Highlands, who were coming
down to Paisley and Glasgow "to take labor and to get
their bread." Manufacturing in the town, he said, had
recently increased more than tenfold. The population,
as reported to the Board of Agriculture in 1793, showed
more than a sixfold increase in forty years.[75]

Although cotton manufacturing gave to Paisley a remarkable increase of wealth and population, the location
and greater resources of Glasgow naturally made it the
chief center of the new industry. As soon as Arkwright's
patent lapsed, the industry at Glasgow expanded so
rapidly as to engage "every eligible situation" in the
city; and in the surrounding district also "cotton mills
on a great scale were erected," the machines being operated by water power where available, and in other places
by horses. "The price of labor rose in every quarter, and
the demand for cotton workers was so great that farmers
could hardly engage men or women servants to remain at
country work. . . . The operation of the manufacturing spirit, issuing from Glasgow, as its central point,
diverged over this county [Ayrshire] in every possible
direction." Similar developments were going on in the

[75] *Parl. Hist.*, XXV, 851; *Min. of the Evidence, Com. of the H. of L.*,
1785 (on Irish Resolutions), 333-339; Fullarton, *General View*, Ayrshire,
76.

Clydesdale region. "Adventurers without stock or experience," aided by the numerous banks that were springing up, eager to share in the profits of industry, were enabled to contend with "people of capital and established credit," and manufacturing enterprises increased immensely in numbers, in size, and in extent of country affected. "The numbers of people already engaged in the manufacturing occupations being insufficient, new ones flocked to the different works, from all quarters and all employments, . . . so that there were perhaps few families in the county [Clydesdale] some part of which was not employed in this extensive manufacture." From England, "all the new machinery necessary for the cotton manufacture were introduced into the county; large quantities of the raw material were imported; and not only all the different kinds of goods formerly made of linen, but imitations of the various manufactures of India [particularly the various muslins, were] formed from that material. The art of dyeing was much improved; and a durable tincture, of various hues, given to cotton. The printing of cloth, too, made great advancement, and large quantities of cotton garments of elegant patterns were executed and exported, with other goods, to the different markets of Europe and America." [76]

These bright pictures of the rise of the new industry were not without darker colors. The reports from which the accounts are taken were written during the period of industrial depression accompanying the outbreak of war with France, and the authors contrasted the period of depression with the immediately preceding period of expansion. The point of view was that of the landlords and farmers, who had suffered, so they believed, from high wages and loss of efficient labor due to industrial

[76] Fullarton, *General View,* Ayrshire, 79, 80; Naismith, *General View,* Clydesdale, 74-76.

competition, and who, at the time of the great depression in 1793, were forced to aid the unemployed. This depression was viewed by some, indeed, as the inevitable collapse of an unsound structure. But the structure was soon repaired. The cotton industry, though destined to meet with recurring vicissitudes due to internal causes as well as to external disturbances, was nevertheless able rapidly to recover the ground lost in 1793 and to enter in Scotland as well as in England upon a new stage of expansion.

The concentration and increase of capital, energy, and population in the relatively new industrial centers constituted a triumph of mechanical technique the more significant because it was a victory won not by destructive but by creative forces. These forces could not be measured simply by increase of machine-made commodities. They called forth new enterprise in various fields. They put into productive use incalculable resources and energies hitherto idle or used merely for current consumption. They found expression "in the creation of new capital, in the increase of buildings and machinery, in the improvement of the soil, and in the opening up of new roads and canals." [77] They increased the demand for farm products and stimulated rural progress, and, though attracting countrymen to the towns, nevertheless increased the population as well as the wealth of country districts, just as emigration from England to the colonies, instead of impoverishing and depopulating England, added to the economic opportunities and therefore ultimately to the wealth and population of England, by creating a colonial demand for English commodities.[78] They opened up new sources of revenue, and enabled the government to meet even the financial demands of war and extravagant administration. "The genius of Watt,

[77] Wilson, *Letter to William Pitt*, 24.
[78] Howlett, *Examination of Dr. Price's Essay*, 6, 15, 16, 153.

Wedgwood, and Arkwright," it was declared, "has counteracted the expense and folly of the American war." The vast increase of wealth and revenue observed by William Pitt in 1792 was attributed mainly by him to the same cause.[79] "A rude country," a witness of the early changes asserted, "in which the operations of industry are carried on by mere manual labor, . . . may be said to be a Hydra, with more mouths than hands. In the modern improved state of manufactures and commerce, produced chiefly by machinery, society is a Briareus; it has more hands than mouths." [80] This multiplied creative power has been obstructed or perverted by war, by excessive or misdirected human passion, by defective sharing of the things created by the modern Briareus, by maladjustment to the rapid changes involved; but its essential beneficence is attested by the fact that its victory has been attended not by a diminution but by an incalculable increase of life-nourishing resources and of life itself.

4. The competitive advance of machine-armed industries

By means of human ingenuity, runs an observation made in 1792, the manufactured commodities of human consumption "can be multiplied to any extent, and by the improvements in mechanism are continually falling in value." [81] It was because of this simultaneous multiplication of quantity and decline in price that constantly increasing amounts of commodities were consumed. In this way the demands for goods were indefinitely enlarged. The manufacturers who continued to depend on

[79] Wilson, *Letter to William Pitt*, 6, 7; *Parl. Hist.*, XXIX, 833 (speech by Pitt); *Increase of Manufactures, Commerce and Finance*, 99; [Hamilton], *Enquiry into the Principles of Taxation*, 205-230.
[80] Eden, *State of the Poor*, I, 443.
[81] Hamilton, *Letter to the People of England*, 7, 8.

the old methods suffered the inevitable consequences of seeing their old and relatively static markets, as well as the newly created markets, absorbed by the manufacturers who adopted the new methods. Nor was this competitive force applicable alone to English markets. It extended as far as the territories that owed allegiance to the English crown; as far as English diplomacy could open the way by treaty rights; as far as English merchants could penetrate the innumerable tariff barriers; as far, indeed, as English adventurers could survive the perils of smuggling. This irresistible competitive advance of English trade was for eighteenth-century England the culminating triumph of the machine.

The competitive power of machinery in the domestic markets naturally found expression mainly in the textile industries. The more conservative potters, iron-masters, and makers of ironwares were soon outstripped and even forced out of business by those who utilized the technical improvements in their respective industries; and their aggregate importance was slight as compared with the manufacturers of woollens and other textiles who tried to maintain their hold by means of the older methods. The most impressive manifestation of the competitive power of the new machines was the outrivaling of old, established, protected, distinctly national textile industries by the cottons, exotic, laboring against tradition, monopoly, and various legal disadvantages, and supported only by superiority of method. The principal sufferers were the woollen manufacturers; they were by far the most important, and in most manufacturing centers they were the least progressive.

A factor other than the conservatism of the woollen manufacturers that has been emphasized [82] was the relative difficulty of expansion in the woollen industry as

[82] For example, by Cunningham, in *Growth of English Industry and Commerce*, II, Pt. II, 642-649.

compared with the cotton industry. It is true that woollen goods already occupied most of the field, whereas cotton goods had practically the whole market to conquer from the woollens. It has also been said that there was greater difficulty in securing added supplies of wool, necessary for expansion, than of cotton; but the point seems to have been overemphasized. The adoption of machinery in woollens would undoubtedly on the one hand have held in check the expansion in cottons and on the other hand have stimulated incalculably the expansion in woollens. For machinery in the woollen industry would have created an effective demand for raw wool available in various parts of the world, and would have opened up inexhaustible markets for English-made woollens by stimulating home consumption and by outrivaling foreign manufacturers. Such were exactly the processes by which the cotton industry expanded, securing its raw materials entirely from abroad and conquering markets strongly entrenched. Granting the adoption by the woollen manufacturers of improvements similar to those which transformed the cotton industry, there seems to have been no insuperable obstacle in the way of a phenomenal expansion of their industry.

But there was an insuperable obstacle in the way of their adopting machinery, and that was their own monopoly-bred inertia. It was "the spirit of monopoly," directing the manufacturers to seek advancement "not by their own improvement" but "by putting an end as much as possible to the troublesome competition of . . . rivals," that called forth Adam Smith's repeated attacks on the manufacturers. Why is it, asked Arthur Young, that the "invention, intelligence, and exertion" that have given to the cotton manufacturers and others an acknowledged superiority, are not to be found in the woollen industry? It is because the woollen manufacturers have too long been fed on "the sweets of monopoly." "Whatever tends to give a great profit without exertion of capital or industry tends strongly to lessen exertion, and to relax vigor. This effect is written in the human heart, and will be true while man exists." [83] With the views of Smith and Young, a host of lesser men concurred.

Under these circumstances, the expansion in the cotton industry was in some degree at the expense of the woollen manufacturers. Complaints concerning the declining state of the industry came from nearly all the important centers where it was carried on with the exception of Yorkshire, and the decline was commonly attributed to the growing popularity of machine-made cottons. Josiah Tucker, Dean of Gloucester, declared as early as 1782 that "the principal cause of the present stagnation of the demand for coarse wools is, beyond all controversy, the prodigious disuse of coarse woollen goods throughout every part of the kingdom. Silks, cottons and linens, combined in a thousand forms, and diversified by names without number, are now almost the universal wear." The "prodigious disuse" of goods made from wool, mentioned by Dean Tucker, was described in greater detail and with a more obvious bias against cottons by an anonymous writer in the same year (1782). "That they [cottons] are sold cheaper for home consumption than the woollens and stuffs, in the opinion of the wearers (assisted by fashion) appears evident, . . . but it must be acknowledged, folly and fashion have got the better of reason and sound policy in dress. . . . Men seem to be cotton mad. . . . As for the ladies, they wear scarcely anything now but cotton, calico, muslin, or silk, and think no more of woollens and stuffs than we think of an old almanack; besides, our furniture now is nearly all of cotton. . . . In short, we have now about our beds scarcely any woollens but blankets, and they would most

[83] *Wealth of Nations,* Bk. IV, Ch. III, Pt. II, and Ch. VIII; *Annals of Agriculture,* VII, 162, 163, IX, 360-363, and many other passages.

likely be thrown aside, could we keep our bodies warm
without them." Others agreed in part with this diagnosis
of the decline in the demand for woollens, but put the
blame in part on the hard times accompanying the war
with America. But the complaints were unabated long
after the passing of the wartime depression.[84]

That conservative futility which so often marked the
attitude of the woollen manufacturers and their
champions was again conspicuous. Indisposed to adopt
the radical but ultimately necessary remedy of revolutionizing their methods, they continued to depend on
monopoly, and to propose futile expedients. Even Dean
Tucker, who in many instances gave evidence of unusual
discernment, suggested as a remedy a system resembling
peonage, having as an aim "the increase of the lower
classes," who should be "obliged by their station in life
to be clad in such garments as are made out of coarse
wools, and to use such sort of goods for their bedding and
furniture." By other writers, local societies were ad-
vised to encourage the use of woollens as against cottons;
and parish officials were urged never to buy "a cotton or
linen gown for the poor instead of a woolsey one."
Further legal protection against the export of wool was
secured, and the direct aid of the government was sought
against the cotton manufacturers, some even intimating
the desirability of checking the use of machines: "Should
those mills and engines be suffered to destroy our woollen
and stuff manufactures, they will prove the most fatal
discoveries ever made in Old England." [85]

[84] Tucker, *Reflections on the Present Low Price of Coarse Wools*,
8, 9; *The Contrast; or a Comparison between our Woolen, Linen,
Cotton and Silk Manufactures*, 13, 14; Nash, *Collections for the History
of Worcestershire*, quoted in *Gentleman's Magazine*, LII, 485-487;
[Mackenzie], *Woollen Draper's Letter on the French Treaty*, 27, 28;
Ruggles, *History of the Poor*, I, 195; McPherson, *Annals of Commerce*, IV, 81.

[85] Tucker, *Reflections on the Present Low Price of Coarse Wools*,
31; Ruggles, *History of the Poor*, I, 99; *The Contrast*, 14.

Hostility to machinery indicated a realization of the fact that the cause of decline was not merely a matter of fashion but a result of the greater attractiveness and the cheaper cost of cottons resulting from the new technique. It gradually became apparent, too, that the woollen industry in Yorkshire, instead of declining, was expanding with a rapidity second only to the cotton industry. The decline was due, that is to say, not merely to the competition of cottons but also to that of Yorkshire woollens. Indeed, Lord Sheffield, as early as 1785, gave first place to the competition of Yorkshire. The causes of the decline of the woollen industry in the west of England, he wrote, were "first, the migration of it to the West Riding of Yorkshire, . . . and second, the use of Manchester goods." The true causes were at length recognized by the manufacturers themselves. The superiority of Yorkshire over the west of England, a manufacturer of the latter region admitted as early as 1779, is "evidently owing to our new inventions." Other factors were involved, but his diagnosis, so far as it went, was correct. Twelve years later another west of England manufacturer confessed that "Yorkshire, by dint of such machines and engines, not only use all their wool, but send down into the west country and buy it up out of the very mouths of the wool dealers and clothiers, and thereby take our trade with it." A woollen manufacturer in the south, drawing a similar contrast between Yorkshire and the southern counties, recognized frankly, in 1803, "the importance and necessity of introducing improved machinery into the woollen manufactory" in his part of the country.[86]

The outrivaling of older industries by the new was an

---

[86] Sheffield, *Observations on Ireland,* 190; *Manchester Mercury,* Oct. 12, 1779 (letter quoting a west of England manufacturer); Wansey, *Wool Encouraged without Exportation,* 69 and *passim;* Anstie, *Observations on Introducing Improved Machinery,* 10-14, and *passim.* See also Billingsley, *General View,* Somerset, 57, 91; Heaton, *Yorkshire Woollen and Worsted Industries,* 270, 272, 275.

impressive demonstration of the competitive power of the machine, and is a fact of great significance in the domestic history of England. But in the history of Greater Britain and of modern industrialism, a fact of far greater significance was the extension, by means of mechanical methods, of England's competitive power in foreign markets. This was indeed to the people of the time the chief justification for their introduction, the chief argument in extenuation of admitted evils of occasional unemployment and maladjustment.

During the early stages of the era of invention, the effects of labor-saving machines were discussed theoretically by various writers, and the consideration most frequently urged in their favor was their value in enabling England to compete commercially with other countries. When the new methods began actually to displace the old, and concrete opposition developed, the same argument became the chief defense of the champions of the new order.

In the early, theoretical aspects of the controversy, it was held that command of trade depends on the relative cheapness of the commodities offered for sale. The use of labor-saving inventions is the easiest way to reduce the price of commodities. By that means England will be enabled to retain markets she would otherwise lose to more progressive nations, or to nations with cheaper labor and other reduced costs of production. Indeed, by this means she will be enabled not only to retain her existing markets but to win new ones now controlled by other nations. This may "starve the rival workmen," but is it not to be preferred to allowing other nations to starve our own workmen? But labor-saving machines are desirable not only because they will enable the inventive nation to supply the existing demand in the world's markets, but also because the cheapening of commodities by means of machinery will increase the demand and lead to enlarged consumption and interchange. No sale can be so sure as that founded upon "cheapness of price," which guarantees "a sure and quick vent." Inventions are "of prodigious use in rendering commodities cheap and in maintaining great numbers of people." Labor-saving machines, in brief, instead of depriving English laborers of work, will ultimately prevent their employment from being taken away by rival nations, and will increase employment by enlarging consumption and demand.[87]

This theoretical justification of labor-saving machines is in accord with the argument of later writers, who utilized it in a multitude of forms, and added the more convincing logic of an appeal to experience. "The competition of Europe," it was affirmed, "is now become rather a contest in skill and ingenuity than in natural strength."—"The principal means by which Britain can now hope to maintain a superiority, or even an equality, among the neighboring nations, consists in the ingenuity and industry of her manufacturers."—Inventions enable us to bring goods to market "cheaper, finer, better. The necessary consequence of this will be, the demand will increase, and *all the world become our customers.*"—"It is entirely owing to the very ingenious designs and mechanical knowledge . . . that we have been able to maintain . . . such an evident and decided superiority in manufactures over all the other commercial states of Europe." [88]

[87] *Laws and Policy of England Relating to Trade* (1764), 42 (quoted in *Political Essays Concerning the Present State of the British Empire,* 213); Steuart, *Inquiry into the Principles of Political Economy,* I, 121-123; Harte, *Essays on Husbandry,* 38; Stone, *Essay on Agriculture,* 146-148 (a survival in 1785 of the view that employment is decreased by labor-saving machines); *Political Essays Concerning the Present State of the British Empire,* 168, 169, 209-219. The author of the last-named work discusses the subject at length and summarizes the views of various contemporaries.

[88] T., *Letters on Employing Machines to Shorten Labor,* 31; *Manufactures Improper Subjects of Taxation,* 2, 3, 17; *Thoughts on the*

On the occasion of the war-time riots in Lancashire in 1779, when there was working-class opposition to machinery, the justices of the peace, in delivering a charge to the grand jury, condescended to advance an argument in support of labor-saving machines which, they said, was "leveled to the comprehension of the meanest capacity." If one of two shopkeepers sells candles a penny in the pound cheaper than the other, to the first the people will go, and the second will face bankruptcy. "It is the same with trade when considered in a more extensive light. If the Dane, the Swede, the Hollander, or the Portuguese can buy cheaper from us than the French, we shall undoubtedly see him in our markets. . . . But if the French, by the introduction of those machines which we refuse to employ, be enabled to undersell us, we shall soon be in the situation of the dear shopkeeper. . . . It has always hitherto been found that the cheaper we can manufacture our commodities, the greater will be the demand, and consequently the greater call for labor." A later writer, using the same logic, sought to clinch the argument by the fact that "it is this which, almost in our own days, has expanded the villages of Lancashire into towns next to the metropolis." [89]

The manufacturers themselves, not only of Lancashire but of the other regions as well where technical advances were being made, soon accepted the logic as valid. Having captured existing markets by means of their superior technique, they sought by the same means to open up new opportunities for trade.[90] Even an op-

Use of Machines in the Cotton Manufacture, 11-14, 17; Manchester Mercury, Oct. 12, 1779 (letter by "Chremes").

[89] Manchester Mercury, Oct. 26, 1779; Annals of Agriculture, IX, 534, 535.

[90] The very significant expansionist policy of the new manufacturers is discussed below, p. 198, ff. The point of interest here is that it was a result of their superior competitive power, depending in turn upon their superior technique.

ponent of machines admitted their competitive power, and based his opposition in part on the excessive influence of the new great manufacturers, who, by means of machines, were engrossing every mart, and engorging "the gainful tide of commerce from all states." [91] But opposition, rapidly waning, gave place to an almost unanimous acceptance of the principle stated by none more clearly than by a belatedly progressive woollen manufacturer in 1803: "In vain will a town, a county, or a nation hope to preserve its manufactures, if a lethargic torpor binds it to an adherence to old modes when other towns, counties, or nations, animated with a spirit of improvement, have found out new methods of manufacturing goods of a similar quality on cheaper principles." [92]

It is true that for a long time there were occasional outbursts of hostility to machinery in the ranks of labor —inevitable, no doubt, because the workers as a class had no opportunity for forming an intelligent, far-sighted judgment, and what was more important, no means of commanding a share of the vast increase of wealth resulting from improved production. They were viewed, as were the machines and their output, as a commodity to be used when needed, to be cast aside (or at best miserably supported by charity) when not in demand, and there is little wonder that they were unable to appreciate or even to understand the argument that machines enabled their employers to dominate the world's markets. But those in authority, alike in the world of industry and of government, being immediate and unquestioned beneficiaries of profits or revenues resulting from the introduction of machinery, could readily appreciate its competitive value.

But even if Englishmen had at first been disinclined to recognize the supreme importance of their new inven-

[91] *Discarded Spinster*, 8, 10.
[92] Anstie, *Observations on Introducing Improved Machinery*, 15.

tions in foreign trade, they would soon have been impelled to do so by the interest of foreigners, and particularly by foreign attempts to utilize them. The cotton manufacturers had become so powerful, a member of the House of Commons told his colleagues in 1785, as to arouse both "the pride of this country and the envy of foreign nations." A writer hostile to the political views of the manufacturers admitted in 1785 that they had "excited the admiration and jealousy of all Europe." [93]

Evidences of a too eager curiosity on the part of foreigners, combined with their own experience with the amazing competitive value of the new inventions, led Englishmen to develop a vigorous policy of trying to retain for themselves the exclusive use of their improvements. The groundwork of this policy was a comprehensive system of laws to prevent the inventions or a knowledge of them from reaching foreigners. Laws of this type were not unknown in earlier times, but the original statutes concerned machines which were distinct forerunners of the great textile inventions: they were for the protection of the stocking-frame and the mechanisms used in the manufacture of silk.

The law prohibiting the export of the stocking-frame (7 and 8 Wm. III, c. 20, secs. 3, 4, in *Stats. of the Realm,* secs. 8, 9 in Pickering's *Stats. at Large*) was based on the fact that by means of this invention "great quantities are wrought off in a little time." Silk manufacturing as well as the hosiery industry had been carried on for a considerable period antedating the factory system by the use of relatively elaborate machinery. This machinery was of Italian rather than English origin, and yet at length in 1750 it also became the subject of protective legislation (23 Geo. II, c. 13). This law, as well as an earlier statute (1719, 5 Geo. I, c. 27), went further than the prohibition of the export of machinery—it forbade

[93] *Parl. Hist.,* XXV, 489; *British Merchant for 1787,* 27.

skilled workers to leave the country, and imposed penalties on any one who induced or aided them to emigrate.

The law of 1750 applied to the woollen industry as well as to the manufacture of silk. This law was but one of many forms of protection secured by the woollen manufacturers. They had long had a monopoly of raw materials and of the home market, and had even secured legislation for the destruction of the industry in Ireland and in the colonies. Their natural and legal advantages, aided by the disruption of the industry in Continental centers,—these circumstances rather than any technical superiority, were the chief sources of their economic strength. They had, in fact, no marked advantage in respect to technique. And yet, in keeping with their general policy of monopoly and dependence upon state support, they secured rigorous legal protection for their tools and the skill of their workmen as against foreign rivals.

When the newer industries developed, particularly cotton manufacturing, their condition in respect to the sources of their strength was the reverse of that of the woollen industry. Having neither such natural advantages as a domestic supply of raw materials nor such legal advantages as a monopoly of the home markets, the strength of the cotton manufacturers depended essentially upon superiority of technique. It was perhaps less incongruous for them than for the manufacturers of other textiles to seek legal protection of their instruments from foreigners. A law of 1774 (14 Geo. III, c. 71) forbade the export of tools or utensils used in manufacturing cotton or cotton and linen mixed.

These various laws proved inadequate, however, for the reason that knowledge of a machine might be secured without the machine itself being exported, and without a single artisan leaving the country. The end might be attained by means of sketches, miniature models, or specifications. To remedy this defect in previous legislation, a law of 1781 (21 Geo. III, c. 37) forbade the use of these and similar methods of exporting knowledge of machines used in the manufacture of the principal textiles.

The printing of cottons and linens had become so extensive by 1782 that those connected with the industry succeeded in procuring legislation of similar character applicable specifically to their field of work (22 Geo. III, c. 60).

By these various laws the textile manufacturers secured protection, but in the meantime in the metal industries a large number of devices and processes had been developed, second only in importance to those in the textile industries. The manufacturers insisted that protection should be extended to these improvements, and in 1785 their demand was granted (25 Geo. III, c. 67). In the following year this act was supplanted by another (26 Geo. III, c. 89) which contained a detailed list of tools and machines to be protected. This law was temporary, but was renewed from time to time till 1795, when a permanent protective law was enacted (35 Geo. III, c. 38).

But the manufacturers were not content to rely for protection on the necessarily imperfect enforcement of the laws: they resorted to measures of their own for maintaining a monopoly in the use of the new inventions. It was naturally due to their initiative that most of the prosecutions were brought under the laws. They investigated suspicious circumstances and reported their findings to the government. They added to the rewards offered to informers. They spread news of convictions in the hope of deterring others from similar offenses and of stimulating officials to be more rigorous against offenders. Working men were urged, on grounds of patriotism and of self-interest as well as because of the legal penalties, to refrain from taking abroad their skill and mechanical knowledge. It was proposed by Josiah Wedgwood, whose views were usually more liberal, to enter into a secret arrangement with the government for opening letters of working men in order to secure evidence against them. Writers and inventors sometimes refrained from making detailed descriptions of inventions from fear of furnishing information to foreign rivals. The government was urged to provide proper rewards for inventors in order to remove occasion for their going abroad to seek recognition; and the same motive was prominent in non-governmental efforts to reward inventive activity. Manufacturers closed their plants against visitors, keeping the outer doors locked in order to prevent the entrance of foreign agents and spies. Mutual warnings were issued by the manufacturers against the approach of suspicious persons. Local and national organizations of manufacturers, then springing up in the new industrial centers, undertook concerted measures of various kinds.[94]

But the curiosity of foreigners, instead of abating, seems to have increased as each new obstacle was thrown in the way of its gratification. Foreign manufacturers

[94] Evidence of these various modes of defense is found in the following sources: *Manchester Mercury*, June 14, Oct. 11, Nov. 29, 1785, Jan. 3, Sept. 19, 1786, and *passim; Corresp. of Josiah Wedgwood*, 15, 16; Wedgwood, *Address to the Workmen in the Pottery on the Subject of Entering into the Service of Foreign Manufacturers; Trial of a Cause to Repeal a Patent Granted to Mr. Richard Arkwright* (1785), 100; [Ogden], *Description of Manchester*, 93; Kenrick, *Address to the Artists and Manufacturers of Great Britain*, 47, 48; *Account of the Manner in Which a Standing General Commercial Committee Was Established at Birmingham*, 15-23; *Owen MSS.*, LXXX, 3, 4; *Manchester Misc. Papers, 1784-1791* (MSS.), No. 125; Boulton and Watt MSS., *Letter Book (Office)*, 1786-1788, 230, 231; *Foreign Office Papers*, 27/18, Dorset to Carmarthen, Apr. 6, 1786; Owen, *Life*, I, 31; Meteyard, *Life of Josiah Wedgwood*, II, 551, 552; Julia Wedgwood, *Life of Josiah Wedgwood*, 228, 229.

resorted to expedients beyond number to secure knowledge of English improvements in iron smelting and manufacturing and in pottery making as well as in the cotton industry. They induced English working men and even master manufacturers and capitalists to go abroad. They offered inducements to English inventors as well as artisans to seek their fortunes in other countries. They sent agents to England with letters of introduction, and secured similar letters from prominent Englishmen, by means of which they tried to secure access to English industrial plants; and when this failed, they sent spies who, under various disguises, attempted to secure drawings and first-hand knowledge. They employed draftsmen to copy drawings and specifications from the official patent records. They offered to purchase English goods on condition that samples of the instruments with which the goods were made were sold with the goods. They resorted to various subterfuges to conceal the smuggling of machinery and tools. They spread a knowledge of English inventions such as they were able to secure by means of public exhibits of models (a policy naturally not encouraged by manufacturers themselves, however). They even used public funds for subsidizing manufacturers who succeeded in securing English machines.

The principal countries involved were France, Austria and the Empire, Prussia, Holland, and the United States. But to Englishmen the chief, or at least the most successful, of sinners against their attempted monopoly of their inventions was France. The French early acquired and put into operation the new cotton machinery in particular. Rouen was called by Englishmen "the Manchester of France," and factories there and elsewhere were established and conducted under the supervision of Englishmen. It was reported, too, that the French were profiting by the skill of Englishmen in metal-working. Iron works were established by

Englishmen; and there was a copper-plate factory "for bottoming the king's ships, the whole an English colony." [95]

Englishmen, formerly less advanced than various Continental peoples, had from time to time resorted to similar methods of stealth and subterfuge to obtain foreign inventions, as when the Lombes made theft of the Italian silk-making machinery. In the absence of international patent laws, or of a system for internationalizing inventions, such methods were perhaps inevitable. It was natural, too, that Englishmen, having learned the competitive advantages of their inventions, should seek to preserve them for their own exclusive use. This, it is true, was difficult, and indeed ultimately impossible, but the policy was long pursued, possibly not without temporary advantages. It was modified, to be sure, by a system of licenses, and in 1825 certain prohibitions were removed. But as late as 1841 a parliamentary committee reported that in respect to spinning and weaving machinery, the original policy had been retained,

[95] Wendeborn, *View of England*, I, 233-235; Owen, *Life*, I, 31; Sheffield, *Observations on Ireland*, 200, 201; Young, *Travels in France*, 523-530, 553; *Corresp. of Wedgwood*, 17-19, 104, 105; Wedgwood, *Address to the Workmen in the Pottery; Journal and Corresp. of Auckland*, I, 516; *Complete Investigation of Mr. Eden's Treaty*, 80; *Manchester Mercury*, June 14, July 19, 1785, Sept. 5, Oct. 3, 1786, and *passim; Lloyd's Evening Post*, XX, 243; Commons *Journals*, XLVII, 559, 560; *Parl. Hist.*, XXVI, 544, 552; *Parliamentary Register*, X, 214; *Min. of the Evidence, Com. of H. of L.*, 1785 (on Irish Resolutions), 148, 149, 249, 250; *Manchester Misc. Papers, 1784-1791* (MSS.), No. 125; *Foreign Office Papers*, 27/17, Hailles to Carmarthen, Aug. 25, 1785, 27/18, Dorset to Carmarthen, Apr. 6, 1786; *Board of Trade Papers*, 6/113, Min. of Mch. 11, 1786, 6/140, Doc. 23, Mitchell to Fraser, Mch. 24, 1788; Letter of Boulton to Watt, June 25, 1787 (on visit of a foreigner to Albion Mill), in Boulton and Watt MSS., Birmingham Free Library; French, *Life of Crompton*, 191, 192 (2d ed.); Wheeler, *Manchester*, 171; Meteyard, *Life of Wedgwood*, II, 551, 552; Axon, *Echoes of Old Lancashire*, 119-126; Dumas, *Étude sur le Traité de Commerce* (1786), 70, 152-157; White, *Memoir of Samuel Slater*, 36, 37, 71, 283-298.

licenses for the export of such machinery never having been granted.[96]

But while England adopted and long tried to maintain a policy of monopolizing her inventions, the influence of this policy in the establishing of her industrial supremacy was probably slight. A sufficient explanation of her supremacy is found in the advantages of originating and first applying the inventions, under the peculiarly favorable conditions of a dominant commercial and maritime position, the possession of immense tributary regions, and the relative freedom of her people from the quarter-century of war that absorbed the energies and ravaged the industries of the Continent. The attempts of England to maintain her monopoly, and of her rivals to destroy it, are significant because they afford cumulative evidence of the early triumph of the machine in the world of competitive industry.

[96] *First Report,* and *Second Report from the Select Committee on the Laws Affecting the Export of Machinery,* 1841, particularly *Second Report,* iv, xx. See also *Report from the Select Committee on the Laws Relating to the Export of Tools and Machinery,* 1825, 2-9, 47-51. It is necessary seriously to modify the view expressed by Dr. Cunningham that "the policy of endeavoring to retain the advantages of machinery for England alone was mooted, but never very seriously pursued, and it was abandoned in 1825." (*Growth of English Industry and Commerce,* II, Pt. II, 609.)

CHAPTER III

1. Origins of the great industrialists

WHEN George III began his reign, in the year 1760, the productive resources of Britain were dominated by landlords and merchants. Manufacturing was carried on by a multitude of petty manufacturers who retained a large measure of control of the processes, but their raw materials were supplied and their output was controlled for the most part by men who were primarily merchants. The power of the landlords was based upon monopoly of land; the power of the merchants, upon monopoly of trade. The great manufacturers, who, toward the end of the century, rose rapidly to a sense of unity and a position of power, were possessed of neither commercial monopoly nor a monopoly of natural resources. Their origin was in the transition to mechanical production; their economic basis was in the productive and competitive power of machines.

The explanation of their remarkable success in utilizing for their individual aggrandizement the productive and competitive power of machines invented by others and invented as a result of influences distinctly social in character, is to be found in the contemporaneous rise of the spirit of *laissez-faire*. During the early stages of the organization of mechanical production, the forces of individualism and private gain prevailed with slight restraint. The latent disadvantages developed somewhat later under the influence of the policy of reaction and

136

repression connected with the French wars into a system of industrial control essentially anti-social. But the disadvantages were at first not fully apparent, and the organization of the system assumed a form that was largely spontaneous, undirected, and unrestrained, and in consequence the benefits derived therefrom by the workers and even by the ruling classes not immediately connected with industry, were secondary and merely incidental to the benefits secured by the manufacturers who fashioned the system.

The individual manufacturers have in most instances remained obscure. Probably the best known members of the group were Josiah Wedgwood of the Staffordshire potteries, and Matthew Boulton, the world-famed founder of Soho and partner of Watt. Richard Arkwright, whose name is most commonly associated with the origin of the factory system, had little to do with the organized activities of the group. Because of his control of patents, a fight was waged against him, which tended to unify the group but to isolate from it the man who, more perhaps than any other, was its creator. Even Arkwright's career is little known and has been the subject of numerous controversies rather than of well-informed discussion. Jedediah Strutt, the Derbyshire hosiery manufacturer, is more frequently mentioned because of his inventions and his association with Arkwright than because of his work as a manufacturer. Samuel Oldknow, the great muslin manufacturer, has been rescued from obscurity by the accidental discovery of letters, account books, and other records left by him in his Mellor township factory.[1] Robert Owen, whose career as a manufacturer began at Manchester, left a remarkable and enduring record of his life in his autobiography, but his fame is based mainly upon activities and views radically different from those of his contem-

[1] Unwin, Hulme, and Taylor, *Samuel Oldknow and the Arkwrights.*

poraries. In later attempts to reorganize the economic system, the influence of his idealism has been strong, but during his life he was as one crying in the wilderness. Thomas Walker, a prominent cotton manufacturer and exporter at Manchester, who represented Manchester in seeking the repeal of the cotton tax in 1785, and who was otherwise active in the new group, is better known because of his political activities as a local Whig leader than because of his position as a manufacturer. Robert Peel, pioneer cotton printer of Lancashire, was also an inventor, but he has been rescued from obscurity mainly by means of the fame of his son, the first Sir Robert Peel, and of his grandson, the prime minister. The first baronet of the name had attained such eminence because of his father's wealth and his own enterprise as to become by 1790 a member of parliament and a "very respectable gentleman," and he, therefore, because of his own career as well as that of his more illustrious son, was able to emerge from the obscurity of the workshop.

As for the manufacturers generally, they belonged to humble families, and most of them probably sought wealth without thought of fame; their relations to the beginnings and organization of a group that was later to acquire dominant political power were for the most part dictated by the prospect of immediate economic advantage. If there were those who coveted a lasting reputation by means of industrial pursuits, they were forestalled in most cases by lack of "respectability," if not by lack of distinctive achievement. The means of attaining distinction in other fields of activity may have been of questionable social value, but in any case, since the motives inherent in the rising industrialism were crassly unsocial, often indeed anti-social, it is perhaps just that society should have rewarded the industrialists with obscurity.

Their origins are further hidden by the flow of capital

from one economic field to another; by the rapid economic change; and by the interlocking and overlapping connections of the new manufacturers with merchants, landlords, and farmers, artisans, and the old petty manufacturers. History, therefore, with few exceptions, has little to record concerning the individual manufacturers of the new era. But our theme is not individual biography but social organization; and out of the changes of the time we may observe with tolerable clearness of detail the emergence of modern industrial capitalism differentiated from all other economic groups.

The members of the new group, and the capitals employed by them, were derived from many sources. The inventions came at a time when wealth was flowing into the country from foreign and imperial commerce; when banking, credit, and international exchange were being rapidly developed; when landed wealth was undergoing changes due to enclosures and engrossing of farms; and when capital generally was unprecedentedly mobile as well as abundant. The promise of rapid gains from organizing and directing enterprises which utilized the improved methods induced many of the gentry to exchange the more or less intangible advantages of superior status for the material enjoyments of industrial profits. Others, aiming to maintain their social superiority by means of continued personal contact with land or with commerce, found indirect means of transferring a part of their capital to manufacturing. But much of the initial capital was supplied by artisans, by the old petty manufacturers, and by yeomen and tenant farmers, who essayed the rôle of capitalist manufacturers. Failure forced many of these into the ranks of the wage workers, but to some of them came an astounding increase of wealth and power. In the earlier stages of mechanical production, before competition reduced profits and increased hazards, and especially as long as the jenny and the hand mule prevailed in the spinning of the finer yarns, very small capitals sufficed in the textile industries for the beginnings of some of the largest of the manufacturing establishments.[2]

2. The differentiation of the great industrialists from other groups

Capital had been employed on a large scale in manufacturing enterprises before the age of machinery. But it was furnished by men who were not primarily manufacturers but merchants, to whom were subject, in one form or another, a host of petty manufacturers. The relations of the former to the latter were varied and intricate, but one fact stands out clearly. The merchants, whether their capital was engaged purely in mercantile enterprises or partly in the organization and utilization of the old petty manufacturing, exerted a greater influence, and enjoyed a higher social status, than the multitude of those engaged directly in manufacturing. In status and influence they were indeed next to the landed aristocracy, and both looked with condescension upon the manufacturers, who were in reality merely artisans. Those merchants whose capital was partly engaged in manufacturing enterprises were connected with industry largely by means of the "putting-out"

[2] *Worsted Small-ware Weavers Apology*, 4; Holt, *General View*, Lancashire, 12 (ed. 1794); Brown, *General View*, Derbyshire, 13; Naismith, *General View*, Clydesdale, 74-76; Fullarton, *General View*, Ayrshire, 79, 80; Wright, *Address to Parliament on the Late Tax Laid on Fustian and other Cotton Goods*, 27; *Min. of the Evidence, Com. of H. of L.*, 1785 (on Irish Resolutions), 227 (case of Joseph Smith, weaver, turned manufacturer); *Annual Register*, 1792, 35 (Chron.) (obituary of Arkwright); *Century of Fine Cotton Spinning*, 8, 9 (case of a noted firm of cotton spinners); Owen, *Life*, I, 22, ff.; Parker, *Sir Robert Peel*, I, 1, ff.; Trevelyan, *Life of John Bright*, ch. 1. The sources of the new group are discussed by Mantoux, *La Révolution Industrielle*, 379-391; by Hammond, *Town Laborer*, 7-11; and by Chapman, *Lancashire Cotton Industry*, 24, 25.

system. They furnished to artisans, either directly or through local dealers, or agents, or master manufacturers, the raw materials to be worked up in the homes or the small shops of the artisans on a wage basis. Sometimes the necessary utensils were also furnished. By a reversal of the process by which the raw materials reached the actual workers, the finished products were returned to the merchants for local distribution through shopkeepers, for sale in other regions by middlemen of various descriptions, or for export by themselves or by merchants engaged exclusively in the foreign trade.[3]

The merchant employer of the "putting-out" system was an important connecting link between the old petty manufacturing and the large establishments of the age of machinery. The "putting-out" system was developed, for instance, by the Glasgow merchants for supplying cargoes of manufactured goods demanded by the colonies; and the system, introduced before the coming of machinery, was continued in modified form even in the spinning of cotton after spinning mills came into use. For example, in Ayrshire "the greatest part of the cotton worked in this manner [that is, spun by machinery in factories as well as by hand in the homes] was furnished to the manufacturers by the Glasgow merchants, who took them bound to return the thread at certain rates, according to its quality and fineness." This, however, was an unusual variation of the "putting-out" system. The system was readily applicable to the spinning jenny and even the smaller hand-operated mule, and in weaving it

[3] On the early industrial and commercial organization of the cotton trade, see Daniels, *Early English Cotton Industry*, chs. 1, 2, and Chapman, *Lancashire Cotton Industry*, 1-17, 113, and *passim*. There is a brief, clear-cut description of the organization of the woollen industry in Webb, *History of Trade Unionism*, 33-35 (ed. 1920). The best account is Heaton's *Yorkshire Woollen and Worsted Industries*. On early connections between commercial and industrial capital, see Unwin, *Industrial Organization in the Sixteenth and Seventeenth Centuries*, especially Introduction and ch. 3.

continued, with diminishing vigor to be sure, till the
handloom was supplanted. With the introduction of
machinery and of factory organization in some of the
processes, there was an inevitable tendency for the
capitalistic manufacturers who controlled these processes
to take over the "putting-out" processes from the merchants and the petty manufacturers in the branches of
manufacturing where it survived.[4] The extension of
"putting-out" to factory spinning under control of Glasgow merchants, though merely temporary, and never
extensively imitated, furnishes nevertheless a significant
illustration of the power of the merchants over the manufacturers under the old system. The superiority of the
merchants of Manchester engaged in foreign trade as
compared with the manufacturers in that region was
noted by the observant young manufacturer, Robert
Owen, during his brief career at Manchester.[5]

The essential significance of the age of machinery in
the reorganization of industrial capital was in giving rise
to a group of large-scale capitalists who were no longer
primarily merchants but manufacturers, and who rapidly,
as manufacturers, acquired financial independence and
an enlarged connection with markets. The manufacturers in the Manchester region were described in 1783
as coming weekly to Manchester "to buy yarn and cotton
and sell goods," and they were dependent on the Manchester merchants, or on the agents of London and
Liverpool merchants, for their markets for buying their
raw materials and selling their products. But they soon
enlarged the scope of their relations to the markets.
Robert Peel told a committee of the House of Commons
in 1785 that the manufacturers in his branch ordinarily
received payment for goods shipped abroad from the

[4] Unwin, Hulme, and Taylor, *Samuel Oldknow and the Arkwrights,*
106-110.
[5] Fullarton, *General View,* Ayrshire, 76-80; Owen, *Life,* I, 37.

English merchants, "unless, which is sometimes the case," he added significantly, "we [as manufacturers] execute an order from those countries." By 1788 the cotton manufacturers had enlarged their relations to the markets by making "frequent trips to London" to exhibit their goods to merchants or agents of merchants. Their rapid rise and growing dissatisfaction with their relations to the markets are observable in their elaborate plan of 1788 for establishing a "general receptacle or hall" in London under national charter. This organization was to have a capital of half a million pounds for financing manufacturers by advances on their goods pending sale; it was to undertake the supervision of sales in order to do away with the necessity of "frequent trips to London" by manufacturers; it was expected to serve as a general clearing house of information concerning markets and to spread a knowledge of English goods abroad, thus promoting world-wide sale.[6]

This ambitious proposal, though formulated by manufacturers, was never carried out, partly because of opposition among the manufacturers themselves. But an increasing number sought a larger measure of independence from the merchants, alike in securing raw materials and in marketing their goods. The case of Thomas Walker, long prominent at Manchester, illustrates the revolution under way in the relations of the manufacturers to the markets. In the Manchester *Directory* of 1781, Thomas Walker and his partner Richard Walker were listed as fustian manufacturers. In 1788, they were classified as manufacturers of fustians, muslins, and calicoes. But by 1794, they had become *merchants* and manufacturers. Colonel Brooke, who put up extensive spinning and cloth-making establishments in Ireland, was described by a

[6] Mrs. H. Ware, *Life and Corresp. of Samuel Hibbert Ware*, 96; *Min. of the Evidence, Com. of H. of C.*, 1785 (on Irish Resolutions), 20, 21; *Board of Trade Papers*, 6/140, Docs. 60, 77.

contemporary Irish writer as desirous of confining himself to manufacturing, but found it expedient, in order to market his goods to best advantage, to assume the functions of a merchant, both wholesale and retail. Wedgwood entered into commercial relations of an extensive character, and early in his career received a large order direct from the Empress Catherine of Russia. Boulton and Watt, as well as others connected with the manufacture of iron and ironwares, established wide commercial correspondence and connections. Manufacturers as well as merchants dealt with the agents of foreign customers in England, and sent their own agents abroad. Various manufacturers, wrote William Eden (later Lord Auckland) from Paris, had agents in France as early as 1786. In that year two delegates of the fustian manufacturers said to the Board of Trade, "We have prospered only since we turned merchants." [7]

The new and enlarged functions of industrial capital are significantly illustrated by the Cornish Metal Company, organized in 1785 in connection with the mining and marketing of copper.[8] Cornwall, an old copper-mining region, depended largely on engines for the pumping of the mines, while the more recently developed and shallower mines of Anglesea were being operated on

[7] Manchester *Directories*, 1781, 1788, 1794; *Thoughts on the Establishment of New Manufactures in Ireland Occasioned by the Late Freedoms We Have Obtained, with an Account of the Manchester Manufactory Established by Mr. Brooke*, 18-24; Jewitt, *The Wedgwoods*, 211; Ware, *Life and Corresp. of Ware*, 17-19; *Journal and Corresp. of Auckland*, I, 143, 144; *Board of Trade Papers*, 6/113, Min., Feb. 22, 1786.

[8] Records of the company's history are in the Boulton and Watt Collection, Birmingham Free Library, and have recently been studied and interpreted by G. C. Allen in an article entitled, "An Eighteenth-Century Combination in the Copper-mining Industry," in *Economic Journal*, XXXIII, No. 129 (Mch., 1923), 74-85. The company is described by him as "an early example of a modern type of combination," presenting "a curious parallel to that of many recent combinations."

a less expensive basis. The mid-century decline in the productivity of the Cornish mines was checked by means of the more efficient engines constructed by Boulton and Watt, but the installation of engines by "adventurers" and the rapid development of mining in both Cornwall and Anglesea reduced prices and threatened the operators with ruin. At this time, Boulton and Watt were dependent largely on the sale of engines for pumping mines and on "engine dues" from the mining regions for their profits from the manufacture of engines; and they, therefore, were vitally interested in the menace to Cornish industry. Boulton at first attempted to safeguard his interests by the purchasing of shares in the mines, and by using his power as a shareholder to promote more conservative and efficient management and cheaper production. It was his influence which seems to have been predominant in a much more ambitious method of safeguarding the profits of the industry, namely, the organization of the Cornish Metal Company, in 1785, for regulating output and prices and for controlling the marketing of copper. The capital of the company was supposedly £500,000, and the considerable sum of £130,000 was actually at the start subscribed. The company was to be the purchasing agent for the operators, who were to sell all their ore to the company, at a price to be fixed by the directors, two-thirds of whom were to be operators' nominees. The company was at first primarily concerned, as the name implies, with Cornish industry, but it soon made a price-fixing and marketing agreement with the Anglesea interests. Serious difficulties ensued, the chief of which were excessive production, foreign competition, and disputes between Cornwall and Anglesea. The arrangements proved ultimately successful, however, after various modifications, and the company continued in existence during the period originally proposed—1785 to 1792. In the latter year the agreements lapsed, due in part to the fact that the enlarging demand for copper made continued centralized control no longer essential to the profitable operation of the industry. Another fact in explaining the dissolution of the company was the change in the attitude of Boulton. Expanding demand for steam engines made those used in the pumping of the copper mines relatively insignificant; and at the same time, his great Soho plant was becoming an extensive purchaser of copper, and he was therefore no longer so vitally interested in keeping up the price of copper.

Among manufacturers of the newer types, there was a general tendency to "turn merchant" or to reduce the merchants to the position of representing them in the larger markets. This was primarily due to the fact that since their enterprises were becoming more highly capitalized and more extensive in scope, they were able to encroach upon the banking and credit facilities previously controlled by the merchants; but the tendency seems to have been accelerated by the disasters to commercial houses resulting from the American Revolution and the European economic coalition against England during the war. It appears, in any case, that soon after the war, the manufacturers commonly "acted as merchants, and shipped their goods on their own account." [9] In brief, a revolution was under way in the relations between merchants and manufacturers—a revolution which indicates nothing less than the rise of a new type of industrial capitalists.

It was a revolution which shows conclusively, also, the differentiation of the group from the older petty manufacturers. There are two phases in the activities of modern, large-scale manufacturers. One phase involves control of the immediate processes of production. The

[9] Wilson, *Letter to William Pitt*, 21-23; Aikin, *Description of the Country Round Manchester*, 182-184; Chalmers, *Estimate*, xxxvi (ed. 1794).

other phase is concerned with the processes by which the manufacturer secures contact with markets for raw materials and markets for finished products. The older petty manufacturers controlled in large degree the immediate processes of production, but frequently under the general supervision of the mercantile interests. As for their contacts with markets, even the wealthier master manufacturers were dependent for raw materials and for the sale of their goods upon gilds, or companies, or corporations, or powerful individual merchants. The great manufacturers of the era of production by machines controlled even more effectively than did the petty manufacturers before them the immediate processes of production. And their operations by degrees assumed such proportions as to enable them at the same time to do what the earlier manufacturers could not do—namely, to bring into subordination to themselves in large measure the mercantile agencies which had formerly controlled the financial and marketing arrangements.

It is obvious that this vital change in the relations between commercial and industrial capital took place with varying degrees of rapidity in different industries. Furthermore, the change was not dependent on the complete supplanting of hand methods and "putting-out" in all processes by machines and factories. In the cotton industry, many great manufacturers who procured their yarns in part from cottage spinning on jennies and mules and who organized weaving partly on the basis of the "putting-out" system without radical break with the older methods of organization, established by degrees their enterprises on such a large scale as to enable them to assume at length the mercantile function. A notable instance is that of William Radcliffe, whose activities have already been mentioned.[10] The origin and rapid expansion of his business resulted in the first instance

[10] See above, p. 109, ff.

from utilization of spinning machinery, partly in cottages, partly in factories. As a "master manufacturer," he employed both spinners and weavers. By degrees his business assumed the modern factory form of organization, and by degrees, also, its expansion led to the more extensive assumption of mercantile functions, including direct dealings with English agents of foreign purchasers and the sending of agents abroad.[11] Furthermore, many individual merchants on the one hand and petty manufacturers on the other hand, instead of allowing themselves to be subordinated to newcomers, merely transferred their capital and oftentimes their personal activities to the new field of large-scale manufacturing. Many individuals who, under the old system, were merchants, or merchant employers, or manufacturers who acted as intermediaries between the merchants and the artisans, now became primarily manufacturers with direct mercantile connections. By these means, the reorganization of manufacturing internally, as well as its change in relation to commerce, was brought about with a minimum of friction,[12] and consequently the change attracted relatively little contemporaneous attention. In fact, no sharply defined boundaries, at least with our present paucity of records of the business relations of that period, can be drawn between the petty manufacturers and the merchants on the one hand, and the great industrialists on the other hand. But it is sufficiently clear that the beginnings of differentiation of the modern type of industrial capitalist from other economic groups is discernible even during the earlier stages of the mechanical revolution.

[11] Radcliffe, *Origin of Power-loom Weaving*, 10, 14-16, 68, 131; Daniels, *Early English Cotton Industry*, Introduction, xxix.

[12] That friction in some degree resulted is apparent. See for instance the pamphlet published in 1785, entitled *Increase of Manufactures, Commerce and Finance*, supporting the manufacturers as against the merchants in respect to facilities for money and credit.

Changes in economic organization are revealed significantly in the woollen industry by an incident in 1794, already alluded to in connection with the transition to mechanical methods in the Yorkshire region. The incident is particularly significant, however, because of its revelation of changes in economic organization. On March 4, 1794, various woollen manufacturers of the West Riding of Yorkshire petitioned the House of Commons for legal intervention to maintain the old system of manufacturing as against recent innovations. Manufacturing had long happily been carried on in Yorkshire, the petition averred, "with a very trifling capital, and by the unremitting labor of themselves, their wives and children, united under one roof." But now, the petitioners complain, this condition is being broken in upon and destroyed by a system developed in other parts of the country and adopted by men of wealth who, with "large capitals," are establishing "great factories" in their midst, and threatening thereby to reduce them "to a state of servitude to gain bread for themselves and their dearest relatives." The petitioners claim that these men of wealth who are attempting to establish a monopoly of manufacturing by the new methods are for the most part cloth merchants turned manufacturers, thereby engrossing the manufacture as well as the sale of cloth. But it appears that the new group of great woollen manufacturers was not recruited entirely from the ranks of wealthy merchants. A wool grower, complaining of the laws against the export of wool, asserted that some of the manufacturers had begun with very small capitals, and had acquired considerable fortunes. The purpose of the manufacturers in petitioning against the merchants was to secure the enactment of a law to separate the functions of the manufacturer from those of the merchant, thereby confining the merchants to their former sphere. The petitioners probably had little hope of legal redress against members of their own group who might desert the ranks of the small manufacturers, and it is not unlikely that some of those who had not yet deserted were hopeful of being able to do so. Under the circumstances, it is natural that their complaints should have been aimed primarily at the merchants rather than at members of their own group who had become manufacturers under the new system. In any case the process of differentiation appears with tolerable clearness.[13]

The most conspicuous differentiation between the older petty manufacturers and the modern industrialists was in the cotton manufacturing districts. There had been master manufacturers in the region who employed dozens and even scores of workers, who enjoyed tolerable incomes, and who occupied positions of local influence. Their wealth seems even to have been so considerable as to subject them to the envy of some of the country gentlemen. But since gentility was often none too intimate with enterprise and prosperity, its occasional alliance with envy is perhaps not surprising.

Many of the more wealthy and influential manufacturers of the period preceding the great inventions owed their wealth and position largely to an earlier mechanical improvement—the Dutch loom for weaving small wares.[14] This loom, introduced as the name implies from Holland, enabled the small-ware manufacturers to rise so rapidly, beginning with its introduction about 1725, that by the middle of the century they could vie with "some of the best gentlemen." But at best the manufacturers of the older type were men of small resources, crude and circumscribed in culture and outlook, and purely local in their influence. "I wonder what any country gentleman can be supposed to envy them for!" ex-

[13] Commons *Journals*, XLIX, 275, 276, 431, 432; *Annals of Agriculture*, XVII, 114.
[14] See above, p. 75.

claimed one of the gentlemen in 1759. "Is it their houses? What country gentleman has reason to envy the possessor of a house of four, five, or six rooms of a floor with warehouses under and warping rooms over?" In similar vein he ridicules the various other pretensions of the manufacturers—an indication, to be sure, of their growing wealth and position such as would suggest even a satirical comparison with the gentry, and yet an evidence of their insignificance in comparison with the "new great cotton lords" of the age of machinery.[15]

It is not without significance that these new men were viewed by their contemporaries as veritable "lords" of industry, whereas the wealthiest manufacturers of the preceding generation were disparagingly compared with the local gentry. Arkwright in his vast accumulation of capital was probably unequaled by his contemporaries, but formidable rivals in spinning, in weaving, in cotton printing, and especially in combinations of these operations, sprang up in large numbers, particularly after the lapse of his patent in 1785. Even at that time there were manufacturers whose operations were so extensive that they paid annual excise duties alone amounting to more than £20,000. In amount of capital employed, in number of workmen, in size of plants, in the regimentation of labor, and in relations to markets,—in these vital respects many of the cotton manufacturers left far behind them the domain of petty industry and entered the realm of modern industrial capitalism.[16]

In the metal and earthenware industries, the changes in economic organization differed in some particulars

---

[15] *Worsted Small-ware Weaver's Apology*, 3, 4; Daniels, *Early English Cotton Industry*, 46, 56, 57 (quoting Thomas Percival's contemporaneous description of the manufacturers).

[16] Owen, *Life*, I, 31, 40; *Min. of the Evidence, Com. of H. of C.*, 1785 (on Irish Resolutions), 8, 18, 30; *Parl. Hist.*, XXV, 838, 852; *Annual Register*, 1792, 35 (Chron.); *Gentleman's Magazine*, LV, Pt. I, 449; [Ogden], *Description of Manchester*, 86.

from the changes in the textile industries. The displacement of small producers by great industrial capitalists was less revolutionary because production, as already stated, had long been organized on a basis differing less from the modern factory system than in the textile industries. Again, natural resources and the need of large capitals to secure control of them played a larger part, while technical improvement was correspondingly less important as a determining factor in the substitution of great capitals for small ones. It is apparent, too, that these industries, in comparison with textile manufacturing, were local and relatively unimportant before the middle of the eighteenth century, and therefore the rise of modern capitalism was less far-reaching in its effects on economic and social organization than in the textile industries. And yet the changes, though less revolutionary, were similar, and were brought about mainly by the same underlying cause—namely, the introduction of technical improvements which could be utilized to best advantage by means of greater capitals and larger plants. The results, also, were similar; for the technical improvements, when introduced, created for the innovators vast fortunes and a new economic and social status. Wedgwood, Wilkinson, Boulton, and various other representatives of these reorganized industries shared with the great textile manufacturers the wealth and honor and influence attending the putting of manufacturing on a new technical and financial basis; and together they formed the nucleus of the modern industrial aristocracy.

This, to be sure, was the incipient stage of the new aristocracy. But its ranks were rapidly recruited, and disciplined by a sense of unity and class interest. Their rapid rise to positions of great wealth, national importance, and international connections gave to the figure of speech by which they were called "lords" of industry a reality rivaling that other figure which designated the commercial aristocracy as merchant "princes,"—a reality which even the lords of royal sanction and ancient lineage reluctantly perceived and at length were forced to recognize.

Indeed, the titled aristocracy of England, with that facile adaptability which peculiarly distinguishes it from the similar groups in other countries, enlarged its foundations by the inclusion of industrial wealth, as earlier it had reinforced its economic power by the absorption of commercial wealth. His Majesty, as head of the aristocracy, with astute graciousness condescended to make a knight out of an erstwhile village barber and itinerant buyer and seller of women's hair for the making of wigs. Nor was the barber-knight loath to identify himself with the group to which he had been raised. "On Sunday last," runs a contemporary account, "Sir Richard Arkwright, Knight, High Sheriff of the County, arrived at Derby, accompanied by a great number of gentlemen, etc., on horseback; his javelin men (thirty in number, exclusive of bailiffs, etc., etc.) dressed in the richest liveries ever seen there on such an occasion. . . . They all rode on black horses. . . . The trumpeters were mounted on gray horses, and elegantly dressed in scarlet and gold. The High Sheriff's coach was very elegant and fashionable, with plated furniture . . . [and rich decorations, designs, and arms]. We must not forget to inform our readers that Sir Richard during the whole of the Assize provided a plentiful table, with the choicest wines, etc., for such gentlemen as pleased to partake of the noble banquet." [17]

Perhaps the astuteness of the aristocracy in seeking an extension of its foundations to include industrial wealth should not be emphasized. Possibly it was a tendency more or less instinctive. But whether rational or not, it

[17] *Manchester Mercury*, Mch. 27, 1787.

was aided materially by the eagerness of manufacturers and tradesmen to adopt the formalism of the landed aristocracy, to secure landed estates, and to invest their sons if not themselves with the "respectability" and if possible the arms, the titles, and the prestige of the "upper classes."

These tendencies, by which the landed aristocracy widened its economic basis and the new industrialism paid tribute to the aristocracy by seeking the prestige of land and titles, undoubtedly softened the rigors of mingled disdain, envy and hostility, and in some degree changed the nature of each group. But the causes of antagonism were by no means eradicated. There is complaint of "the inundation of *new men*," who "expel the ancient families, destroy the venerable mansions of antiquity, and place in their stead what seemeth good in their own eyes of glaring brick or ponderous stone"; and the country is urged "to preserve the memory of those persons and those houses whose light is in its wane." The direct connection of manufacturing with this tendency in the Lancashire region was observed by a writer who, instead of lamenting, rejoiced in the rewards of industry in the form of elegant houses rivaling and even supplanting the old mansions. Preston he described as "the most beautiful town in the north of England," a town which, because of the number of "genteel families" formerly in the region, "got the epithet proud." But the town had undergone a revolution, for "aristocratic ideas" failed to assimilate with manufacturing. Turning punster, he added: "Instead of cards, therefore, for killing time, cards are used by which thousands may live." [18]

The disdainful attitude, not unmixed with envy, assumed by the upper classes, "proud of their exemption

[18] *The Topographer*, I (for 1789), Preface, iii, iv; *European Magazine*, XX, 216, 217.

from commerce and manufactures," finds illustration in the experience of Edmund Cartwright, who, when he turned manufacturer, was viewed by many "as having deserted his caste." A "great *mill-monger*," we are told in reference to Arkwright, "is newly *created* a knight, though he was not *born* a gentleman." The great manufacturer upon his death was accorded faint praise, criticized for his crudeness, and described as a useful, though not a great character. A noted moralist of the time, observing the tendency, condemned "the aristocratic prejudices and the envious contempt of neighboring peers and country gentlemen, proud of their rank and ancient family, who even in these days occasionally disgrace themselves by looking down on the man raised by merit and industry from obscurity to eminence." [19]

Arrogance had indeed long characterized the attitude of peers and gentry toward merchants and manufacturers, but their envy, at least of manufacturers, was of recent origin. Out of the growing wealth and power of the manufacturers and the growing jealousy of the landed classes was engendered a reciprocal hostility. "Our landed gentlemen," wrote James Watt to a French correspondent in 1787, reckon "us poor mechanics no better than the slaves who cultivate their vineyards." Another manufacturer (for Watt was writing as a manufacturer) expressed the desire of members of his group to bring "nearer to their own level" the "gentlemen of landed property," "the proud and bigoted landowners [who] look down with contempt on the merchant or manufacturer." Their measureable success was attested by the complaints of Lord Sheffield in connection with the corn-law controversy of 1791 that "the alacrity of the manufacturer"

---

[19] [Strickland], *Memoir of Edmund Cartwright*, 84, 85; *Humble Petition of the Poor Spinners; Annual Register*, 1792, 35, 36 (Chron.); Gisborne, *Duties of Men*, 571.

had triumphed over "the supineness of the landed interest." [20]

At Manchester the reciprocal antagonism of the two groups was early apparent. Curious literary (perhaps some would prefer the term pseudo-literary) memorials of early class relationships have survived in the writings of a Manchester clergyman, Rev. Thomas Bancroft, giving expression to the hostility between the manufacturers and the aristocracy, and to the growing class consciousness of the former, and foretelling the destined preeminence of the industrial group. Bancroft, as early as 1777, in poem-letters to a friend at Cambridge, described industry at Manchester ("Mancunium"), and continued:

> This is fustian, rank fustian, I hear you exclaim;
> But be gentle, my friend, ere you damn it to fame.

And concerning Manchester's busy industrial leaders, whom the aristocracy looked upon as "servants around," he wrote:

> Such are England's true patriots, her prop and her pride;
> They draw wealth from each state while its wants are supply'd;
> To mankind all at large they are factors and friends,
> And their praise with their wares reach the world's farthest ends. . . .
> Is it then, ye vain lordlings! ye treat us with scorn,
> Because titles and birth your own fortunes adorn?
> What worth to yourselves from high birth can accrue?
> Are your ancestors' glories entailed upon you?
> And is your lazy pomp of much use to a nation?
> Are not parks [21] and wide lawns a refined devastation?

[20] Boulton and Watt MSS., *Letter Book* (*Office*), 1786-1788, 147; [Anstie], *General View of the Bill for Preventing the Illicit Exportation of British Wool and Live Sheep*, 65; *Parl. Hist.*, XXVIII, 1380.

[21] The writer refers, of course, to the private parks of the aristocracy. It is a sad commentary on the devastating influence of the industrialism that was possessing the city that no provision was made for public parks.

But peace—'tis presumption,—too much would demean 'em
To hold converse with upstarts, *a vulgus profanem.*
Their blood in pure currents thro' ages conveyed
It were impious to taint with the contact of trade.

In a succeeding letter he describes the early vicissitudes
and later triumphs of industry in Venice and Holland,
and in prophetic strain foresees the shifting of power in
England to the industrialized north of England:

At length (thanks to heav'n) she is freed from her thrall,
And her weeds has thrown off to reign empress o'er all.
Yet her mansions in chief she has fixed on our shore,
Where freedom and justice maintain her in power.
See around—but around it were needless to roam;
For the climax reversed, we may look nearer home. . . .
For thy glory, Mancunium, these tributes are paid.[22]

The government of the industrial city of Manchester
itself was a picturesque survival from the days of landlord supremacy. On November 20, 1787, appeared the
following advertisement of the proffered sale of the city:
"To be sold by private contract all that the ancient
Manor of Manchester, in the County of Lancaster, with
its rights of markets, royalties, members and appurten-
ances, the property, and now in possession of Sir John
Parker Mosley, Baronet." Sir John seems to have received no satisfactory offer, however. "This is to give
notice," runs a typical advertisement of later date, "that
the Court Leet, or View of Frankpledge, of Sir John
Parker Mosley, Bart., Lord of the Manor of Manchester,
in the County of Lancaster, will be holden at the Exchange, in Manchester aforesaid, on Wednesday, the 29th
day of April, 1789, at nine of the clock in the forenoon, at
which time and place all burgesses, inhabitants, and other
persons who owe suit and service at the said court, are

[22] Quoted in Harland, *Collectanea Relating to Manchester,* II, 216-218.

required to attend." Signed by the Deputy Steward of the Lord of the Manor.[23]

Two full sessions of the Court Leet were held each year, one at Easter, the other at Michaelmas. At the latter session, town officers were elected, from borough-reeve (equivalent to mayor) to swineherd and beadle for rogues. It was by means of this election that the interests of a "town of trade" found expression, but not without conflicts with the landed interests. Attempts on the part of the Lord of the Manor to influence elections and to enforce his ancient privileges and prerogatives as to markets, tolls, and control of the highways, were opposed with increasing vigor. The land steward of the Lord of the Manor was in 1786 publicly censured by members of the Court Leet for attempting to control elections. In 1788 subscriptions were raised for the purpose of enabling a committee to combat Sir John's authority and "for asserting the rights of Manchester." Sir John on his part maintained also a belligerent attitude, declaring in response to proposed compromises that "my manorial rights [are] fully ascertained and secured by the laws of the country." But the committee continued its activities, reinforced by the fact that the town officials, almost continuously, were prominent manufacturers who were able and willing to support them. The controversy continued till at length at least partial victory was gained in the form of legislation increasing the powers of the elected officials and authorizing the reconstruction and enlargement of the city. In connection with these controversies and other matters affecting the interests of the industrial classes, a significant change is observable in the attitude of the professional classes.

[23] *Manchester Mercury,* Nov. 20, 1787; *Manchester Chronicle,* April 25, 1789. The city (that is, the manorial rights and prerogatives) was bought by the Manchester authorities in 1846 for the sum of £200,000. (Hammond, *Town Laborer,* 10, n. 1.)

Naturally sensitive to economic changes because of economic dependence upon the dominant group, it is not surprising that in spite of supposedly superior status conferred by alliance with the landed aristocracy, they rapidly shifted their connections and their support to the industrialists.[24]

In Manchester and in other localities, the new manufacturers were beginning seriously and not without measureable success to challenge the long-unquestioned local supremacy of the landed aristocracy, and to assume a position as a distinct and powerful group. In lesser degree the same is true of their national status and influence. It was no longer possible for "the indolent and ignorant Great"—as the aristocracy were described in an earlier complaint—to class them with "men possessed of no property and capable of nothing but labor," and "confound them indiscriminately with the refuse of mankind." [25]

Many of the manufacturers had in fact come from what the "Great" were often disposed to look upon as "the refuse of mankind," and their very emergence from the ranks of common labor tended to raise higher the barriers already existing between employers and employees in manufacturing enterprises. The further separation of these two groups is another manifestation of the early differentiation of the new manufacturers from other groups. The idyllic pictures of the state of labor

[24] Roberts, *Charge to the Grand Jury of the Court Leet for the Manor of Manchester* (Michaelmas, Oct. 15, 1788); Walker, *Review of Some of the Political Events Which Have Occurred in Manchester during the Last Five Years*, 23, and *passim; Manchester Mercury*, Nov. 7, 14, 1786, Nov. 7, 14, 21, Dec. 12, 1788; *Manchester Chronicle*, Jan. 17, 1789; *Manchester Misc. Papers, 1784-1791* (MSS.), Nos. 128-131; Manchester *Directories* (on personnel of city government and reconstruction of city); Tait, *Medieval Manchester*, 35, 58, 59, 72; *Memoirs*, Manchester Lit. and Phil. Soc., I, 80.

[25] Kenrick, *Address to the Artists and Manufacturers of Great Britain*, 20, 21 (quotation applied in a slightly different but similar sense).

preceding the rise of modern industrialism painted by its opponents must be largely discounted. In mining, in domestic manufacturing, in lace making, in hosiery making, and most notoriously of all, perhaps, in agriculture, the distressing conditions caused multitudes to seek refuge in factories and allied industrial enterprises. In many cases this proved to be a jump from the frying pan into the fire, due in part to war, political reaction, and other influences for which the new system of industry was not responsible. In any case, the concentration and regimentation of labor had early the consequence of giving to the industrial workers a greater unity and distinctness as a class, and a greater opportunity for developing group consciousness and concerted action.[26]

3. The relation of the great industrialists to politics

The opportunity which the new system gave was for a long time nullified by other influences. One of these was the united action of landlords and manufacturers, who, however divergent their interests in other respects, were bound together as employers and exploiters of labor, and as adherents to the same general conception of the impropriety of allowing to their employees any share whatsoever of economic or political authority. The direct political authority of the manufacturers themselves was at first not recognized, but their indirect influence in national and especially in local affairs found immediate and vital expression. Their rapid rise to power in economic life and economic policy as officially expressed was deplored by many but denied by none.

Many of the manufacturers were truly described as men of "great wealth and opulence, and of great power

[26] For discussion of these and related subjects, see Ch. IV.

and influence arising from that wealth and opulence."
They employed workmen "amounting in some instances
to several thousand"; they were able to employ in some
cases "single capitals of two or three hundred thousand
pounds"; their enterprises and investments were so extensive as to enable them "to give credit almost everywhere [in foreign markets as well as at home] from
twelve to eighteen months." They were rising rapidly to
a position of international economic importance. "Go to
France," exhorts Arthur Young with characteristic
exuberance, as early as 1787 when the great capitalists
were daily waxing greater, "and look for an Arkwright,
a Wedgwood, a Darby, a Wilkinson, a Boulton, a
Parker: there are no such men to be found in that kingdom. . . . Can one man, with 6 or £8,000 capital, bear
the rivalry of another with £100,000?" In the debates of
the time on taxation, the corn laws, the navigation
system, and commercial laws and treaties generally, the
economic status and interests of the newly risen lords of
industry were reiterated in various forms. A member
of the House of Lords asserted that if weighed in the
balance with men of such ingenuity and enterprise,
"ministers and anti-ministers would together kick the
beam." [27]

In view of their status and the recognition of their
importance, and in the light of the current agitation for
the reform of parliament, it is naturally to be supposed
that the new manufacturers would have sought to bring
about a change in the electoral and representative system
such as would have given them a proportionate voting
power in the House of Commons. The press and political

[27] *Whole Proceedings on the Trial of an Action Brought by Thomas
Walker*, 81; *Thoughts on the Causes of the Present Failures*, 13;
Howlett, *Insufficiency of the Causes to Which the Increase of our
Poor and the Poor's Rates Have Been Commonly Ascribed*, 33;
Wilson, *Letter to William Pitt*, 23; *Annals of Agriculture*, VII, 272,
273; *Parliamentary Register*, XVIII, 34 (2d part).

leaders in favor of a reform of parliament were not slow to utilize the growth of the industrial class as an argument for reform. It was indignantly asserted that "the monied interest is not represented at all." The greatest manufacturer or merchant "has not the privileges of a beggar in a Cornish borough. Accordingly the great manufacturing towns of Manchester, Birmingham, Sheffield, etc., have no representation in parliament." Similar contrasts were repeatedly made by Wilkes, Fox, and various others.[28]

And yet it is a singular fact that the manufacturers themselves were indifferent in respect to reform. During the period of most vigorous and most general agitation, when petitions in large numbers from nearly every part of the country assailed the House of Commons, the new industrial centers were not enough interested to send petitions.[29] The absence of such petitions, in spite of many appeals to these regions to support reform, afforded the opponents of reform an opportunity which they cleverly utilized. A speaker in 1783 (Mr. Powys), in opposing Pitt's motion for a reform bill, minimized the importance of various petitions. "Manchester and Birmingham, however, he was determined to hear, and to pay particular attention to. They were great trading towns, and their petitions ought not to be slightly passed over, in the usual manner. . . . He must have the whole of what they contained explicitly and distinctly made known to the House, and for that purpose desired the clerk to read them. The clerk turned over and over

---

[28] *Political Register*, II, 224, 225; *Parliamentary Register*, III, 439; *Parl. Hist.*, XVIII, 1292, XXIII, 863, XXIV, 999, XXX, 789; *Gazetteer*, May 4, 1785.

[29] Commons *Journals*, XXXIX, Jan. to May, 1783, XL, Feb. to April, 1785. During the revival of reform agitation in connection with the French Revolution, they continued indifferent to the movement. A petition from Sheffield in 1793 (*Parl. Hist.*, XXX, 776) is an exception, but the tone of the petition indicates that its basis was not economic but political—an outgrowth of revolutionary sympathies.

again; but no such petitions being found, he told Mr.
Powys that neither Manchester, Birmingham, nor
Sheffield were in the list. Not in the list! said Mr.
Powys—good God, what a misfortune!" Lord North
also called attention to the lack of petitions from these
regions, and twitted the proponents of reform for having
taken great pains to secure petitions with the result that
they were able only to say: "What horrid sound of *silence*
doth assail mine ear?" [30]

Fox, who at the time was representing himself as a
champion of the industrialists, and who would eagerly
have availed himself of any evidence of their interest in
parliamentary reform, explained their indifference on the
ground that they were "threatened with ruin" by the cotton tax of 1784 and by the Irish Resolutions of 1785, and
were "on the eve of emigration" to Ireland and foreign
countries, and for that reason considered it "no time . . .
to set about making improvements in the constitution."
As a matter of fact, there is evidence that the manufacturers resented attempts to involve them in political controversies. They experienced a species of pride in their
aloofness from politics, other than for the promotion of
economic policies directly involving their interests. This
aloofness existed in some degree even in local politics.
They prided themselves on desiring to wear no "party-
colored robes," and it was frequently held that the lack of
national representation and the absence of local chartered
and gild regulations were among the chief advantages of
the northern and midland towns. "For thereby the attention of the industrious manufacturer can seldom be
called off, by the interference of party interest; and that
grand principle which should ever animate a flourishing
commercial establishment universally pervades the great
body of the inhabitants, that of the uninterrupted appli-

[30] *Parl. Hist.*, XXIII, 837, 850, 851, XXIV, 988, XXV, 458, 459, 463,
466, 467. See also Langford, *Century of Birmingham Life*, I, 314.

cation of each individual who composes it to his own peculiar concerns."[31]

It is apparent that the industrial communities were little interested in parliamentary representation, or even in local politics. For the most part they desired to be let alone and allowed "uninterrupted application" of their energies to their "own peculiar concerns." But when these "concerns," that is, their economic interests, were directly involved in affairs of politics, they were not slow in bringing to bear their influence for the directing of public policy. It was the connection between their economic interests and public policies that counteracted their individualistic tendencies and furnished the incentive for organizations at first local and at length national.

4. Early organizations

The history of these early organizations is in many cases extremely obscure, and it is difficult in some instances to distinguish between informal or temporary groupings for concerted action in specific cases, and formally constituted bodies for exerting continuous influence on economic policies. In other cases, it is not possible, perhaps, to say whether a given organization was for business purposes only, for example, to construct and operate a cloth hall such as the Muslin Hall at Stockport,[32] or for purposes analogous to the modern chambers of commerce, manufacturers' associations, and similar bodies. The General Chamber of Manufacturers

[31] Parl. Hist., XXV, 466, 467; Journal and Corresp. of Auckland, I, 92, 93; Corresp. of Wedgwood, 29, 125; Companion to the Leasowes, to Which is Prefixed the Present State of Birmingham, 15, 16. See also Walker, Review of Political Events in Manchester, 23, 24; Campbell, Political Survey of Britain, I, 322; [Ogden], Description of Manchester, 93, 94; Sinclair, Lucubrations during a Short Recess, Containing a Plan for a More Equal Representation, 42, 43; Billingsley, General View of the Agriculture of Somerset, 167.

[32] Referred to by Radcliffe, Origin of Power-loom Weaving, 14.

of Great Britain, organized formally and in permanent form in 1785, was unquestionably of the latter type, as were certain local groups of an earlier date. One local group apparently of this kind was in existence at Norwich as early as 1736. When the so-called "Manchester Act" was passed in that year to legalize the use of "stuffs" made of cotton and linen as well as of worsted, "the committee of trade" at Norwich, unable to prevent the competition of cotton and linen fabrics by law, took steps to encourage the introduction of such manufactures at Norwich.[33]

But the effective beginnings of such organizations were in the last three decades of the eighteenth century. The woollen clothiers and manufacturers [34] of the West Riding of Yorkshire, Lancashire and Cheshire formed an organization in 1777, in accordance with the provisions of a law passed by parliament in that year, having as their initial purpose the supervising of the administration of the laws against alleged frauds and embezzlements incident to the "putting-out" system, and against combinations of employees. But the "worsted committee," as the organization was known, soon assumed other functions. It opposed the export of wool and of machinery, encouraged invention by means of rewards (in imitation of the Society of Arts), sought to allay hostility to ma-

[33] James, *History of the Worsted Manufacture*, 224 (quoting *Gentleman's Magazine*, 1736, 169).

[34] Strictly speaking, the worsted manufacturers. The technical distinction, in the words of Dean Cunningham, is that "the worsted, as distinguished from the woollen, manufacture works up wools with long staple, the fibers of which are straightened out as in the linen or cotton manufacture; while the woollen manufacture, properly so-called, is dependent on wools with a short staple, the fibers of which have much tenacity, and which can thus be matted into a thick material like felt." (*Growth of English Industry and Commerce*, II, Pt. II, 651.) There were also differences as to location, and the worsted industry was generally more highly capitalized. In this work, the popular and comprehensive term "woollen manufacture" has in most cases been used.

chinery, promoted the legislative interests of the manufacturers, and in brief became a forerunner of later manufacturers' and employers' associations.[35] Our relatively clear knowledge of this organization is accounted for in part by the fact that it had an official status, and in part by the fact that its activities in opposition to the export of wool brought it into conflict with the landed interest and gave it a publicity which would otherwise have been denied. There is fugitive evidence, nevertheless, of organizations before 1785 among the iron masters of the counties of Salop, Worcester, Stafford and Warwick, and the potters of Staffordshire;[36] and there is information concerning organizations at Manchester and Birmingham in tolerable clearness of detail. They were without official status or sanction, being purely a result of private initiative; and since they were more directly connected with the origins of modern methods of manufacturing and industrial capitalization, they are more significant in the history of industrial evolution than is the worsted committee.

The Manchester "committee for the protection and encouragement of trade" (a comprehensive term applied primarily, however, to manufactures) was organized in 1774. At the annual general meeting of those interested, called together by advertisement on June 26, 1781, there appears to have been a reorganization. A new committee was elected by ballot, representing the cotton, linen, silk,

[35] 17 Geo. III, cc. 11, 56; Commons *Journals*, XL, 78, 611, 1024; Heaton, *Yorkshire Woollen and Worsted Industries*, 418-437; James, *History of the Worsted Manufacture*, 292-299 (an unduly favorable account of the activities of the committee. Arthur Young and other champions of the wool growers, in the *Annals of Agriculture* and in various pamphlets, went to the other extreme in their intemperate denunciations).

[36] Commons *Journals*, XL, 867; Langford, *Century of Birmingham Life*, I, 114, 316, 320, 321; *Corresp. of Wedgwood*, 15, 16; *Papers Relative to Mr. Champion's Application to Parliament for the Extension of the Term of the Patent*.

and small-ware industries. Subscriptions were solicited from citizens of the town for "securing and maintaining its manufactures." About seventeen months later (on December 10, 1782), the committee reported that it had met more than thirty times and had carried on varied activities. From this report, it appears that the purposes of the organization included taking steps to oppose the patent system, particularly in the case of Arkwright's patents, and to devise other methods of encouraging and rewarding inventors; to secure the repeal of restrictions on the use of cotton goods; to obtain larger and cheaper supplies of raw materials by modifications of restrictions on imports; to facilitate the punishment of buyers and receivers of stolen goods; to aid employers in their dealings with employees, by preventing alleged abuses and sabotage, checking emigration of workmen abroad, and fighting combinations of workers; and to bring the manufacturers into more effective relations with other industrial centers and with public officials.[37]

It is apparent, therefore, that the organization and objects of the committee put it distinctly in the category of modern business men's associations. Furthermore, there were organizations for special branches of industry, as the fustian manufacturers, the dyers and crofters, and the calico manufacturers and printers. These special committees, however, gave evidence of the difficulties of maintaining a general and harmonious organization at Manchester. The city's industries early developed a diversity of interests as well as an excess of individualism and ambition accompanied by frequent controversies.

[37] Owen MSS., LXXX, 3, 4; Manchester Misc. Papers, 1784-1791 (MSS.), 149, 149a; Manchester Mercury, June 23, 1781, April 20, May 11, Sept. 21, Oct. 5, Dec. 14, 1784, and passim; Commons Journals, XXXVII, 773, XXXIX, 250, 455. See also Daniels, Early English Cotton Industry, 100, 101; Chapman, Lancashire Cotton Industry, 206; Helm, Chapters in the History of the Manchester Chamber of Commerce (extremely deficient as to the earlier organizations).

There is a curious document in the national archives which picturesquely illustrates this tendency. In 1788 the calico and muslin manufacturers and printers sought the aid of the government against the competition of the East India Company. This aroused the jealousy and hostility of the fustian manufacturers, whose stronger competitive position in the markets perhaps accounts for their more rapid advance toward ideas of economic liberalism.[38] At a meeting of both groups, "Mr. Thomas Walker (fond of popularity) took the lead," we are told, "and speeched away for the fustian makers; Mr. Robert Peel and others for the printers; at last they were so warm that Mr. Lawrence Peel and Mr. Walker collared each other, and all was violence." [39] But the eruptive tendencies were at least occasionally quieted by the pressure of a common external danger, and after 1794 a continuous and more or less general organization was maintained.

Birmingham, following the example set by Manchester, organized a "general commercial committee" in 1783. The occasion for its formation was furnished by the proposed repeal of the laws against the exportation of brass. This committee gave such satisfaction to its constituents that at a public meeting presided over by "one of the leading manufacturers," it was "resolved that it is the sense of this meeting that it is highly expedient to establish a standing General Commercial Committee for the purpose of watching over and conducting the public interest of this town and neighborhood." It might be inferred, from their own statement of their

[38] And yet Thomas Walker, connected with the fustian industry, led the Manchester opposition to the French commercial treaty of 1786 for the reciprocal lowering of duties. He was apparently influenced mainly by his bitter hostility to Pitt, and his views were overwhelmingly repudiated by his fellow manufacturers at Manchester.
[39] *Board of Trade Papers,* 6/140, Doc. 45 ("A letter from Manchester about the Calico and Muslin Business").

purpose, that they intended to assume the functions of the town government. Their activities in their organized capacity were to be sure more modest, but the characteristic and perhaps naïve way in which they identified their own group interests with the interests of the entire community is not without significance. The work of the committee was so similar to that of the Manchester Committee, already described, that further details are unnecessary.[40]

5. The early history of the General Chamber of Manufacturers

In these and other local organizations there was at first no clear distinction between merchants and manufacturers. But circumstances arose in 1785 which led to a differentiation and to the formation by the manufacturers of a national organization—the General Chamber of Manufacturers of Great Britain. Their individualistic tendencies, and the diversities among them, raised up serious obstacles, and the stimulus necessary for organized unity was the desire to ward off what were believed to be common dangers. These dangers, which the manufacturers persuaded themselves were threatening them with ruin, were the tax laws and the Irish policies of the government of William Pitt. United by common opposition, they utilized their organization successfully for the defeat of the policies in question. The first triumph of union was the repeal of the cotton tax of 1784.

Among the urgent and difficult problems confronting the youthful Pitt when the magic of his father's name and his own ambition elevated him to the premiership in

[40] *Account of the Manner in Which a Standing General Commercial Committee Was Established at Birmingham;* Langford, *Century of Birmingham Life,* I, 314-330, 348, and *passim.*

1783 was the reorganization of finance.   As a part of his fiscal policy, he secured the enactment in 1784 of a new excise by which the taxes on dyed stuffs of cotton and linen mixed or of cotton were considerably increased. Bleachers and dyers were required to purchase licenses. The taxes were to be collected by special excise commissioners.   Manufacturers were required, under heavy penalties, to give detailed information concerning their utensils and methods; excisemen might enter a plant day or night to secure information, and any obstruction offered subjected the manufacturer to a fine of £200. Requirements as to marking the cloth at different stages of the manufacture for identification by the excisemen were rendered obsolete, it was claimed, by changes in technique.   Counterfeiting of the exciseman's stamps was punishable by death; and the seller of goods marked in counterfeit incurred the double penalty of a fine of £100 and two hours in the pillory.   Arrears of taxes might be collected by confiscating the machinery.[41]

The administrative features of the law, minute and inquisitorial, were similar to those of earlier excise laws. These older methods were no longer applicable to the more complicated and advanced technique of manufacturing then being introduced, nor did the government in attempting to utilize them take into account the fact that many of the manufacturers, in wealth and influence, were far superior even as early as 1784 to those of former generations.   The government of William Pitt, like political governments generally, responded slowly to eco-

[41] 24 Geo. III, c. 40; Baines, *History of the Cotton Manufacture,* 279-281. Dowell's *History of Taxation* contains (IV, 343, ff.) a brief summary of early laws as well as a discussion of the law of 1784.   See also Wright, *Address to Parliament on the Late Tax Laid on Fustian and Other Cotton Goods,* an exhaustive though somewhat biased analysis, and Percival, *Short View of the Grounds and Limits of the Obligation to Pay Taxes.*

nomic changes, and the old system of excise, once looked upon as a natural and unavoidable part of fiscal policy and public control, was now considered by the manufacturers to be so meddlesome and mischievous as to be intolerable. Nor were they slow to inform the government as to their sentiments.

The new excise (called the fustian tax because it applied primarily to the various fabrics known as fustians[42]) aroused the united opposition of the cotton interests, led by the fustian manufacturers, who appointed a special committee to go to London for the purpose of conducting negotiations with the government. An appeal for funds in August of 1784 soon resulted in 350 subscriptions in support of the committee's work. The dyers and bleachers voted to shut down their plants till parliament should grant relief, but this threat of direct action (to use more recent terminology) was vigorously opposed by the fustian manufacturers, who favored "constitutional" methods in place of attempts "to inflame the minds of the public," and who began to erect dyeing plants of their own.

At Glasgow, similar opposition developed, subscriptions were raised, and decision was made "to join the powerful opposition at present forming in Lancashire and elsewhere." Nor was the movement confined to the cotton men. Others, taking alarm, and fearing an extension of new excises, joined the forces of opposition. The iron founders and manufacturers of the counties of Salop, Worcester, Stafford, and Warwick, at their quarterly meeting at Stourbridge, January 7, 1785, passed vigorous

[42] The term fustian comprehended a large variety of fabrics. See *Board of Trade Papers,* 6/112, two documents endorsed "Dyed fustians R/30th May 1786 from Mr. Hilton," and "White fustians R/30th May 1786 from Mr. Hilton," the former containing samples of twenty-four types, including velvets, denims, satinettes, etc., and the latter containing samples of twenty-three types, in plain and figured weaves, including muslinettes, sateens, etc.

resolutions condemning the government's policy. The Birmingham Commercial Committee took similar action and directed its Committee of Correspondence to seek the cooperation of other manufacturers.[43] The committee of the fustian manufacturers, backed by united opposition to the government and by adequate financial support, conferred in London with various government officials, but without promise of relief. They were treated with a humiliating condescension, which would perhaps have been effective in earlier generations when the manufacturers were insignificant as individuals and unorganized as a group, but under the new conditions hostility was thereby aggravated, and the tendency toward general united opposition was given powerful impetus. While the government, blind to the newly rising power of the manufacturers, was needlessly embittering them by its inconsiderate treatment of their delegates in connection with fiscal policy, it opened the way for a still more extensive opposition by the publication of the terms of its Irish policy.[44]

The Irish problem, ever a thorn in the side, was rendered acutely piercing in the case of Pitt's government by pressure of disturbed conditions inherited from the preceding ministry. Pitt, recognizing Ireland's newly acquired legislative independence, was at once confronted with the problem of establishing economic relations on a basis acceptable to the Irish parliament as well as to the

[43] The principal source of information concerning early organized hostility to the excise policy is the *Manchester Mercury*. See in particular the issues of July 27, Aug. 10, 31, Sept. 7, 21, 28, Oct. 12, Nov. 2, 9, 1784, and Feb. 15, 1785. See also Langford, *Century of Birmingham Life*, I, 320-322, and *Parl. Hist.*, XXV, 365, 366.

[44] On the relations of the government to the representatives of the Manchester manufacturers, see *Min. of the Evidence, Com. of H. of L.*, 1785 (on Irish Resolutions), 185-190; *Min. of the Evidence, Com. of H. of C.*, 1785 (on Irish Resolutions), 6, 47, 53-64, 70-90; *Report of the Lords of the Com. of Council Relating to Trade and Plantations*, 1785 (on Irish Resolutions), 53-61; *Parl. Hist.*, XXV, 837.

parliament at Westminster. His policy, formulated in the so-called Irish Resolutions, or Propositions, having been accepted by the Irish parliament, came up for consideration in the English House of Commons in February, 1785, in the midst of the agitation against the excise laws.

According to Pitt's own interpretation, his policy embraced two "capital points." He proposed to allow Ireland to share England's colonial and foreign trade (with certain important restrictions favoring English merchants); and to reduce tariffs on manufactured goods from either country into the other to the rate in that country where existing duties were the lower. Various important exceptions were made, however, in favor of the English landed classes, merchants, and older types of manufacturers, while no attempt, apparently, was made to conciliate the manufacturers of the newer type. Here again, as in the case of the excise legislation, the ministers seem to have been blind to the most significant industrial development of their generation. Pitt himself, in a private letter written at the time, quite frankly admitted the possibility of certain unprotected industries shifting to Ireland in consequence of the Resolutions. Many of the manufacturers were of the same opinion— an attitude ill-adapted to reconciling them to the government's policy. It must be remembered that in the development of large-scale manufacturing in progress in 1785, water power was at the time of utmost importance, and that in this connection many places in Ireland offered superior inducements. These attractions had already led certain English gentlemen who had secured models of the new textile inventions to set themselves up as manufacturers in Ireland, or to invest in enterprises there. In view of the fact that most of the so-called Irish manufacturers were in reality English gentlemen—"captains, colonels, and the relations of great families," so Arthur

Young averred [45]—the complacency with which William Pitt and the Lord Lieutenant of Ireland viewed the possible shifting of unprotected English industries to Ireland assumes an unexpected significance. English manufacturers repeatedly asserted that the government's policy was really intended to promote the fortunes of these favored gentlemen rather than to aid native Irish industries.[46]

It was believed that the most important attraction offered by Ireland was relative freedom from taxation. Pitt himself admitted the force of the argument, first in private, and later in consenting to the modification of the excise laws. The vital relation believed to exist between the Irish Resolutions and the question of relative tax burdens in the two countries was set forth in resolutions of Manchester manufacturers, providing for the appointment of delegates to go to Ireland to negotiate for the transfer of their enterprises to that country. They desired "to justify their conduct to their countrymen for adopting a measure so repugnant to their feelings, and so ruinous to the nation, as transplanting the cotton manu-

[45] *Annals of Agriculture*, III, 272, 283.
[46] The text of the Resolutions as they passed the Irish parliament is in *Parl. Hist.*, XXV, 312-314. The text of the Resolutions as revised by the English parliament is in *Ibid.*, 934-942. The Resolutions were explained and interpreted in *Report of the Commissioners of Excise*, 1785, to the House of Commons; in *Report of the Commissioners for His Majesty's Customs* on the same subject; and in *Corresp. of Pitt and Rutland*, particularly Pitt's letter of Jan. 6, 1785, pp. 55-75. See also *Minutes of the Evidence Taken before a Committee of the House of Commons*, and *Minutes of the Evidence Taken before a Committee of the House of Lords*, on the subject of Irish relations, each in the year 1785. An interesting pamphlet on Irish attempts at industrial revival: *Thoughts on the Establishment of New Manufactures in Ireland, Occasioned by the Late Freedoms We Have Obtained, with an Account of the Manchester Manufactory Established by Mr. Brooke*. General accounts, such as Rose's *William Pitt and National Revival*, ch. 11, and McNeill's *Constitutional and Parliamentary History of Ireland till the Union*, ch. 17, are unsatisfactory in respect to the relations of the manufacturers to Pitt's Irish policy.

facture," and to this end they set forth the evils of the excise laws. They contrasted "these destructive and obnoxious systems" with the "unbounded profusion" of advantages offered by the governments of both countries to manufacturers in Ireland. Taxes were in fact much lower in Ireland, and in addition the new Irish government had made extensive grants of money and privileges for encouraging industry. Various English manufacturers received attractive offers from Ireland, and many of them, including Robert Peel, asserted that if the Resolutions were adopted by parliament, they intended to transfer their enterprises to Ireland.[47]

Admirers of Pitt have commonly described the Resolutions as a liberal and far-sighted attempt to solve the Irish problem; and the opposition has been looked upon as an outburst of prejudice, animosity and partisanship wholly unjustified, and explicable only on the ground that Irish relations then, as in most other instances, were fashioned in the heat of prejudice and passion. This judgment should be modified. A magnanimous public spirit probably would have dictated a self-sacrificing acquiescence on the part of the manufacturers; but in a politico-economic society accustomed for centuries to monopoly and public protection, and actuated by profit-making dependent upon group conflicts and compromises, opposition to the Resolutions was the natural course for them to pursue. In respect to the interests of English landlords, merchants, and woollen manufacturers, as well as of most of the other older types of manufacturers, the Resolutions were far from liberal in granting concessions to Ireland; such liberality as they possessed was mainly in granting concessions at the expense of the newer types

[47] *Corresp. of Pitt and Rutland,* 62-64 and *passim; Gazetteer,* April 15, 18, 1785; *Min. of the Evidence, Com. of H. of C.,* 14, 16, 17, 19, 21, 29, 32, 49-51, 59, 60, 66, 67; *Min. of the Evidence, Com. of H. of L.,* 6, 10, 57, 172-174.

of manufacturers, concerning whose rising importance the government seems to have been uninformed.[48] Nor can the attitude of these manufacturers be dissociated from the government's fiscal policy. It was not unnatural, under the circumstances, for the cotton manufacturers in particular, who felt themselves discriminated against and humiliated by the government, to utilize anti-Irish prejudices in unifying the manufacturers against the government's policy in reference to excise. "Manchester and its neighborhood," wrote a member of the House of Commons, "being out of humor with the late tax on fustians, and mixing their politics with their resentment, have been very discontented." A more accurate statement of the situation was made by a member of the House of Lords. "The Manchester people," wrote Lord Lansdowne, "have contrived artfully enough to confound the taxes lately imposed on manufactures with the Irish propositions." [49] They had genuine objections to the Irish Resolutions, but it is true that their chief concern was the repeal of the cotton tax. The government made a serious tactical error in allowing the two policies to be so closely associated, for thereby the easily aroused anti-Irish prejudices were cleverly welded into a unified opposition to both policies. Out of the situation thus created emerged the General Chamber of Manufacturers of Great Britain.

The potters, the iron masters, and the Birmingham manufacturers shared with the cotton interests the initiative and moving force in the formation of the General Chamber, and these groups together contrived to enlist the support of the more numerous but less powerful manufacturers in various other industries less affected by the technical and economic changes of the time.

[48] Concerning the relation of the Irish Resolutions to the question of commercial liberalism, see below, pp. 198, 199.
[49] Hist. MSS. Com., *Rutland MSS.*, III, 201, 202.

Wedgwood the potter had formulated a plan in 1784 which contemplated concerted action by the various local organizations for the purpose of preventing the emigration of workmen, and when the Irish Resolutions came before parliament, his idea of a general union became more definite. He wrote to Matthew Boulton in February of 1785, saying that it was his intention to recommend the formation of "a Committee of Delegates from all the manufacturing places in England and Scotland to meet and sit in London" while the Irish Resolutions were pending, and he hoped that such a step would result in a permanent association. He even had his designer, John Flaxman, make drawings for "the manufacturers' arms." [50]

The interest of the Birmingham group in the question of concerted action found expression in 1783 when the Commercial Committee was organized. Representatives of the Committee were "expressly enjoined . . . to correspond with any commercial committees that are or may be established in any other commercial cities or towns," and particularly to seek the cooperation of the industrial centers in the Black Country, on which Birmingham depended for coal and iron. When Manchester sounded the alarm against excises, the Committee, through its sub-committee on correspondence, sent circular letters to other manufacturing centers "to invite them to withstand what they conceived to be a fixed plan to introduce the excise laws by degrees into all private houses." [51]

Glasgow manufacturers, in September, 1784, voted to enter into correspondence with other industrial centers, and "to join the powerful opposition" of Lancashire. The manufacturers of the Manchester region were indeed

[50] *Corresp. of Wedgwood*, 15, 16; Meteyard, *Life of Wedgwood*, II, 485, 495, 539.

[51] Langford, *Century of Birmingham Life*, I, 316, 320-322; *Parl. Hist.*, XXV, 365.

the heart and center of the movement for general union as well as for opposition to the excise laws. This was later recognized by the Birmingham chamber, which called upon its members to emulate the citizens of Manchester in their liberal support of the General Chamber. The Committee of Trade had carried on correspondence with other industrial centers as early as 1782, and its activity in that connection was described as "a great advantage" to the city. After the cotton manufacturers met with rebuffs at the hands of the ministry in connection with the excise laws, the question of securing the support of other manufacturers became all-important, and they resolved on March 3, 1785, that "it is highly necessary to correspond with every manufacturing body in this kingdom." [52]

Results were soon apparent. It was reported in London on March 12 that "manufacturers are assembling" from various parts of the kingdom. A meeting had already been held in London on March 7; and the cotton manufacturers, having the advantage of a committee of delegates already in touch with the situation, secured action at this meeting which at the outset connected the Irish policy with the question of excise and committed the manufacturers to a joint consideration of the two questions. A committee was appointed, with Josiah Wedgwood as chairman, but the cotton men predominated. This committee met on March 12 and called a general meeting for March 14. At this general meeting, the idea of a union merely temporary to deal with the existing political situation was abandoned, and decision was made to form a permanent national organization, to be called the General Chamber of Manufacturers of Great Britain. It was resolved unanimously that the

[52] *Manchester Mercury,* Sept. 21, Oct. 12, 1784, Mch. 8, 1785; *Gazetteer,* Mch. 9, 1785; Langford, *Century of Birmingham Life,* I, 328, 329; *Owen MSS.,* LXXX, 3, 4.

association "do not cease with the present business," and to that end steps were taken to perfect the organization. The plan adopted was presented by a Manchester manufacturer. The Chamber was to consist of manufacturers only, a sharp distinction being made between manufacturers and merchants. It was expected that the members would normally be members also of local chambers. A permanent secretary was appointed; a standing committee was chosen; offices were engaged at 38 Fenchurch Street; and financial support was arranged by membership fees and by subscriptions. Plans were made for special activities during sessions of parliament, but the central office was to maintain constantly a clearing house of information and legal advice. Briefly, the Chamber was a forerunner of modern associations of manufacturers, identical in spirit, and not dissimilar in form.[53]

The nation-wide activities of the Chamber in opposition to the Irish Resolutions and the excise laws produced a flood of more than sixty petitions, deluging the House of Commons,—petitions representing in most cases local groups of manufacturers, and containing such similarities as to prove their common inspiration. They usually denounced both the Resolutions and excises. The government first yielded on the question of taxes by repealing the more obnoxious features of the cotton tax of 1784. But it was now too late for the government to break up the united opposition of the manufacturers. The cotton men, having had the support of the General

[53] The principal sources of information concerning the early history of the General Chamber are contemporaneous newspapers, particularly the *Gazetteer and New Daily Advertiser* (cited herein as the *Gazetteer*), which published official resolutions and other statements emanating from the Chamber, with extensive comments. See in particular the issues of March 9, 12, 14, 15, 17, 18, 23, April 6, May 2. See also *Manchester Mercury*, April 5 (Supplement), August 16, 1785; *British Merchant for 1787*, 10, 11; and *Public Proceedings of the General Chamber of Manufacturers of Great Britain on the French Treaty*, 70-78.

Chamber against the excise law, stood by it in its continued war on the Irish Resolutions. Pitt again yielded, introducing the Resolutions in a new form, including several changes demanded by the manufacturers. Immediately thereafter the General Chamber held a full meeting and resolved to notify its constitutents and to ask them to petition parliament for further delay. Then followed a second deluge of petitions conforming closely to the recommendations of the General Chamber. Although Pitt secured the adoption of the revised Resolutions, the revision itself was a virtual defeat at home, and the cause of the not unexpected rejection of the entire plan in Ireland. Thus ended in defeat, at the hands of the organized manufacturers, a policy which had engaged the utmost power of the government, and which had been regarded by Pitt as vital to his own position and to the empire.[54]

After this twofold triumph of union, the General Chamber of Manufacturers was held in high esteem by local groups of manufacturers. Membership and subscriptions increased rapidly. Enthusiastic meetings of the local organizations were held, particularly at Manchester and Birmingham and in Staffordshire, at which funds were voted and support was pledged. The Chamber itself was active in the establishment of new local groups as branches of the central body. Its activities included a study of excise laws with the purpose of securing further modifications and preventing extensions; the furnishing of aid to manufacturers in guarding their improvements and inventions against exportation and against foreign spies; the enforcement of the laws prohibiting the emigration of workmen; the dissemination of pertinent information; the granting of legal advice

[54] Commons *Journals*, XL, 576-1088 (texts of the petitions); *Gazetteer*, Mch. 9, 15, 16, 17, 18, 23, Apr. 6, 15, May 2, 14, 1785; *Corresp. of Pitt and Rutland,* 57, 75.

wherever needed; and the study of British and foreign tariffs in the hope of securing reciprocal trading relations.[55]

6. *The General Chamber of Manufacturers and the French Commercial Treaty (1786)*

It was in connection with the last-named subject—the reciprocal readjustment of tariffs—that the General Chamber came once more into significant contact with public policy. The occasion was furnished by the revision of commercial relations with France called for by the Treaty of Versailles (1783). According to this treaty, a new commercial agreement was to be concluded not later than January 1, 1786. The English government under Pitt was not eager to take up the task of carrying out the agreement. This was due, however, not so much to lack of interest as to the unsettled condition of English politics. The insecurity of the young minister's power, the violent tactics of the opposition, and especially the economic disruption of the empire involved in the separation of America and the legislative independence of Ireland—these circumstances combined to force the government to focus its attention on problems more vital to its own existence. As a result, the English were forced to ask for an extension of time beyond the first of January, 1786. To this the French reluctantly consented, for the French government desired immediate action. The leading English manufacturers represented in the General Chamber were also eager for treaty arrangements to be made, for their productive powers were increasing so rapidly as to demand an expansion of mar-

[55] *Manchester Mercury*, May 24, June 28, Aug. 23, Nov. 22, 29, Dec. 13, 27, 1785, Jan. 3, 1786; Langford, *Century of Birmingham Life*, I, 327-329; *Corresp. of Wedgwood*, 17-19, 37-40.

kets. Under this twofold pressure, the government was at length impelled to take action.[56]

The treaty, which was signed at length on September 26, 1786, marked a notable advance in the direction of commercial liberalism. It provided for reciprocal liberty in respect to residence, travel, the purchase and use of consumption goods, and the practice of religious faiths, within the European dominions of the two countries, "freely and securely, without license or passport, general or special, by land or by sea." The principal commercial advantages gained by France were in respect to wines and other commodities wherein she excelled by virtue of superior soil, climate and natural resources. The English, on the other hand, benefited chiefly by means of reductions in tariffs on articles in which England excelled not because of natural advantages but because of superior skill and business enterprise, particularly cottons, irons, and pottery.[57]

During the negotiation of the treaty and the formula-

[56] *Foreign Office Papers*, 27/17 (letters of Hailles to Carmarthen, Aug. 4, 11, Oct. 6, 1785); Dumas, *Étude sur le Traité de Commerce*, 30-32; *Corresp. of Pitt and Rutland*, 111, 112. On the attitude of the manufacturers toward reciprocal treaties, see *Min. of the Evidence, Com. of H. of C.*, 1785 (on Irish Resolutions), 181-183; *Min. of the Evidence, Com. of H. of L.*, 1785 (on Irish Resolutions), 150-152, 176, 177; *Report of the Lords of the Com. of Council*, 1785 (on Irish Resolutions), 81; Commons *Journals*, XL, 647; *Gazetteer*, Mch. 23, 1785; *Manchester Mercury*, Nov. 29, 1785.

[57] The texts of the treaty and the supplementary convention are in Commons *Journals*, XLII, 266-274, 289, and *Parl. Hist.*, XXVI, 233-255, 268-272. The treaty is also printed as an appendix to the first volume of the *Journal and Corresp. of Auckland*. These three references contain extensive records of the general history of the treaty. The principal manuscript records are in the *Foreign Office Papers* and *Board of Trade Papers*, cited herein from time to time. For general accounts, mainly diplomatic and political, see Dumas, *Étude sur le Traité de Commerce de 1786 entre la France et l'Angleterre;* Rose, *William Pitt and National Revival*, 328-339, 343; Rose, "The Franco-British Commercial Treaty," in *English Hist. Rev.*, 1908, XXIII, 709-724; Browning, "The Treaty of Commerce between England and France in 1786," in *Trans., Royal Hist. Soc.*, 1885, n.s., II, 349-364.

tion of details, the General Chamber of Manufacturers continued its activities. Numerous committee meetings were held, the Lords of Trade were interviewed, answers to various questions were secured from William Eden (later Lord Auckland), who negotiated the treaty, and extensive correspondence and interviews were conducted with manufacturers of various parts of the country. The letters received were in general favorable to the treaty, though it appears that special weight was given to the sentiments of the cotton, iron, and pottery manufacturers, who were enthusiastic in support of the treaty, and who from the first had been leaders in the General Chamber. On the basis of its investigations, the committee in charge of the Chamber's relations to the treaty met in London on December 9, 1786, and adopted resolutions favoring the treaty. It was resolved that "from the best information the committee can collect from the Chambers of Commerce and Manufactures" and other sources, the treaty, based on "liberal and equitable principles, promises to be advantageous to their manufacturing and commercial interests by opening a new source of fair trade to both nations," and by "securing a continuance of peace and good offices between two great and neighboring nations, so advantageously situated for availing themselves of the blessings of peace and an extended commerce." [58]

Although the committee asserted that its action was based upon the carefully ascertained views of the constituents of the General Chamber, the resolutions of December 9, when published, gave rise to a controversy which divided the organization into hostile factions. It was maintained by the opponents of the treaty that the resolutions favoring the treaty were not representative of the sentiments of the manufacturers generally, and the

[58] *Gazetteer,* Dec. 12, 1786, Feb. 17, 19, 21, 1787 (including accounts of activities earlier than the dates given).

resolutions were ascribed to the fact that "the Manchester, Birmingham, and Staffordshire manufacturers have, of course, great sway in that body." Other manufacturers, it was declared, opposed the treaty, and had trusted the General Chamber to represent their views. But since those favoring the treaty controlled the Chamber, the opposing manufacturers, having been misrepresented till the treaty had been signed, "do not know where to communicate their thoughts, or how to collect the general sense and convey it with force to the minister." But they resolved not to yield without a struggle. In order to give effect to their views in the approaching discussion of the treaty in parliament, they decided to contest the control of the General Chamber by the cotton, iron, and pottery men. The older, more conservative manufacturers, though far less powerful individually, were more numerous, and they succeeded in outvoting their progressive opponents. They were aided by a small minority from the newer industrial centers, notably by Thomas Walker, a Whig leader at Manchester, who seems to have been moved largely by his extreme hostility to Pitt. The group favoring the treaty was severely criticized, hostile resolutions were adopted, and the House of Commons was petitioned to delay action in order to allow further consideration. The controversy continued for some time, and, although those favoring the treaty later for a time regained control, the disruption of the General Chamber was a serious blow to the prestige of the organization. Proponents of the treaty, having gained their ends for the time being in its adoption, were less eager, apparently, to press the fight in the Chamber than were those who sought to defeat the treaty.[59]

It is a fact of significance that the end which the cot-

[59] *Gazetteer*, Jan. 12, Feb. 7, 12, 13, 19, 21, 27, 28, Mch. 19, 30, 1787; *Manchester Mercury*, Feb. 27, Mch. 6, 1787; *Public Proceedings of the General Chamber on the French Treaty*.

ton, iron and pottery men sought was the establishment reciprocally of virtual free trade in their commodities; while the other manufacturers were generally either opposed to reciprocal trade even with high tariffs, or else in favor of it only under serious restrictions. The manufacturers of silks, ribbons, paper, clocks, leather, paper hangings, hats (except in Lancashire), saddlery, and plate glass are on record as in general opposed to reciprocal tariffs, and were in any case insistent that English import duties be high enough to afford protection in the home market.[60] The woollen manufacturers in some cases opposed and in other cases favored reciprocal tariffs, but generally opposed free trade; and they unanimously demanded, as the price of reciprocity, that "none of our raw materials be allowed to be exported and . . . great care be taken to prevent our manufacturing instruments and mechanical machines and improvements from being exported." It was desired, also, that the woollen trade with Portugal, already on a favorable basis, be safeguarded. Their liberalism, therefore, was of a very dubious kind.[61]

Among the manufacturers of cotton, iron and pottery, such reservations were seldom made. Almost without exception they desired the elimination of all duties and the introduction of reciprocal free trade. At Manchester, the day fixed for opening trade under the treaty (May 10, 1787) was celebrated by the ringing of bells and by banqueting. Some of the toasts offered by the banqueters reveal the spirit that animated the community: "May the prosperity of free trade, wise government, and constitutional revenue be the extinction of smuggling, peculation and excise laws."—"May near neighbors never

[60] *Board of Trade Papers,* 6/111, Docs. 52, 53, 57, 61, 62, 6/112, Doc. dated Dec. 11, 1786, endorsed "Answer of the Watch and Clock Makers," 6/113, Min. of Feb. 22, Mch. 3, 11, 13, 16, Aug. 10, 1786.

[61] *Ibid.,* 6/111, Docs. 25, 27, 30, 33, 35, 6/113, Min. of Jan. 20, 21, Feb. 10, Mch. 9, 14, 1786. (Transcripts in B. T. 6/114).

have cause to consider each other as enemies."—"May the pending treaties with Spain, Portugal and Russia have a speedy and happy conclusion." [62] The enthusiasm of those connected with the iron industry rivaled that of the cotton manufacturers. Their delegates told the authorities at London that "the duty should not be more than 5%, but the lower the better." The action of the General Chamber of Manufacturers in opposing the treaty was repudiated by the Birmingham Commercial Committee, and the spirit in which the treaty was accepted is embodied in the lines of a local rimester:

> The prospect how pleasing—of commerce I mean,
> When Eden returns from the banks of the Seine.
> May kingdom 'gainst kingdom no more be at spite;
> For both 'twere much better to trade than to fight;
> And whilst mutual friendship and harmony reign,
> Our buttons we'll barter for pipes of Champaigne.[63]

The potters, led by Josiah Wedgwood, were also ardent advocates of reciprocal reduction of duties,—"the lower the duty the better,"—and they, too, desired similar arrangements with countries other than France.[64]

It is apparent that there was coming to be a significant cleavage among the manufacturers in respect alike to

[62] On the attitude of the cotton manufacturers, including those of Scotland, see Board of Trade Papers, 6/113, Min. of Feb. 8, 11, 22, 24, Mch. 14, 1786 (Transcripts in B.T. 6/114), 6/140, Docs. 2, 3; Foreign Office Papers, 27/17, Doc. endorsed "Memorial of Wm. and Robt. Fulton and John McKerrell & Son to Lord Carmarthen"; Manchester Mercury, Nov. 22, 1785, Oct. 17, 1786, Jan. 30, Feb. 27, Mch. 6, May 8, 15, 1787.

[63] Quoted by Langford in Century of Birmingham Life, I, 329. See also Board of Trade Papers, 6/111, Doc. 75, 6/113, Min. of Feb. 3, Mch. 11, 14, 1786; Boulton and Watt MSS., Letter Books (Office), 1786-1788, 155, 156.

[64] Board of Trade Papers, 6/112, Wedgwood, Warburton and Neale to the Customs Commissioners, Oct. 19, 1786, and Resolutions of Staffordshire potters, Oct. 10, 1786, 6/113, Min. of Feb. 24, 1786.

their economic position and to their views of public policy. The situation seems at length to have been sensed by the prime minister. The haughtiness and condescension of Pitt's early relations to the manufacturers now gave place, in his dealings with the great industrialists who had organized the General Chamber of Manufacturers, to a recognition of their power. His new attitude found expression, however, in a most artful manner. "It cannot be too generally understood," he wrote on December 16, 1785, to Eden, his appointee for negotiating the treaty, "that our sole object is to collect, from all parts of the kingdom, a just representation of the interests of all the various branches of trade and manufacture which can be affected by the French arrangement, and that we are perfectly open to form an unprejudiced opinion on the result. I probably need hardly add, however, that there are many reasons which make it desirable to give as little employment or encouragement as possible to the Chamber of Commerce [65] taken collectively." Again, in his speech of February 12, 1787, in the House of Commons in support of the treaty, he said that the manufacturers "merited every respectful attention," and that in matters involving their interests, "their representations must indeed carry the most powerful weight." But as for the General Chamber of Manufacturers, this body he referred to contemptuously, as if its existence had just been called to his attention. Its petition against the treaty he mentioned as coming from "a few manufacturers collected in a certain Chamber of Commerce," a body which was absurdly wandering "into the paths of legislation and government," and attempting to take from parliament "the trouble of legislation." The minister's purpose was plain if somewhat disingenuous. He knew, from the bitterness of the defeat of some

[65] The General Chamber of Manufacturers was sometimes thus designated in spite of its membership being confined to manufacturers.

of his most earnestly championed policies, something of the power of the great manufacturers who had cleverly organized the industrial interests of the country against those policies. He was forced to recognize them, but he desired at the same time to discredit their organization.[66]

But his deference to the leading members of the General Chamber as originally organized was as pronounced as was his desire to discredit their organization. The negotiation of the treaty of 1786 with France affords the first but by no means the only significant instance of this attitude on the part of Pitt's government. Such an attitude was evident in the initial step in the negotiation of the treaty—the appointment of William Eden to represent the English government. As a prominent member of the opposition, he had fought the Irish Resolutions and the cotton tax, and he was generally looked upon as a champion of the industrial interests. Eminent manufacturers expressed their pleasure, and Matthew Boulton even stated that had the choice been left to him, he would himself have appointed Eden. Lord Sheffield stated that it was not Eden's "system" to knock his head "against any knot of manufacturers." His constant attention to the views of the manufacturers and the cordiality of his relations with them afford ample evidence in support of Sheffield's statement.[67]

It will be remembered that Pitt instructed Eden to ignore the General Chamber of Manufacturers as far as possible, but to secure full information from the manufacturers individually as a basis for the treaty. That Eden adhered at least to the latter part of the instructions is apparent. A short time before leaving for France he wrote familiarly to Morton Eden that he was "passing

---

[66] *Journal and Corresp. of Auckland,* I, 90, 91; *Parl. Hist.,* XXVI, 379-382, 390, 392.

[67] *Journal and Corresp. of Auckland,* I, 92, 93, 164.

every morning and all the morning" in securing information from the merchants and manufacturers. "I do not
yet foresee," he continued, "precisely when I shall be
able to proceed to the Continent. . . . It is some satisfaction, however, that our inquiries go forward pleas-
antly," with "much liberality and good temper." That
Pitt made use of the views of the manufacturers in fram-
ing his draft of the treaty is evident from his letters to
Eden written in April, 1786. "The evidence of the manufacturers," he wrote, "will furnish some tolerable ground
to go upon." And again: "The general knowledge from
the examination of the manufacturers and from other
sources is enough to satisfy me that the general principle
[of the treaty] is right." There is evidence, also, that
the government kept in close touch with the views of the
manufacturers during the progress of the negotiations in
France. Consultations with them continued after Eden's
departure for France; and Eden himself, while in
France, not only corresponded with manufacturers in
England, but also held interviews with their agents at
the place of conference. In view of the intimate relations
between the government and the leading manufacturers
during the various stages of the making of the treaty,
their influence may be stated fairly in the words of a
writer of the time who referred to the treaty as having been "framed in concert with the manufacturers
themselves." [68]

The government conferred repeatedly with manufacturers of various types, but it should be noted that it
was the interest of the newer industrial groups that found

[68] *Journal and Corresp. of Auckland,* I, 94, 110, 114, 143, 144, 158, 166,
167; *Foreign Office Papers,* 27/17, Carmarthen to Hailles, Dec. 9,
1785, 27/19, Instructions to Eden, Mch. 10, 1786; *Letter from a
Manchester Manufacturer to the Right Honorable Charles James Fox
on His Political Opposition to the Commercial Treaty with France,* 14.
Records of the conferences with the manufacturers are for the most
part in the *Board of Trade Papers.*

recognition in the treaty. The importance of these groups is evidenced not so much by their prominence in the process of securing information as by the objects of the treaty. Pitt in private letters and more cautiously in parliament declared that "the chief immediate advantage" desired was "that of encouraging industry and raising the demand for our manufactures"; and that the "great and leading" manufactures "which we wish to send to France are cotton, some sorts of woollens, hardware, and earthenware." Again, in writing to Eden, he stated that the idea of a duty as high as fifteen per cent. "on the essential article of cottons cannot be listened to," and should the French insist on such a high rate, "it would in fact be breaking off the treaty." But as for glass and certain other articles, he was willing to make concession, "a little adventurously," which he hoped would assist in carrying the point on cottons. The French wanted a duty of twenty per cent., "and some went as high as thirty per cent." Eden wrote to Pitt of his sense of triumph when, "after much dispute," he secured an agreement for ten per cent., which, however, was later raised to twelve. Supporters and opponents of the treaty alike agreed that the chief beneficiaries would be the cotton, hardware, and pottery manufacturers.[69]

The men who had organized the General Chamber of Manufacturers now found their power and interests recognized, while at the same time their organization had been disrupted and seriously discredited. These circumstances led to the virtual abandonment for the time being of attempts at national organization. The heart of the difficulty, so far as the method of organization was con-

[69] *Parl. Hist.*, XXVI, 385; *Journal and Corresp. of Auckland*, I, 129, 148, ff., 484, ff.; *Necessity and Policy of the Commercial Treaty with France Considered*, 44, 60; [Mackenzie], *Woollen Draper's Letter on the French Treaty*, 5, 26, 27; *View of the Treaty of Commerce with France*, 13, 20-35, 45-68.

cerned, lay, according to Wedgwood, in the fact that "a man who should get a delegation from the tooth-brush makers of London would have a vote equal with a delegate sent from Birmingham or Manchester." The General Chamber survived for some time, and its formal reorganization was discussed but never effected. But the local organizations in the cotton, iron and pottery districts were effectively maintained, and among leading manufacturers there was an accord perhaps more effective because less formal and less subjected to the criticisms of hostile groups.[70]

The General Chamber came somewhat prominently before the public in 1787, when the faction opposed to the treaty with France sought vindication of its attitude by publishing the debates, but in general its policy had been opposed to publicity except among the manufacturers themselves. During the progress through the House of Commons of the Irish Resolutions and the bill to modify the excise on cottons, the Chamber was so desirous of keeping itself behind the scenes that it refused even to petition the House. Yet the initial impulse behind its formation, it will be recalled, was to influence the government in the consideration of these measures; and it did exert a determining influence. Its method was indirect, through local bodies, and by means of correspondence and consultations. It was the publication of its debates on the treaty with France that was assigned by some of the prominent manufacturers as one reason for withdrawing their support. The indirect, behind-the-scenes methods probably account in large part for the obscurity of the organization, which prevented his-

[70] Letter of Wedgwood to Watt, Mch. 27, 1787, in Boulton and Watt Collection; Boulton and Watt MSS., *Letter Books (Office)*, 1786-1788, 159, 222, 225; *Manchester Mercury*, July 31, Aug. 7, 1787; *Journal and Corresp. of Auckland*, I, 429; Meteyard, *Life of Wedgwood*, II, 550, 556, 561; Langford, *Century of Birmingham Life*, I, 330; Julia Wedgwood, *Life of Wedgwood*, 224.

torians for more than a century from discovering its influence. Its very considerable power and importance would otherwise undoubtedly have elicited more extensive contemporaneous comment.[71]

The comments that have survived are mostly so hostile in nature as to justify the fear of publicity. Arthur Young, as might be expected from the wide range of his observations and his agrarian connections and sympathies, wrote at length concerning the Chamber, and looked with suspicion on the concerted action of the industrial group as a menace to "the landed interest." The Marquis of Lansdowne, as a public official, spoke with irony and yet not without apparent apprehension concerning an organization which he would probably have denounced, had he been familiar with later political terminology, as a "soviet" of capitalists. He had no doubt, he said, that "the Chamber of Manufacturers of Great Britain was very respectable," but he hoped its members "would keep themselves to their simple object, and not harbor the idea of setting themselves up as a body to overawe parliament, or interfere with the political measures of the country." The prime minister himself spoke in similar tone, as has been seen, of the Chamber's desire to relieve the government of "the trouble of legislation." [72]

Contemporaneous comments hostile and friendly alike are rare, but the General Chamber was an organizaztion far more significant than its obscurity would indicate. Its own immediate influence on public policy was a manifestation of the forces which, though checked by wartime reaction toward aristocratic rule, culminated nevertheless in the indirect domination of the state by

[71] *Gazetteer*, Apr. 6, 1787; Boulton and Watt MSS., *Letter Books (Office)*, 1786-1788, 155; *Corresp. of Wedgwood*, 15, 16.

[72] *Annals of Agriculture*, III, 452-455 (see also pp. 260, 388); *Parl. Hist.*, XXV, 858, XXVI, 390.

the industrial oligarchy.[73] It promoted the formation of local business organizations which have had practically continuous existence and have exerted decisive influence. Its own organization broke down due to an internal defect, but even in form it was a forerunner of modern associations of business men for maintaining committees, attorneys, information bureaus, and lobbies for promoting their interests as affected by politics and by other economic groups.

7. The rise of economic liberalism

The fact of greatest significance in the history of the Chamber is suggested by its failure. Its disruption in 1787 was the result of the great and growing divergence between the older petty manufacturers and the great modern industrial capitalists. The former continued to rely on primitive methods and state support and regulation; the latter were tending rapidly toward the technique of the age of machinery and of factories, and toward the commercial liberalism and the *laissez-faire* policies of the nineteenth-century Manchester school.

The illiberal spirit of the older manufacturers as well as of the merchants is so well known as to need little comment. Their objection to reciprocal tariff reductions in connection with the French commercial treaty was in harmony with their traditional attitude. Their fight for the adoption in 1788 of more rigorous measures against the export of .raw materials in the woollen industry is typical of their continued dependence on monopoly. The spirit prevailing among them and the merchants was bitterly assailed by Adam Smith in well-known passages

[73] A recent conservative observer writes: "It is very generally admitted that the most powerful organization in Britain is not Parliament but the Federation of British Industries." (H. N. Casson, in Phila. *Pub. Ledger,* Dec. 17, 1923, Bus. Sec., p. 1.) This body is the present-day counterpart of the General Chamber of Manufacturers.

advocating freedom of trade. The interests of the landed class, he asserted, with curious lack of discernment for so keen an observer, are "strictly and inseparably connected with the general interest of society." But merchants and manufacturers make up a class "whose interest is never exactly the same with that of the public"; members of this class, indeed, "have generally an interest to deceive and even to oppress the public." The "sneaking arts," the "impertinent jealousy," the "mean rapacity," the "monopolizing spirit," and the "interested sophistry of merchants and manufacturers [have] confounded the common sense of mankind." To expect freedom of trade in Britain "is as absurd as to expect that an Oceania or Utopia should ever be established in it," for "the monopoly which our manufacturers have obtained against us" is too strong; they are able to "intimidate the legislature." [74]

Adam Smith's invidious contrast between the landed class and the merchants and manufacturers is obviously untenable. But the fact of the "monopolizing spirit" of the latter at the time when the *Wealth of Nations* was written is beyond question. Smith's view, however, took no account of the transformation which was then in its initial stage. He was no herald of the rising industrialists. He seems to have had no conception of that profound change by virtue of which the manufacturers were to become the champions as against the landlords of free trade and *laissez-faire*. But while the *Wealth of Nations*, even in the later editions, is singularly silent concerning the change, other writings of the time afford striking recognition of the growth of liberalism among the great manufacturers. The merchants, as well as the older types of manufacturers, were contrasted with the men in control of the cotton, iron, and pottery industries in respect to their attitude toward monopoly. Concerning

[74] *Wealth of Nations,* I, Bk. I, ch. 11, II, Bk. IV, chs. 2, 3 (8th ed., 1796).

the manufacturers, a contemporary advocate of monopoly observed two "factions" among them. One faction, we are told, is interested essentially in maintaining control of the home markets; the members of the other faction are possessed of a "desire of an open trade," because they, "from their present ascendancy of skill, have nothing immediate to fear from competition, and everything to hope from the speculation of an increased demand." The latter faction the author identifies as consisting of the cotton, iron, and pottery manufacturers. Essentially the same distinction was made by other writers, including Sir Joseph Banks, president of the Royal Society, and Arthur Young. Young at various times condemned what he characterized as the narrow, monopolizing spirit of the older manufacturers, and praised the liberal and progressive spirit which he found in the newer industries. "The food that is wholesome and nourishing at Birmingham and Manchester," he wrote in 1792, "will not be poison at Leeds and the Devizes." [75]

The early development of free-trade and *laissez-faire* tendencies is observable in connection not only with the French commercial treaty but with various other public policies as well. The *laissez-faire* attitude of the newer types of manufacturers was a principal cause of their opposition to the government's excise policy. This attitude found expression in a large proportion of the statements, petitions, and resolutions issued in opposition to excises. It was declared by the "principal manufacturers" of Manchester that of all methods of taxation, "those under the excise laws are most obnoxious," and that the cotton tax in particular "operates more vexatiously and produces more evils than any heretofore enacted." The

[75] *British Merchant for 1787*, 8, 12, 28; *Annals of Agriculture*, VII, 159-175, IX, 498, 499, XVI, 352, XVIII, 327, 328; *Historical and Political Remarks upon the Tariff of the Commercial Treaty*, 166-169; *View of the Treaty of Commerce with France*, 75-83. See also above, pp. 121, 184, 185.

reasons for the peculiar evils of the cotton excise, it was stated, are "the complex nature of that manufacture," and "the amazing number of excise officers necessary to enforce" the law. It is declared that "such an influx of those gentry [the excisemen] to disturb the harmony and arrangements of their manufactures, to deprive them of personal liberty and the free exercise of their property, is UNWISE, IMPOLITIC, and UNJUST." The amount of the tax, though considerable, was declared to be a minor objection. In a petition to the House of Commons, the boast was made that although they "have never received or solicited any parliamentary aid," nevertheless they "have always been, and still are, ready on all occasions to contribute to the general exigencies of the state." They object to the extent of the taxation, but mainly to "what is still worse," the fact that their "liberty and property," by means of the excise laws, are "fettered and embarrassed." To the same effect was a resolution of the General Chamber of Manufacturers, which denounced the excise methods as "calculated to lay open the secrets of trade, to lock up in excise [by advance payments of excise before sales could be made] the capital before usefully employed, and to infringe upon the liberty of the subject." Birmingham manufacturers, though not so immediately affected, declared in resolutions of the Commercial Committee that "every excise law is irreconcilable with the freedom and secrecy every manufacturer has a right to demand in his own workshop and in the exercise of his business." [76]

In view of the prevalence of high taxes and of excise methods not essentially different from those embodied in the cotton tax, the extreme hostility that this tax aroused is explicable only on the grounds that it was in the first place ill-adapted to the changes in technique and busi-

Gazetteer, Mch. 9, Afr. 6, 15 18, 1785; Commons Journals, XL, 642, 760; Langford, Century of Birmingham Life, I, 320.

ness organization in the cotton industry; and in the second place, out of harmony with the rising tide of individualism and *laissez-faire* which was rapidly overwhelming the old system of governmental relations to industry.

The opposition to restriction and control by the government in connection with the excise laws was supplemented by hostility even to governmental patronage of a favorable character. There was a crisis in 1788 due to a temporary excess of English-made cotton goods beyond the power of the markets to absorb, which was aggravated by importations by the East India Company. This induced some of the manufacturers, particularly about Glasgow, where manufacturing remained more largely under control of the great merchants, to propose a national cloth hall with the backing and under the regulations of a royal charter. This proposed organization, in common with the older chartered companies, involved a highly centralized system, supported and at the same time controlled by the government within the conditions of the charter. It gained considerable favor among the temporarily embarrassed manufacturers, but was discarded at length due to its public character. Among the objections urged against it by the Paisley manufacturers was the belief that it would interfere with "private trade" and the making of "private bargains." At Manchester resolutions were adopted declaring that "any attempt to restrain the freedom of the commerce of this country" should be opposed; ingenuity and industry should be left without restraint.[77]

Other aspects of the tendency toward *laissez-faire* were connected with the relations of the manufacturers toward their work people, particularly the breakdown of the laws relating to settlement and apprenticeship. The shifting and concentration of economic opportuni-

[77] *Board of Trade Papers*, 6/140, Docs. 60, 70, 77, 85-88.

ties, the increasing demand for unskilled labor, and the rapid internal reorganization and specialization of industry, made the old regulations, both legal and traditional, no longer applicable. These conditions inevitably led to dissatisfaction with governmental regulation of economic life. And yet the manufacturers, in their attitude toward their workers, were far from consistent in their advocacy of *laissez-faire*. What they demanded for themselves they were unwilling to concede to their employees. They were eager to avail themselves of old laws and to secure the enactment of new regulations for shifting from their own shoulders the burden of poor rates, for preventing their workers from forming combinations analogous to their own organizations, and for denying to their employees the privilege of going abroad while vigorously asserting on many occasions their own right to leave the country and to take with them their capital and their technical equipment. They were willing to accept for themselves the benefits of legal protection against their employees, while at times they invoked the principle of liberty to prevent similar protection being accorded the workers, and at other times invoked the contrary principle of public control to restrict even attempted self-help by the workers themselves.[78]

The attitude of the early manufacturers of the new industrial era toward that phase of economic liberalism associated with international trade, while not entirely consistent, was on the whole inclined toward liberalism, not only in connection with the treaty with France but as well in various other instances. Even their opposition to the Irish policy of William Pitt, although resulting in part from anti-Irish prejudices far from liberal, gives evidence at the same time of a tendency toward free trade. In place of Pitt's policy of discriminations in favor of the English woollen manufacturers, merchants,

[78] For further discussion of this subject, see below, p. 216, ff.

and landlords, they proposed that "all articles, which are the natural growth, product, or manufacture of either country . . . be imported into the other duty free." Manchester petitioners asserted that "a complete union in commerce, policy, and legislation is the most probable means of establishing a lasting harmony and good will between the two nations"—a proposal far more liberal than the traditional policy of monopoly and discrimination. In another respect their opposition was not wholly illiberal. The Resolutions provided for preferential duties on certain Irish products, particularly linens, to the exclusion of these commodities from other countries. This was probably a well-intentioned measure of justice to Ireland to compensate in some slight degree for the ruin of her woollen and other industries, but it was none the less a perpetuation of the principle of monopoly. It was opposed by the leading manufacturers in England on the ground that it prevented the making of reciprocal trade agreements with other countries which were seeking a market, particularly for their linens, in England. Such a policy of reciprocal treaties based on mutual tariff reductions was clearly in harmony with free-trade tendencies. It was this policy that was later adopted by Pitt, worked out in conference with the manufacturers, and made the basis of the treaty with France, as well as of other proposed treaties, negotiations for which were interrupted by the war.[79]

These were indeed halting steps, oscillating between the old monopolistic, protective system and a new conception of freedom and private initiative in the domain

[79] Commons *Journals*, XL, 647, 749; Lords *Journals*, XXXVII, 312, 323; *Min. of the Evidence, Com. of H. of C.*, 1785 (on Irish Resolutions), 179, 181-183; *Min. of the Evidence, Com. of H. of L.*, 1785 (on Irish Resolutions), 150-152, 176-178; *Report of the Lords of the Com. of Council Relating to Trade and Plantations*, 1785 (on Irish Resolutions), 81; *Gazetteer*, Mch. 23, 1785; *Manchester Mercury*, May 24, 1785; Mrs. H. Ware, *Life and Corresp. of Ware*, 17-19, 95-98.

of international trade. But economic forces were pressing the manufacturers more and more decisively in the latter direction. A most potent factor was the need for new markets to absorb the ever-increasing output made possible by invention. The anticipated expansion of markets was the source of their enthusiasm for the treaty with France; and the favorable results of the treaty inspired a desire for the extension of reciprocity. When the delegates of the Birmingham Commercial Committee avowed their desire for reciprocal free trade with France, they were asked if they thought a similar arrangement with Spain would be advantageous. "Yes—with all the world," was the response. Similar sentiments were expressed by the potters and by the cotton manufacturers. Representatives of the latter petitioned the government in 1788 to enter into agreements with Continental powers and with the Turkish Empire "to open new channels of consumption for the increased quantity of . . . cotton goods which have been and will be made in Great Britain in consequence of the great extent of the powers of machinery and human labor which have been applied to this manufactory." [80]

The manufacturers found a demand for their goods in other countries, but they discovered that as long as England maintained her high tariffs and her navigation acts as a wall against reciprocal trade except on her own terms and in her own ships, these countries would be loath to allow entrance to English goods. Josiah Wedgwood stated that French retaliatory measures against England's protective system were preventing the sale of earthenware in France except by illicit methods; and he complained frankly that illicit trade in an article so bulky was too costly and dangerous to be profitable. Other manufacturers were more fortunate as to the phys-

[80] *Board of Trade Papers,* 6/113, Min. of Mch. 11, 1786, 6/140, Doc. 42; *Corresp. of Wedgwood,* 9, 10, 188-194.

ical character of their commodities, but they, too, desired "an open trade" with reciprocal duties as low as could be secured, in place of resort to indirect routes, false labels, and other expensive and hazardous expedients for reaching the French markets. Complaints were made concerning similar difficulties encountered in reaching the markets of Spain, Russia, Germany, and other countries. Because of these obstacles in the way of legitimate trade, and because of the expense and danger of illicit methods of putting their goods into the hands of foreign consumers, the great manufacturers were literally forced to recognize the desirability of reciprocal concessions in the direction of a more liberal system of international trade. Protected as they were by machines and superior methods, they no longer needed legal monopoly, which, instead of being an advantage, had itself become an obstacle to expansion of markets by inciting retaliatory measures.[81]

Another economic factor was the question of access to raw materials. This impelled first the cotton manufacturers, and later others, in the direction of commercial liberalism. The monopoly conferred on English shippers by the navigation system led the manufacturers to attack that seemingly impregnable fortress of protection, defended even by Adam Smith. The increase of the demand for cotton beyond the supply available from the British colonies made the question a vital one. Less than a third of the cotton imported in the year of the French commercial treaty came from the British dominions. Much of it was supplied by the French possessions. Attempts were made by the manufacturers, the East India Company, and the government, to stimulate cotton

[81] *Board of Trade Papers*, 6/111, Doc. 4, 6/113, Min. of Jan. 21, Feb. 22, 24, Mch. 11, 1786; *Foreign Office Papers*, 27/17, Hailles to Carmarthen, Aug. 4, Sept. 15, 1785, 27/19, Eden to Carmarthen, Apr. 25, 1786; Langford, *Century of Birmingham Life*, I, 322-324. See also above, p. 199.

growing within the empire, but without adequate results.[82]

The monopoly held by English shippers was rendered the more serious in the view of the manufacturers by the complications growing out of the wars and the economic alliance against England during the period of the American Revolution, which added to the difficulty of supplying the rapidly increasing consumption demands. They had been encouraged in opposing the shipping monopoly by the benefits derived from an earlier slight relaxation in the navigation system made by the "free-port law" of 1766, which opened certain ports in the British West Indies to foreign vessels, and which is said to have enabled them to purchase French colonial cotton at a rate thirty per cent. cheaper through the "free ports" than through France. This law, which was to expire in 1774, they persuaded the government to renew. It was in that year that the Manchester Commercial Committee was organized, one of its objects being to facilitate the importation of cotton. Another organization was formed there in the same year for the purpose of bringing about a more satisfactory connection between the manufacturers and the sources of raw material. The Commercial Committee in 1780 petitioned the House of Commons to allow importation of cotton in neutral ships on the ground that the cotton industry was menaced by the shipping monopoly. The government, in the face of strong opposition by the merchants and the West India planters, acceded to the demand of the manufacturers to the extent of allowing imports contrary to the Navigation Act of 1660 till the conclusion of hostilities. The relief was merely temporary, but it appears that methods were found for violating the rights of monopoly conferred by law on English

[82] *Board of Trade Papers,* 6/113, Min. Feb. 22, 1786, 6/140, Docs. 7-16, 42, 92-95, 98; *Important Crisis in the Calico and Muslin Manufactory Explained,* 7, 8; Edwards, *History of the British West Indies,* II, 273; Owen, *Life,* I, 32, 33.

shippers. This is indicated, for instance, by complaints to the Board of Trade in 1790 to the effect that a "very alarming inroad (not permitted in the importation of any other extraneous production) is made upon our navigation act." [83]

.With the growth of industrial population and industrial influence, there arose a demand for a breach in another part of the protective system—the corn laws. England had normally produced food in excess of her own requirements, though the surplus of some other countries was even larger. The government had for a long time attempted to encourage agriculture and to maintain a high level of prices by putting protective regulations and tariffs in the way of foreign competitors, and had even paid large sums in the form of bounties on exports of grain. As early as 1765 the pressure of home consumption brought about slight modifications in the laws, but by 1790 it was recognized that these minor relaxations in the control of the grain market were inadequate. The rapid increase of population in the industrial centers, the loss of self-sufficiency, and the resulting problems of public policy were recognized even by spokesmen of the landed class. The increase of population due to industrial development was generally admitted. Moreover, the opportunities for profit-making were so great in manufacturing as to draw capital and energy away from the production of food supplies. Nor were these the only causes of loss of self-sufficiency. The increase of industrial wealth had been accompanied by "an advance in the manner of living and diet." The problem resulting from these circumstances was the problem of "the safety and propriety of relying on dis-

[83] *Owen MSS.,* LXXX, 3, 4; Commons *Journals,* XXXVII, 763, 764, 772, 773, 786, 795, 853, XXXVIII, 814; 20 Geo. III, c. 45, sec. 1; 21 Geo. III, c. 26, sec. 6; *Board of Trade Papers,* 6/140, Doc. 97. See also Chapman, *Lancashire Cotton Industry,* 3, n. 3; Daniels, *Early English Cotton Industry,* 101, n. 1.

tant countries (dangers of sea and enemy included) for the necessaries of life." The landed interests were inclined to view the situation with alarm. "The island of Great Britain is becoming more and more a manufacturing country every day," it was declared, and, having lost its self-sufficiency, "the moment it loses its superiority at sea, every creature within may be starved, who cannot be supported by the natural produce of the island." [84]

The remedy generally proposed by the champions of the landed classes was the stimulation of home production by increasing the rigors of the corn laws and by a general policy of encouraging agriculture in preference to manufacturing. But the manufacturers were beginning to clamor for access to foreign supplies of food. Petitions for more liberal laws regulating imports came from Manchester, Birmingham, Sheffield, Glasgow, and other industrial centers. These in general agreed with the Manchester petitioners' view that because of industrial progress, "this country cannot raise corn sufficient for its own support." A town council committee at Glasgow went so far as to demand that there should be "a free importation and exportation of corn at all times, with the exception of stopping exportation altogether in times of extreme dearth." The committee was also of the opinion that no distinction should be made between British and foreign vessels—a significant attack on the acts of trade as well as on the corn laws. The remedies proposed by other petitioners, while more moderate, were in the direction of free trade. The conflict over the question, declared Lord Sheffield, was between the industrialized and populous northwest and the agrarian south and east of England. And "the alacrity of the manufacturer," he added,

[84] *Annals of Agriculture,* XVIII, 68, XX, 133, 134; Robertson, *General View,* Perthshire, 12-14; Holt, *General View,* Lancashire, 13 (ed. 1794), 206 (ed. 1795); Sheffield, *Observations on the Corn Bill now Depending in Parliament* (1791), 12; *Parl. Hist.,* XXVIII, 1381.

had triumphed in connection with the corn law of 1791 over "the supineness of the landed interest." The acrimony of the discussions, the general nature of the arguments advanced, and the alignment of groups remind one of the more famous corn-law controversy of half a century later.[85]

The tendency of the great manufacturers of the new industrial era to dispense with monopoly and to depend upon their own initiative and resources, particularly in connection with the treaty of commerce with France, was observed by the Marquis of Lansdowne in a notable speech in support of the treaty. After praising the principle of free trade in general, and its embodiment in the treaty in particular, he said that "he was not the man to flatter any body of manufacture, or to court them for the sake of popularity or any such idle purpose; he despised the idea; but at the same time he was ready to do justice to the manufacturers. . . . When he looked at the commercial treaty, he said he was proud of the conduct of the manufacturers. . . . [They,] seated as they had been on the throne of monopoly, had generously descended from it; and seeing the true policy of the measure, consented without a murmur to give up all their prohibitions, to meet the foreign manufacturer in his own market, to travel abroad with their manufactures, and to

[85] Commons *Journals*, XLV, 348; 349, 461, XLVI, 85, ff., 200, 376, 387, 444, 653; *Board of Trade Papers*, 6/132, Petition of colliery owners, Dec., 1790, Petition of the Glasgow Chamber of Commerce, Dec. 21, 1790, and Petitions of the Magistrates, *et al.*, of Greenock, Dec., 1790, 6/133, *Report of the Committee of the Town Council of Glasgow, Appointed to Consider the Corn Bill; Parl. Hist.*, XXVIII, 1380. Some further references to contemporaneous discussion of the subject: *Parl. Hist.*, XXIX, 98; Smith, *Tracts on the Corn Trade and Corn Laws;* Mitford, *Considerations on the Opinion Stated by the Lords of the Committee of Council upon the Corn Laws* (the Committee of Council paper referred to is in the last preceding reference, Appendix, p. 8, ed. 1804); Hamilton, *Letter to the People of England;* Sheffield, *Observations on the Corn Bill* (1791); *Observations on the New Corn Bill,* by an Essex Farmer.

bring home wealth in one hand and revenue in the other." [86] In view of the monopolies retained by many of the manufacturers, and in view of the benefits others expected to derive from the treaty because of their technical superiority, the praise accorded them may seem exaggerated. But praise or blame is beside the point, namely, that in connection with the French commercial treaty and in many other policies, they were moving rapidly in the direction of nineteenth-century economic liberalism. The treaty was in fact viewed as a radical departure, a "revolution" in England's age-long policy, and its proponents were dubbed "citizens of the world." [87] But the spring of action by the manufacturers in advocating free trade with France and in supporting other policies involving economic liberalism was far removed from abstract theory and from altruism. They were not without a laudable hope, to be sure, of promoting the national welfare and of encouraging international good will; but their generosity in descending from "the throne of monopoly," and in venturing into new economic relationships without the safeguards of the old protective system was prompted primarily by a sense of their "unmatched superiority" in methods of production.

The prime minister himself soon recognized the technical superiority of the English manufacturers and its economic significance. Pitt, at first a proud aristocrat with physiocratic and agrarian sympathies intensified by Adam Smith, was rudely awakened as we have seen to the rapidly rising power of industrialism. He soon became keenly aware of the nature of the new economic

---

[86] *Parl. Hist.*, XXVI, 555-557.

[87] *Short Review of the Political State of Great Britain at the Commencement of the Year 1787*, 46-50; *Reply to a Short Review of the Political State of Great Britain*, 56 (6th ed.).

forces, and of their source in the transition to mechanical production. The terms of the treaty with France he made to conform almost meticulously to the views of the principal manufacturers. In his great speech in parliament in support of the treaty, he declared that it was based upon Britain's art and enterprise by virtue of which she was "confessedly superior in her manufactures and artificial productions." His change of attitude is evident as well from his later policies and speeches. In his address of February 17, 1792, on the state of the public finances, he enlarged upon the vast increase of commerce and industry since the misfortunes of the late wars, and asked, Why this unprecedented economic expansion? The first reason he assigned was "the improvement which has been made in the mode of carrying on almost every branch of manufacture, and the degree to which labor has been abridged, by the invention and application of machinery." Accompanying this was the development of credit in the operations of industry; the spirit of enterprise in the expansion of markets; and the rapid accumulation of capital by the reinvestment of profits in productive undertakings. In this comprehensive speech on the resources and revenues of the country, agriculture was virtually ignored; it was mentioned in a merely incidental manner. His attitude aroused against him the bitterest criticism of Arthur Young, who charged that the minister, in his zeal for the industrial interests, "overlooks everything connected with land," and that because of his favoritism, "the agricultural interests of this kingdom perhaps never found themselves in so contemptible a position." Pitt's views and policies mean nothing less, in fact, than a recognition by him that out of the transition to mechanical production a new economic era was emerging.[88]

[88] *Parl. Hist.*, XXVI, 384, 385, 395, XXIX, 832-834; *Annals of Agriculture*, XVII, 373.

The great industrialists of the new era were the product not of monopoly but of ingenuity and enterprise; and they found it impossible to fit themselves into the grooves of the old system. They were impatient of public restraints, and even indifferent to public favors. The essential tendency of the reorganization of industry accompanying the development of the new methods of manufacturing was away from the old monopolistic, stratified system, and in the direction of a fluid, or elastic, or dynamic condition. This tendency involved a new conception of the relation of government to industry, namely, that government should conform to economic conditions, rather than attempt to create or to mold them. This conception, radically different in origin, nevertheless approximated the physiocratic and Smithian doctrine of *laissez-faire*. It was indeed the industrialist who forced the translation of Adam Smith's theories, particularly in reference to commerce, into practical policy. Smith's darling agrarians, whose interests he believed to be identical with public interests, and upon whose influence he relied for the changes he advocated, became the "last-ditch" opponents of free trade; and the despised industrialists became the relentless champions of liberalism, champions more liberal than even Smith himself, who tried to justify both the navigation system and countervailing duties. The work of introducing free trade and *laissez-faire* was mainly the work neither of the agrarians nor of the theorists, but of the industrialists. And their influence, as we have seen, was felt distinctly even in Adam Smith's own life time.

The teaching of the theoretical free-traders, in contrast with the illiberal spirit imputed to the manufacturers by Adam Smith and others, has commonly been assigned as the basis of the early free-trade movement. Adam Smith said, Let there be free trade. And at length there was free trade. Therefore, Adam Smith is the

father of free trade. Such, in hyperbole, is the logic that
has gained wide acceptance. The influence of an idea
or of a personality is attractive, perhaps in part because it
is intangible and elusive. But the force of an event is
manifest and inescapable. The chief sources of the
liberalism of the new industrial groups were not ideas
but events.

Of these, the primary event was the transition to mechanical production. Connected therewith were secondary developments of the utmost importance in the history of economic liberalism. Those who utilized the
improved technical methods were drawn thereby at once
into a new economic system in which the old regulations
and restrictions, being inapplicable, were necessarily discarded; and the slow-moving machinery of government,
instead of creating new regulations and restrictions
adapted to the new conditions, allowed virtually free play
to the mobile economic forces of individual initiative and
ambition. By the same means (the utilization of technical improvements) English manufacturers acquired a
productive and competitive superiority which enabled
them to laugh at their rivals, and which removed the
need of the old protective and monopolistic safeguards.
It was not long till the new instruments of production
created commodities in excess of available markets, and
in consequence there arose a positive desire for the removal of the old restrictions which had become fruitful
alone in retaliatory measures abroad, and for the substitution therefor of a system of reciprocity and ultimately of complete free trade by which new markets
might be opened up for the output of the new technique.
There was a parallel tendency of production to outrun
the supply of raw materials available at home or by the
use of shipping as limited by the acts of trade; and in
consequence there arose inevitably the idea of securing
increased supplies by relaxations in the navigation sys-

tem and by concessions of a liberal nature to those who controlled the supplies. The rapid expansion of industry and of foreign trade resulting from the new methods of production involved also a disproportionate growth of population engaged in manufacturing and commerce as compared with agriculture, and this led in turn to a demand for the breaking down of the barriers raised to protect English agrarians from the competition of foreign food producers.

These tendencies toward a general policy of *laissez-faire* and economic liberalism were distorted and repressed by the quarter-century of wars and political reaction. But in the case of free trade, the forces which were active and influential even before Europe was devastated by the cataclysm of war and reaction were destined to find expression, during the reassertion of power by the industrial group in the nineteenth century, in an unprecedented system of commercial liberalism.

CHAPTER IV

THE INDUSTRIAL WORKERS

1. *Economic control in relation to the workers*

THE most important and most promising single fact that emerges from a study of the transition from primitive methods to modern industrial technique is the well-nigh inconceivable increase of the productivity of human energy. There is but one event in the modern history of mankind that is comparable to the transformation of British industrial technique in respect to the opening up of economic opportunity, and that event was the discovery of the New World. The inventions and improvements in eighteenth-century England led to a veritable new world of opportunity less limited in scope and possibility, in fact, than the New World of sixteenth-century geographers. For the latter was circumscribed by the fixed boundaries of continents and islands, while the former was restricted only by the expanding boundaries of man's intelligence.

It is apparent that by means of the intervention of mechanical power and improved technique, a given unit of human energy could either be made to produce the same amount of commodities and services in a fraction of the former time, thus releasing human energy for non-economic activities; or, the given unit of human energy could be kept in action long enough to produce, by the aid of technical improvements, a larger quantity of commodities and services. It is naturally to be supposed that in a free and rational society, interested, as is the normal individual, not merely in the use of economic goods but as well in the pursuit of non-economic activities and in the enjoyment of the refinements of civilization,—it is naturally to be assumed that under these circumstances men would utilize improvements in the methods of production by transferring a portion of their energies from economic activities to other fields. But such was not the result, for compulsory drafts came to be made upon the energies of the users of the new instruments of production in many cases even greater than upon the energies of the older workers. Again, it might naturally be assumed that a society which found itself possessed of such vastly increased productive power as to be able to satisfy its economic needs by the exercise of a fraction only of the energies formerly devoted to such needs, would devise a system for the distribution of labor by which no individual, least of all the immature and dependent child, would find it necessary to exhaust his entire store of energy in economic productivity. But in this respect also the possibilities of improved methods of production were not utilized. Frail women, feeble men, dependent children of tender age, toiled machine-like, manipulating machines, more than half the hours of each day in the week, while others lived idly and luxuriously, and others still lived meagerly by means of charity because of lack of opportunity for work. The assumption may be carried one step further. It is naturally to be supposed that Englishmen would have sought out some method of controlling the vast increase of wealth resulting from mechanical and technical improvements so that all members of society, or at the very least, those whose energies were being utilized to carry on economic processes, might have enjoyed a comfort-giving portion of the increased output. But instead of utilizing the obvious possibility of greater economic well-being, society permitted a declining standard of living even in the case of those workers whose energies were being most completely drafted for the multiplication of economic goods. In earlier periods, poverty and its attendant consequences may be accounted for in part by scarcity of the means of material well-being due to crude methods of production and transportation. During the period beginning with the transformation of economic technique, the well-nigh unlimited productive powers of human energy render this explanation invalid.

To the rational student of events of the later period, the opportunity for directing the new economic energies into channels of social control for purposes of the common welfare seems to have been so obvious and so magnificent that the utter failure to do so seems tragic if not inexplicable. In the history of the workers of the period, this failure is the central fact. However difficult it may be to explain the failure on rational grounds, it is the first duty of the historian not to criticize but to understand. With that end in view, let us examine the attendant historical circumstances.

A frequently accepted explanation of the wretchedness of the industrial workers during the transition period is the alleged displacement of hand workers by labor-saving machines. But the explanation is discredited by the facts of labor displacement. It is based on *a priori* grounds rather than on historical evidence. In eighteenth-century England (runs the thought) labor was a commodity. The introduction of labor-saving machines decreased the demand for human labor. Consequently wages declined and unemployment increased. This explanation was occasionally offered by contemporary writers. John Howlett, for instance, a writer whose observations are in general well worth consideration, noted in 1788 the "increasing poverty and wretchedness of our laboring classes," due, he said, to decline of real

wages, the decline in wages being, in turn, due to the
increase in population and "the abridgement and facili-
tation of the work itself, partly from the greater dexterity
of the workmen, in consequence of the division and sim-
plification of their labors, still more from the invention
of machines." But when he departed from *a priori*
generalizations and entered the field of observable facts,
he discovered that Manchester, Birmingham, and Liverpool, regions most vitally affected by the invention of
machines, were growing rapidly by drawing the surplus
laborers from the districts where primitive hand methods
continued to prevail. Among observers of actual conditions, there is a remarkable agreement as to the fact of
increased employment due to the introduction of technical improvements.[1]

In the later stages of the transition, particularly in
connection with the introduction of the power loom, displacement of hand labor by machines assumed a more
serious aspect. But even here the difficulty was due
largely to attendant circumstances, such as the fluctuations of trade during the quarter century of wars; the
difficulties, partly legal and partly economic, in the way
of the shifting of labor; and the conservatism of the
semi-independent hand-workers, who in many cases
preferred starvation wages at their accustomed tasks to a
higher income under factory conditions.[2] As for the
"discarded spinsters," [3] their lot was undoubtedly rendered more difficult by the introduction of machines for
spinning wool, but it should be remembered that most

[1] Howlett, *Insufficiency of the Causes to Which the Increase of Our
Poor and the Poor's Rates Have Been Commonly Ascribed*, 73, 74;
Howlett, *Examination of Dr. Price's Essay*, 22; *Gentleman's Magazine*,
LII, 475; *Annals of Agriculture*, XVIII, 571. See also above, p. 95, ff.,
and below, p. 253, ff.

[2] Hammond, *Town Laborer*, 21.

[3] *The Discarded Spinster* is the title of an anonymous booklet in
rime, published in 1791.

of this class of workers were not primarily connected with manufacturing but rather with agriculture, spinning by the women and children being utilized to supplement the inadequate wages of the agricultural laborers. The chief difficulty, therefore, was the failure of the landlords and farmers to pay a subsistence wage for the work done by their laborers. With minor qualifications, the truth of the matter is that the introduction of machines resulted, in general, in an increase of opportunities for finding work. This was due, to be sure, to no conscious effort at social readjustment, but to the expansion of demand growing out of the competitive power of the new methods of production. But the point of the matter is that we must look elsewhere than to the displacement of hand laborers by labor-saving machines for the fundamental cause of working-class wretchedness during the transition.

As a matter of fact, we might assume that there was an actual decrease in the number of persons engaged in economic productivity,—we might assume that there was an actual decrease in the total of human energy expended in producing economic goods,—and still have no satisfactory explanation of the decline of well-being among the workers. For the hypothetical decrease of human energy was obviously more than made good by the increased productive power of machinery. The vital question still remains unanswered: Why did a society which was admittedly rapidly increasing its means of gratifying economic needs permit a large proportion of its members, particularly those most actively engaged in the productive process, to suffer simultaneously a serious decline in an already wretched standard of economic well-being? The question is fundamentally not a question of an increase or a decrease in human energy expended in production; it is essentially a question of control.

The control of industry in early centuries had been largely a group control, by means of gilds. Town governments, and during recent centuries the national government, had assumed more and more authority, till governmental control had come to be regarded as natural and normal. But, as has already been observed, the state as an agency of social control came at the end of the eighteenth century under the sway of an extreme individualism having as its aim the unfettered utilization of the instruments of production by their owners. To this end, the restraining hand of the state was removed from the owners of the instruments of production, while at the same time it was used by them to keep themselves freed from the restraints of working-class influence. This was in a measure true of all employers, but it was particularly characteristic of the new industrial employers. For the great manufacturers acquired an extreme and hitherto unknown individualism as well as great power. Their power grew out of their control of the technical improvements of the time, but their individualism was independent of the transition to mechanical methods. That transition was not a creation of individualism; it was essentially a social phenomenon. The inventions, as has been seen, were the result of a prevailing spirit of technical progress, consciously recognized and fostered by various instrumentalities of public opinion and public action, by the government, and by various non-profit-making organizations. These extensive manifestations of public spirit in promoting the transition gave promise of a public-spirited control and utilization of the new inventions.

The "public" of that time was to be sure not very comprehensive, for the masses, the "vulgar and common sorts" of people, were not included. Their welfare was believed to consist in poverty-bred ignorance and subjection. Wages above a subsistence level were regarded as abnormal and demoralizing. The public welfare, therefore, in so far as it was supposed to enable individuals or classes to exercise power or utilize the means of gratifying varied wants, had a very limited meaning, since only the classes who already had economic power and independence were included.

But even in this limited sense, the influence of government in promoting the public-spirited utilization of the new inventions was largely frustrated by forces tending in the direction of an organization of the new system of manufacturing and economic life on the basis of private initiative and private profit-making little restrained by the action of the government. Prominent among the prevailing forces were the discrediting of the government during a crucial period of the transition by the failure of George III and his ministers in dealing with foreign and colonial affairs and domestic reforms; the acuteness of party and factional conflicts, which focused attention on political issues and maneuvers; inability or unwillingness to adapt the old system of public control of industry to the rapidly changing conditions; and the acceptance by the younger Pitt and his followers of *laissez-faire* doctrines, in respect to the traditional restraints that had been imposed by the government upon the merchant, the landlord, and the manufacturer. It is important to remember, in connection with the general question of the control of industry as related to working-class welfare, that neither Pitt's government nor any later government for many decades adopted the policy of *laissez-faire* in respect to the removal of restraints on the working classes. It was Pitt himself, aided largely by the philanthropist Wilberforce (whose mental reactions afford an interesting illustration of upper-class thinking in relation to other groups), who, instead of removing existing restrictions as in the case of employers, set about the forging of new governmental fetters for the workers in the form of the Combination Acts of 1799 and 1800.[4]

Thus it came about that the government was no longer an effective agency in the control of industry; and, in so far as it retained regulatory functions, these were almost without exception conceived in the spirit of upper-class philosophy, and were intended to restrain the workers but not the owners of lands and ships and factories. It is apparent, therefore, that the laboring classes could not depend on the government, the chief existing agency of social control, but must work out their own salvation. The original question, as to why there was no advance in working-class well-being corresponding to the unparalleled increase in the productivity of labor, assumes the form, therefore, Why did the laboring classes fail to work out their own salvation? Why were they able neither to check the devastating individualism of their employers, nor to put in the place of the abdicated government of the time, so far as the control of industry on their behalf was concerned, an effective influence of their own?

2.   The reservoirs of the new industrial labor

The most important phase of the answer to this question is to be found in a study of the sources of industrial labor. The new groups of industrial workers were composed of laborers recruited from the older industries and from the farms of England, Scotland, Wales and Ireland. "A good many [came] from the agricultural parts," said an observer who began his career as a textile employee in 1780; "a many from Wales; a many from Ireland and from Scotland. People left other occupations and came

[4] The contrast in the policies of the government as here suggested is discussed more fully in Hammond, *Town Laborer*, particularly in chs. 7, 10.

to spinning for the sake of the high wages. I recollect shoemakers leaving their employ and learning to spin; I recollect tailors; I recollect colliers; but a great many more husbandmen left their employ to learn to spin."[5] This account by a Bolton cotton spinner is true in a remarkably literal way of the sources of working-class population in most of the newly developing industrial centers. The process by which the cotton, iron, pottery, and more progressive woollen centers tapped these labor reservoirs has already been described.[6] Our present purpose is to examine the reservoirs themselves to discover if possible whether the sources of industrial labor were pure or polluted.

Perhaps the most important question in this connection concerns the income of the workers who furnished recruits for the new industries. As for the farm workers, those in England seem on the whole to have been much better paid than the Irish, the Welsh mountaineers, or the Scotch Highlanders. Arthur Young, who probably was better informed on the subject of English farm wages than any other person, wrote that "the average price of [agricultural] labor in England twenty years ago, when I made my tours [1767-1770], was 7s. 6d. a week, or 1s. 3d. a day." He was of the opinion, in 1793, that very little change had taken place in nominal wages—a judgment with which thorough students of the subject concur. Young's point of view held at the time his observations were made should not be overlooked in connection with his wage calculations. His belief, repeatedly expressed with characteristic vigor, was to the effect that the workers were generally receiving an income larger than was necessary to support themselves with frugality appropriate to their station in life, and that their wages should be kept as low as possible. A "reasonable" wage

[5] *Factories Inquiry Commission, Suppl. Rep.* (1834), Pt. I, 169.
[6] See above, p. 95, ff.

he considered much lower than the above estimate of average wages. The scale prevailing about Witney, for instance, in 1767, which he deemed "very reasonable," ranged from 8d. to 10d. a day, during most of the year, with slight additional pay during the busiest season. Young seems to have been in general an honest and dependable if somewhat superficial observer; but his belief that existing wages were too high would naturally incline him to emphasize and criticize the upward rather than the downward variations in making his calculations. In other words, it seems reasonable to assume that the level of wages was not higher than the estimate made by him.[7]

The bare statement of a wage in terms of money means little without an interpretation in the light of living costs and conditions. The majority of farm workers had in fact been semi-independent producers. The wage-earner's income had consisted of several elements in addition to money wages. He could cultivate a plot or strip of ground; he could keep a cow and perhaps a pig and poultry on the common pasture; he could secure fuel in the form of wood from the waste or turf from the common; he could increase his food resources by the gleanings of his wife and children after harvest; and by means of domestic industries, he could even add to his money

[7] Young, *Travels in France,* 446 (a passage summarizing the elaborate statistical evidence contained in his various English *Tours*); Young, in *Annals of Agriculture,* XLIII, 38 (approvingly cited by Hasbach, in *English Agricultural Laborer,* 119, 120); Young, *Farmer's Letters,* I, 194, ff.; Young, *Southern Tour,* 91, 232; Davies, *Case of Laborers in Husbandry;* Howlett, *Insufficiency of the Causes to Which the Increase of Our Poor and Poor's Rates Have Been Commonly Ascribed;* the budgets cited below, p. 226, n. The principal evidence as to the state of wages in the early years of the last decade of the century, when there was an upward trend in nominal wages, more than counteracted, however, by rising prices and the depressing effects of enclosures, is in Young's *Annals of Agriculture,* Eden's *State of the Poor,* and particularly the reports sent to the Board of Agriculture from the various counties.

income. Furthermore, his employer frequently made grants of food and drink, especially during harvest, and sold him wheat and other commodities in small quantities at relatively low prices. There was of course no sudden or universal obliteration of such rights and customs. Thus in Hertfordshire, in 1795, laborers who were employed regularly by the same master were ordinarily allowed 7s. and small beer, and during "the haying month," 9s. and ale. In Staffordshire, wages ran from 1s. to 1s. 6d. a day with beer, and in the summer, 1s. with meat and drink and "the draft or carriage of a load of coals." In Devonshire, "wages are one shilling a day, and a quart of cider. In harvest, the wages [are] much the same, with as much cider as they choose to drink." In Huntingdonshire, during harvest, the day laborers were allowed beer "in times of carrying"; and regular workers could grow their own potatoes.[8]

Supplementary items in the laborer's income had given his money wage a meaning radically different from what it acquired during the second half of the eighteenth century. With the progress of enclosures, of large-scale farming, and of more highly commercialized marketing of farm products, he became increasingly dependent upon his money wage.

The old customs of granting food, drink, and minor articles, and of selling wheat and other commodities directly to the laborer, were disrupted by large-scale, commercialized farming and marketing. "The sources of the market which used to feed him are in a great measure cut off since the system of large farms has been so much

[8] Walker, *General View*, Hertfordshire, 83; Pitt, *General View*, Staffordshire, 107; Fraser, *General View*, Devonshire, 43, 67; Maxwell, *General View*, Huntingdonshire, 18, 19. The status of the farm laborer preceding enclosures and attendant changes is discussed in some detail by Hammond, *Village Laborer*, ch. 6, and by Hasbach, *English Agricultural Laborer*, 71-103.

encouraged," we are told by Nathaniel Kent, a leading contemporary student of agricultural changes. The same writer observes in another place, in respect to the farm laborers, that "formerly they could buy milk, butter and many other small articles in every parish, in whatever quantity they wanted. But since small farms have decreased in number, no such articles are to be had; for the great farmers have no idea of retailing such small commodities, and those who do retail them carry them all to towns. A farmer is even unwilling to sell the laborer who works for him a bushel of wheat, which he might get ground for three or four pence a bushel." The effects of changing market conditions are described in detail by another writer (Davies): "Formerly the laborer could have corn of different kinds mixed in any proportion, in exchange for his labor, even more readily than he could get money. His wife carried it to the mill, had it ground and dressed, and then brought it home, and baked it for the family. There was no intermediate person, except the miller, between the farmer and the consumer, to receive a profit. But now it is out of the course of business for the farmer to retail corn by the bushel to this or that poor man; except in some particular places, as a matter of favor, to his own laborers. The great farmer deals in a wholesale way with the miller; the miller with the mealman; and the mealman with the shopkeeper; of which last the poor man buys his flour. . . . In short, the poor man buys *everything* at the highest price; at a higher price than the rich do." The statement, made by various writers, seems not unfounded that town workers could often purchase provisions more readily than could the farm laborer. We are told, for instance, that in the North Riding of Yorkshire the milk supply was better in the towns than in the country, the farmers selling the better grades in the town markets, and as for the surplus, they desired to "make of it old milk cheese, or maintain with it their pigs and calves." [9]

Contemporaneously with these changes, the immemorial customary right of gleaning was gradually broken down by the opposition arising out of the new type of large-scale, enclosed farming; and by a decision of the Court of Common Pleas in 1788, gleaning was declared illegal.[10]

More important elements of the auxiliary income of the farm laborer were his garden plot, and his fuel and pasturage rights in the commons. These were commonly swept away by the tide of enclosures. This result, while not universal, was so general and so serious as to effect a vital change in the status of a large proportion of farm laborers. Arthur Young, who had at first denied that enclosures adversely affected the poor, was later convinced of his error, and he frankly wrote in 1801 that "by nineteen enclosure acts out of twenty, the poor are injured, and in some grossly injured. The poor in these parishes may say, and with truth, *Parliament may be tender of property, all I know is, I had a cow, and an act of parliament has taken it from me.*" [11]

These changes are discussed here primarily to indicate their relation to the question of farm wages. They had the effect of reducing farm laborers to dependence on money wages, putting the rural workers in this respect practically on the same footing as town laborers. Large-scale, commercialized farming, and improved market and

[9] Kent, *Notes on the Agriculture of Norfolk*, 165, quoted by Hammond, *Village Laborer*, 111; Kent, *Hints to Gentlemen of Landed Property*, 263, ff., quoted by Hasbach, *English Agricultural Laborer*, 127, 128; Davies, *Case of Laborers in Husbandry*, 44, 45; Tuke, *General View*, North Riding of Yorkshire, 84; Holland, *General View*, Cheshire, 299.

[10] Hammond, *Village Laborer*, 107-109.

[11] Hammond, *Village Laborer*, chs. 5, 6; Hasbach, *English Agricultural Laborer*, 103-147; Slater, *English Peasantry and the Enclosure of the Common Fields*, 128 (quoting Young).

transportation facilities probably benefited the town workers by giving them readier access to country products; while the same changes injured the farm workers by depriving them of supplementary income. At the same time, their economic deterioration was accelerated by rising prices.

We have seen that according to the best informed observers of the time, a tolerable calculation of the average weekly wage of farm laborers, from about 1770 to 1790, was the sum of 7s. 6d. We have observed, also, that the workers were becoming increasingly dependent on money wages. But the question remains, What was the relation of such a wage to the actual necessary expenses of the ordinary farm laborer's family? To be sure, one might labor indefinitely to define the term "necessary expenses," so greatly do standards vary among individuals, among peoples, and from age to age. But one who patiently examines the facts of eighteenth-century working-class conditions is not likely to cavil unduly at the absence of agreement as to the meaning of the term.

Among these facts, especially significant are the family budgets collected by David Davies, an Anglican clergyman, beginning in 1787, in his own county of Berks and in various other districts where he made detailed inquiries. We may profitably examine one of these budgets, here reproduced as it was set down by the rector in the course of his parochial visits in 1787.

Weekly expenses of a family, consisting of a man and his wife, and five children, the eldest eight years of age, the youngest an infant.

	£	s.	d.
Flour, 7½ gallons at 10d. per gallon.....................		6	3
Yeast, to make it into bread, 2½d. and salt, 1½d........			4
Bacon, 1 lb. boiled at two or three times with greens; the pot-liquor, with bread and potatoes, makes a *mess* for the children			8
Tea, 1 ounce, 2d.; ¾ lb. sugar, 6d.; ½ lb. butter or lard, 4d.		1	
Soap, ¼ lb. at 9d. per lb...............................			2¼

	£	s.	d.

Candles, ⅓ lb. one week with another at a medium, at 9d.   3

Thread, thrum, and worsted, for mending apparel, etc....   3

The expenses already set down are only *weekly outgoings* exclusive of house-rent, fuel, clothing, lying-in, sickness, and burials; these being best allowed for by the year, may be called *annual outgoings,* and are as under:

Rent of a cottage, or part of an old farm-house, with a small piece of garden ground, for a family, is from two pounds to two guineas: say............................   **2**

Fuel: this is turf from the Commons,[12] and when bought costs 12s. per family; but as a man can cut in a week nearly enough to serve his family all the year, and the farmers (if the distance be not great) will give the carriage for the ashes, let this be charged at a little more than one week's wages.............................   **10**

Clothing: 1. *The man's:* wear of a suit per annum, 5s.; wear of a working jacket and breeches, 4s.; two shirts, 8s.; one pair of stout shoes nailed, 7s.; two pair of stockings, 4s.; hat, handkerchief, &c., 2s. Sum, £1 10s. 2. *The wife's:* wear of a gown and petticoats, 4s.; one shift, 3s. 6d.; one pair of strong shoes, 4s.; one pair of stockings, 1s. 6d.; two aprons, 3s.; handkerchiefs, caps, &c., 4s. Sum, £1. 3. *The children's:* their clothing is (usually) partly made up of the parents' old clothes, partly bought at second-hand; what is bought (supposing three children to a family) cannot well be reckoned at less than £1; where there are more than three children, 7s. may be added, and where there are fewer, 7s. may be deducted, for each. Let the whole be estimated at **3 10**

(Note.—Very few poor people can afford to lay out this sum in clothes; but they should be enabled to do it. Some cottages breed a few fowls, with which they buy what sheets and blankets they want; but those who live in old farmhouses are seldom allowed (to use their own words) to keep a pig or a chick).

Lying-in: the child's linen, 3 or 4s.; the midwife's fee, 5s.; a bottle of gin or brandy always had upon this occasion, 2s.; attendance of a nurse, for a few days, and her diet, at least 5s.; half a bushel of malt brewed, and hops, 3s.; to the minister for churching, 1s.; call the

[12] This item mentioned by Davies is a survival, it will be noted, of rights of commons, very generally but not universally destroyed by enclosures.

£ s. d.

sum £1, and suppose this to happen but once in two
years, this is, per annum   10

Casualties: 1. In *sickness,* there is the physic to be paid
for, and the loss of time to be allowed for. 2. *Burials:*
Poor people having many children sometimes lose one.
For both these together it seems moderate to allow
per annum   10

It will be observed that in the case of the "weekly outgoings," the expenses of a particular family are given;
in the case of the "annual outgoings," much more stable
in amount, the average for the poorer class of the community is given. Dividing the "annual outgoings" by
the number of weeks in the year, and adding the result
to the "weekly outgoings," we find that the weekly expenditures of this particular family totaled 11s. 7½d. The
earnings of the entire family amounted to 8s. 6d. a week.

This detailed account of a Berkshire peasant's budget
is quoted because of the clear picture it paints of the
manner of life of a typical farm laborer, as well as because of the fact that it is a fair illustration of the relation between farm wages and the costs of the simpler and
cruder human needs. Numerous other family accounts
that have come down to us are similar.[13]

David Davies, who was responsible for collecting many
of these accounts of the incomes and expenses of farm
laborers, proposed as remedies for the discrepancies between earnings and elemental needs such moderate and
conservative policies as the more general employment of
women and children and the revival of the Elizabethan
statute, unrepealed and yet unenforced, for fixing wages

[13] The budget quoted is in Davies, *Case of Laborers in Husbandry,*
10, 22. Other budgets collected in the same parish are on pages 10-28;
while the Appendix, pages 169-240, consists of budgets secured in
various parts of the country outside of Berkshire. See also, for similar
budgets, Eden, *State of the Poor,* III, cccxxxix, ff. (reproduced in part
in Hasbach, *English Agricultural Laborer,* 141, ff.) ; Young, *General
View,* Sussex, 91, 92; *Chatham Papers,* CCCVIII, Account of family
budgets of farm laborers in Bucks, reported by Rev. John Drake.

in accordance with fluctuations in the cost of provisions. And yet Davies looked not without sympathy upon the plight of the laboring poor, and in a certain sense may be regarded as their advocate. Arthur Young, on whose observations we are so largely dependent for our knowledge of wages, could hardly in any sense of the word be regarded as a champion of the agricultural workers. His observations, therefore, concerning the relation between wages and necessary expenses could hardly be suspected of assigning to the laborer a less favorable status than he actually occupied. As has already been stated, Young believed, at the time of his English tours, that farm wages were too high. To prove his point, he formulated a "model" budget, showing what he considered to be the necessary expenses of a farm laborer's family. His discussion throws so much light on the status of farm workers and on the point of view of the members of his class as to justify a summary of it.

The family of Young's "model" budget consisted of five members—the parents and three children, one an infant, one fifteen, and another ten years old. What are the expenses that such a family may reasonably incur? He first outlines a weekly "bill of fare" for the head of the family. His first day's fare is to consist of two pounds of bread made of equal parts of wheat, rye, and potato; cheese, two ounces; and two parts of beer. The second day he is made to consume three messes of soup made of lean beef, peas, mealy potatoes, ground rice, onions and celery (or a double portion of onions without the celery), salt and water. The third day's lone dish consists of rice pudding, made of one-half pound of rice, two quarts of "flet" (skimmed) milk, and sugar. On the fourth day, he is to dine on a quarter pound of fat meat and a pound and three-quarters of potatoes baked together, and there is once more an allowance of beer. The fifth day's portion consists of two-pence worth of rice milk. On the sixth day there is to be a repetition of the first day's fare. And at the end of the week, our proletarian epicure is made to dine on potatoes and fat meat, two and a half pounds, with beer and two ounces of cheese. The wife is supposed to eat two-thirds as much as the husband; the share of the oldest child is three-fourths of his father's fare; the ten-year-old child is to consume half as much as the father; while the food of the infant, not described, is to cost a shilling. This food allowance for the family totals for the year £15 12s. Other items are: house rent, £1 10s.; clothes, £2 10s.; soap and candles, £1 5s.; and loss of time, and expenses due to sickness, £1. The total is £21 17s., or a weekly average of about 8s. 5d.

It is to be observed that among various items that naturally occur to one, nothing is allowed, in particular, for fuel. Young states that there are wide variations in this item, but he thinks the average will not exceed £1 15s. or £2. As for other items: "It may be said," he comments, "that wheaten bread, that beef, that mutton, that tea, that sugar, that butter are dear; but do not in the height of an argument jumble these and *the neces-saries of life* together." The consumption of such things as tea by the workers was regarded by Young as a veri-table economic crime. Their staple diet, he believed, should consist of potatoes and rice.[14]

Certain conclusions of importance may be drawn from a study of Young's "model" budget. To begin with, it is apparent that the necessaries of life as interpreted not by the workers themselves but in accord with Young's extremely meager standards required, as early as 1770, an income considerably larger than the average wage as estimated by Young in connection with his English tours. The apparent inconsistency was due to Young's putting not only expenditures but income as well on a family

[14] *Farmer's Letters*, I, 194-213.

basis; the wife, according to his estimate, was expected to earn one-fourth as much as the husband, a child of ten the same sum as the mother, and a child of fifteen a sum equal to half the father's wage. The system preceding the modern industrial régime based the family economy by the sternest necessity upon the labor of the mother and of the children of tender age as well as upon the labor of the man.

A second inference one may deduce from a study of the budget is that no provision was made for an income sufficient to secure even the necessaries as interpreted by Young except by average families. Young frankly admitted that it was not expected "that all the poor should be able to maintain themselves; that would be impossible." [15] The larger families, those in which the mother and children for any reason could not work, those who were afflicted with unusual periods of illness, those affected by even casual unemployment, would almost inevitably fall below the line of self-support, even on the basis of a family income, expended with the most rigorous economy and frugality.

Still another conclusion may be drawn from Young's most interesting "model" budget. He was merely giving definite, concrete expression to the subsistence theory of wages.

The economists who in the nineteenth century developed the wages-fund theory and the "iron law" of wages were preceded by a long succession of writers who held similar views. The chief difference was in the fact that earlier writers based their views on moral grounds. They contended that a wage at or near the level of vigorous physical existence was desirable and proper. The later economists put the theory on the basis also of natural and inescapable "laws"—laws of their own making which have since been discredited, but which were

[15] *Farmer's Letters*, I, 210.

creations fittingly emerging out of eighteenth-century conditions.

The subsistence view of wages was based in the first instance on the century-old conception of class relationships defined by few more clearly or bluntly than by Rev. William Harrison in the time of Elizabeth, when he wrote that the various classes of workers, the day laborers, poor husbandmen, shopkeepers, copyholders, and all artificers, "have neither voice nor authority in the commonwealth, but are to be ruled and not to rule other." [16] The dominant attitude found frank expression in one of the greatest of English poems. Spenser in the *Faerie Queene* describes a conflict between Artegall (Justice) and a giant. The giant had proposed to restore equality in nature and among men, and "the vulgar did about him flock." Artegall defied the giant, declaring that differences in the status of classes are decreed by man's "great maker," who has created also the lowly vales and the lofty hills. The giant is overwhelmed, whereupon the people, who had hoped to gain "wondrous riches by his innovation," rose in revolt. Artegall, seeing the uprising, was loath to soil his noble hands with "the base blood of such a rascal crew," and sent his retainer, who dispersed them "like a swarm of flies." [17]

In the eighteenth century, a practically universal distinction, explicit or implied, was made between those who have "surplus labor in store," that is, property, and those who "must labor for subsistence." It was agreed as "an axiom not to be disputed," that the latter group should receive enough to insure propagation as well as mere individual subsistence, "otherwise this useful class could not last beyond a single generation." But without poverty necessitating work on the part of the class, its

[16] Harrison, *Description of England*, ch. 1, "Of degrees of people in the Commonwealth of England."
[17] *Faerie Queene*, Canto V.

usefulness to society would be lost: "there could be no riches, no refinement, no comfort, and no benefit to those who may be possessed of wealth." It is urged by another writer, also in a vein typical of nearly all the writings of the time, that as for "mere labor, though it should not be, as Virtue is said to be, left merely to its own reward, it certainly should be, as Virtue generally is, rewarded but moderately. Men possessed of no property, and capable of nothing but labor, are entitled to nothing but the means of daily subsistence. Were they possessed of more, they would remit their daily labor; so that a numerous body of industrious poor is a fund of real wealth to the community." The point of view here expressed is typical of the writings of the time in another respect, namely, the implicit, apparently unconscious confusion of the "community" with the possessors of property, and of its interests with their interests. The other assumption, namely, that poverty among the masses is useful, indeed necessary, as a stimulus for productive work, was used by both landlords and master manufacturers as an argument for low wages, and at the same time as a justification of high prices. It was held that when the prices of the necessaries of life were low, the workers were enabled to spend part of their time in "idleness," and to treat their masters disrespectfully. But "when provisions are so dear that they are obliged to stick close to their work for a maintenance," this evil spirit of working-class independence is cast out.[18]

[18] Colquhoun, *Treatise on Indigence*, 7-14; Kenrick, *Address to Artists and Manufacturers*, 20; Young, *Farmer's Letters*, I, 33-42; Sheffield, *Observations on the Corn Laws*, 23; Townsend, *Dissertation on the Poor Laws*, 15, 28; Ruggles, *History of the Poor*, I, Preface, xiii-xv, II, 60, 61; Davies, *Case of Laborers in Husbandry*, 157; *Annals of Agriculture*, VII, 473-477; *Vindication of Commerce and the Arts*, 29, 30, 33; Furniss, *Position of the Laborer in a System of Nationalism*, chs. 6, 7; Hasbach, *English Agricultural Laborer*, 100, n. 1.

Those who advocated poverty as a necessary compulsion to labor in the case of the workers might have been reminded of the absence of any positive attractions. When it was generally understood, by workers as well as by masters, that the utmost possible toil would be recompensed by nothing more than a subsistence, it is obvious that no trial was made of any motive save the compulsion of poverty. But such views would have fallen on deaf ears. The worker had his proper and legitimate place in society, according to the dominant view, and that place, so far as the production, control, and utilization of wealth were concerned, was hardly distinguishable from that of the beast of burden.

The subsistence wage was originally to be determined by the "scarcity or plenty" of provisions, fluctuations to be taken into account by the local officials in their assessment of wages. Any employer who braved the scorn of his class by offering wages higher than the officially authorized wage could be punished (according to the Elizabethan statute) by ten days' imprisonment and a fine of £5; and a laborer receiving higher pay was to be imprisoned twenty-one days. The Elizabethan law was preceded by various others going back to the time of the freeing of the serfs, in the fourteenth century. The measures were initiated not by a statute enacted by parliament but by an ordinance of the king in 1349, during the Black Death, and it was frankly issued "because a great part of the people and specially of the workmen and servants has now died in this plague," and because the surviving workers are trying to secure higher rewards as a result of "the necessity of lords and the scarcity of servants." These laws, with supplementary statutes for forcing the lower classes to labor, constitute the legal basis for the view, sometimes exaggerated, and yet not unfounded, that the modern workers, instead of becoming really free, merely emerged from serfdom into "wage-slavery."[19] Their enforcement, to be sure, had by the end of the eighteenth century largely lapsed; but not because of the trend of wages above the subsistence level, for the tendency, at least during the latter part of the century, was in the opposite direction, and enforcement would have been a boon to an increasing proportion of the workers.[20] The theory and practice alike of eighteenth-century employers and writers thus outran the policy of the laws.

That is to say, the non-enforcement of the laws which had previously attempted to maintain wages at a subsistence level was accompanied by a very general decline of agricultural wages below the subsistence level, and by the consequent extension of private charity and public poor relief. "It is manifest," wrote David Davies, "that the poor rate is now [1787] in part a *substitute for wages.*" The fact that "the price of labor has not advanced in proportion to the advance in the price of provisions," wrote John Howlett, is "alone sufficient to have raised the complained of expenses [of poor rates] much higher than they have yet risen, in order to place the poor in a situation equally comfortable with that they possessed forty or fifty years ago." Charles James Fox, in a parliamentary debate in 1795, stated that the original purpose of the poor law had been to provide a fund accessible to those who, because of exceptional circumstances, were unable to support themselves. "But he feared that the reverse was the case; that the exception was with respect to the few who derived sufficient means of subsistence from their labor, and that the great mass of the laboring part of the community are under the necessity of applying to this fund for relief." It is

[19] The more important examples of the long succession of such laws are to be found in Bland, Brown and Tawney, *English Economic History: Select Documents.*

[20] For indications of this attitude on the part of the working classes, see *Ibid.*, 547-553.

obviously impossible to determine accurately the proportion receiving aid. Howlett, whose keen and extensive observations led Arthur Young to describe him as a "celebrated political arithmetician," was of the opinion that in rural parishes, "very nearly a third" of the inhabitants received either constant or occasional aid; and that in the larger towns and manufacturing centers, the proportion was probably less than a sixth.[21]

The consequences of this deficiency of income on the character of the farm laborers, and indirectly on the character of the industrial workers largely drawn from the rural sections, are too obvious for elaboration. The one point that needs to be emphasized is the fact that the deficiency of wages occurred throughout the agricultural sections, independently of the industrial progress of the time—or, more accurately, in spite of the rise of new industries; for the expansion of industrial population not only enlarged the markets and increased the prosperity of the employers of farm labor, giving them an economic basis for higher wages, but, as we shall see later,[22] served, by the withdrawal of workers from the farms, to maintain farm wages at a higher level in the vicinity of industrial centers than elsewhere.

The deficiency of income was the more disastrous because it was an income based upon the labor of women and children as well as of men. The consequences of the dependence of the family on the wage-earning work of the mother and young children have commonly been associated with the rise of the factory system; but they were connected as well with agrarian society preceding and during the rise of factories.

[21] Davies, *Case of Laborers in Husbandry*, 35, 36; Howlett, *Insufficiency of the Causes to Which the Increase of Our Poor and the Poor's Rates Have Been Commonly Ascribed*, 53; *Parl. Hist.*, XXXII, 701; Howlett, in *Annals of Agriculture*, XI, 6-8, XVIII, 574, 575. See also below, p. 257, ff.

[22] See below, p. 253, ff.

The agricultural workers were subjected to other adverse conditions as well as deficiency of income and the forced labor of women and children. As for hours of labor, the spirit of the eighteenth as well as of earlier centuries is illustrated by the following passage from the Elizabethan Statute of Artificers: "All artificers and laborers being hired for wages by the day or week shall betwixt the midst of the months of March and September be at their work at or before five of the clock in the morning, and continue at work until betwixt seven and eight of the clock at night . . . [except at meal times]; and all the said artificers and laborers between the midst of September and the midst of March shall be at their work from the spring of the day in the morning until the night of the same day." [23] This provision, like the one for fixing wages, was allowed to lapse; and while the hours of labor, toward the end of the eighteenth century, were not so exacting as the letter of the earlier law would indicate, they remained such as left the farm laborer virtually no time save for sleep. The prevailing hours seem to have been, in summer, from six to six; in winter, "from light to dark"; and during harvest, "as early and late as they can see." The relatively short working day of from six to six in summer and from sunrise to sunset in winter and harvest had recently been secured in some regions, as a result of a certain independence due to opportunity for industrial labor, which had led farm workers to insist on these "gentle hours." There were complaints that the accustomed hours were too short: "The want of more hours of work in the summer months greatly retards the business of the country, and occasions great dissoluteness among the workers." Among the remedies proposed and frequently adopted was the more extensive resort to a primitive form of "speeding up,"— the substitution of payment by piece work for fixed wages,

[23] 5 Eliz. c. 4, sec. 9.

—a practice which was recommended because it induces the workers to "work earlier, faster, and later," and "less money is paid in this way for the same quantity of work." [24]

Such scant leisure as fell to the lot of the rural worker was spent amid surroundings far from enviable. The rural hovels, made frequently of turf or moss and thatch, may have presented superficially to the casual observer a picturesque appearance; but in them, even more than in the equally picturesque overhanging timbered town habitations, lurked deadly enemies of comfort and of health. "The dwellings of the laborers," runs the report of the Board of Agriculture's correspondent from the North Riding of Yorkshire, "are generally small and low, consisting only of one room, and very rarely of two, both of which are level with the ground, and sometimes a step within it. This situation renders them damp, and frequently very unwholesome, and contributes, with the smallness of the apartments, to injure the health both of parents and children, for in such contracted hovels, numerous families are frequently compelled to reside." Available evidence indicates that rural housing conditions in England as a whole were somewhat better on the average than in the North Riding. As for Scotland, Ireland and Wales, particularly in those regions which furnished the largest proportion of recruits for the new industries, conditions were even more serious than in the North Riding. Fairly typical of many authentic descriptions of the habitations of rural workers in many parts of Scotland is Sir John Sinclair's account of the hovels of Sutherland. "The estates furnish some wood,"

[24] Clark, *General View*, Herefordshire, 29; Lowe, *General View*, Berwick, 54; Vancouver, *General View*, Cambridgeshire, 175; Johnson, *General View*, Dumfries, 58, 59. The reports from the various other counties to the Board of Agriculture also, in a large proportion of cases, contained information concerning hours of labor agreeing substantially with the ones cited.

he writes, "with which, and the swarded surface of the ground, cut into the form of large bricks, they make houses and offices for themselves, covering them with the same swarded turf, cut thinner, and resembling slates in their form. Once in three years, all the earthy part of these houses is thrown on the dunghill, and new houses built again of the same materials. The cattle commonly occupy one end of the house, during the winter season. Some holes in the walls and roofs serve for windows and chimneys. An iron pot, for boiling their food, constitutes their principal furniture." In the light of such conditions, one is not unprepared for Adam Smith's appalling confession that in parts of his country, "it is not uncommon . . . for a mother who has borne twenty children not to have two alive." Arthur Young's extremely vivid description of the hovels of Irish workers indicates a condition even more degraded than in Scotland, a condition alleviated only by the somewhat milder climate.[25]

One of the most serious of working-class problems in the modern industrial world grows out of the transient, fluctuating nature of a large part of industrial employments. Similar conditions exist, to be sure, in modern agriculture, but they are diffused and more remote from the centers of population, and, while the resulting problem is perhaps none the less grave, it is not so readily observed and subjected to criticism. Comparable condi-

[25] Tuke, *General View*, North Riding of Yorkshire, 80, 81; Sinclair, *General View*, Northern Counties, 130; Adam Smith, *Wealth of Nations*, Bk. I, ch. 8; Young, *Tour in Ireland*, II, 47, 48. See also Robertson, *General View*, Midlothian, 33, n. (where it is stated great improvements are being introduced, as straw thatching, and "in some cases" a "timber floor"); Donaldson, *General View*, Nairn, 20, 21; Webster, *General View*, Galloway, 15; Sinclair, *General View*, Northern Counties, 50, 211; Lloyd, *General View*, Cardigan, 14, 15; Ruggles, *History of the Poor*, II, 79; McPherson, *Annals of Commerce*, IV, 80; Smollett, *Humphrey Clinker*, II, 138, 139 and *passim* (Jensen Society's ed.).

tions existed at the time of the emergence of modern industrialism.

Probably the principal cause of casual, floating labor was the demand for additional labor during the harvest season, especially in the grain regions, but there were various other causes. Intensive gardening in summer for the town markets; planting seasons; cattle feeding during winter; variations from year to year in the amount of produce to be harvested; variations in the amount of improvements, such as draining and fertilizing; and changes in the types of farming, particularly in connection with enclosures and the enlargement of farms: these and other circumstances swelled the floating population of the rural districts.

Laborers from Ireland were described as "pouring in" whenever there seemed to be a chance for employment. From the mountains of Wales every year came troops of harvesters and cattle feeders to the Welsh lowlands and the western counties of England, and even market gardeners to the region of London. In Scotland, large numbers of "strangers" are reported as coming each spring to the Carse of Gowrie from the north, returning about Martinmas. To East Lothian, hundreds of reapers came each year during the harvest season. Because of the "perpetual influx of the unemployed from the north [that] pours into Edinburgh and its vicinity," we are told that "there is perhaps no county in Great Britain better supplied with work people than Midlothian"; and it appears that casual, floating labor had become so definite a part of the agricultural economy of the region that these migratory workers had acquired a "roving disposition," seeking new employments "on the least lure of emigration." In spite of the obstacles raised by the acts of settlement, there were many migratory Englishmen as well as Scotchmen, Welshmen and Irishmen. In the East Riding of Yorkshire, for instance, harvest work was done "by day laborers, men and women, who, during harvest, come in great numbers to Malton to be hired, from the North and West Ridings." In Leicestershire, "many laborers are called in from other counties." In Bedfordshire, the absence of manufactures to enable the workers to supplement their farm wages resulted in seasonal emigrations. "The laborers continue with the farmers during the winter season, to thrash out their grain, and on the approach of summer many of them set off for more cultivated counties where labor is more required." [26]

The flow of casual laborers was directed largely by chance, without any coordinated method or agency for regulating and distributing it. In some regions, to be sure, a form of contract labor existed. In Herefordshire, for instance, "the grain is cut by persons who come from the mountainous parts of Wales annually for that purpose, mostly from Cardiganshire. A foreman generally agrees for a whole farm at a stated price per acre, who finds the requisite number of hands to fulfill his contract, at whatever price he can." To the south, in Wiltshire, the current names for such workers were "taskers" and "laborers by compact." A crude method of distributing migratory laborers was utilized in some sections by recognizing certain places as "markets," as in East Lothian, where there were two markets for reapers, to which

[26] Adam Smith, *Wealth of Nations*, Bk. I, ch. 10, Pt. I (a passage in which he states that employment in the commoner sorts of manufactures "is more steady and uniform" than employment in agriculture); Howlett, in *Annals of Agriculture*, XVIII, 566-572; Webster, *General View*, Galloway, 15, 16; Sinclair, *General View*, Northern Counties, 209, 212, 213, and Appendix, 33; Donaldson, *General View*, Carse of Gowrie, 22; Robertson, *General View*, Midlothian, 26; Leatham, *General View*, East Riding of Yorkshire, 31, 32; Monk, *General View*, Leicestershire, 49; Stone, *General View*, Bedfordshire, 56; Walker, *General View*, Hertfordshire, 12, 83; Driver, *General View*, Hants, 65; Hassall, *General View*, Pembrokeshire, 21; Hasbach, *English Agricultural Laborer*, 82, n. 2.

Highlanders and others resorted in hope of meeting employers.[27]

The term "market" is not without significance as an indication of the condition of these laborers. Our means of picturing to ourselves the manner of life and social status of these masses of migratory farm workers is limited to such inferences, and to our knowledge of the obviously more favorable conditions prevailing among the class immediately above them—the regularly employed farm laborers. It is interesting to observe by comparison that even in later times, supposedly better informed and more democratic in spirit, the casual workers, though performing vitally important economic functions, are seldom able to secure from other classes of society the recognition which their services no less than their needs seem to justify.

Casual, shifting types of work necessarily involved alternating periods of unemployment. The amount of unemployment was increased by other factors, and chiefly by the progress of enclosures and the process of enlarging or engrossing of farms. The amount of unemployment resulting from these changes varied from place to place, and in some cases an increase of land under cultivation or the adoption of more intensive methods of farming may have even created opportunities for work. But in general, even the advocates of enclosures and of engrossing admitted the decrease of employment as a result. "Plain facts must be admitted," wrote no less an authority than Sir John Sinclair, "and that when two or three farms are thrown into one, it must affect the population in some degree." He opposed the view that "every sacrifice [should] be made to population," and believed that the landlords were justified in taking steps "to turn their lands to the best possible advantage." As

[27] Clark, *General View*, Herefordshire, 29; Davis, *General View*, Wiltshire, 89; Buchan-Hepburn, *General View*, East Lothian, 96, 97.

to enclosures, he was even more positive. "In regard to the effect of enclosures on population, it certainly has a tendency to diminish the number of hands employed in agriculture." [28]

Sinclair's justification of enclosures and engrossing is even more significant than his admission that unemployment resulted therefrom. "It compels the cottagers," he wrote, "to reside in villages or towns, where they are more usefully employed, both for themselves and for the public, than if they remained idling away their time in the country." This view was merely one expression of an idea very generally held among landlords and farmers, to the effect that cottagers and others with small tracts of land of their own and rights of common were too independent. Cultivating their own gardens, collecting fuel for their own use, caring for their own stock, —all this was not "work" in the eyes of those who desired to gain control alike of the land and of the labor of the cottagers, and the latter were therefore naïvely charged with "idling away their time," their labor being "lost to the community,"—that is, of course, the "community" of landlords and farmers. Another writer put the matter even more plainly: "Let not the mistaken zeal of well-disposed but ignorant people persuade the man of sense that it [that is, enclosing for purpose of engrossing or enlargement of farms] is prejudicial to the poor. . . . The benefit which they are supposed to reap from commons, in their present state, I know to be merely

[28] Sinclair, *General View*, Northern Counties, 30, 31, 207, and Appendix, 41; Robertson, *General View*, Perthshire, 64; Johnson, *General View*, Tweedale, 18; Wedge, *General View*, Warwickshire, 21, 22; Crutchley, *General View*, Rutland, 31; Davis, *General View*, Wiltshire, 87, 88; Walker, *General View*, Hertfordshire, 51, 52. Principal later students of the subject, as Slater, Hasbach, the Hammonds, and Cunningham, are in substantial agreement as to the resulting unemployment and suffering. Particularly significant is Cunningham's change of view as stated in the revised edition of his *Growth of English Industry and Commerce*.

nominal; nay, indeed, what is worse, I know that, in many instances it is an essential injury to them, by being made a plea for their idleness; for, some few excepted, if you offer them work, they will tell you, that they must go look up their sheep, cut furzes, get their cow out of the pound, or perhaps say they must take their horse to be shod, that he may carry them to a horse-race or cricket-match." Still another writer frankly avows that one of the main purposes of the advocates of enclosures was "to have the laborers more dependent upon them." Whether or not this was the general intent of the farmers and landlords who carried on the process of enclosing, the process was in fact accompanied by the disappearance of the last vestiges of economic independence on the part of the agricultural workers. The loss of independence was extending rapidly also to the yeomen. This class, traditionally as vigorous in character as it was large in numbers, had long been declining, but it had survived in many districts, as in Westmoreland, where it was described by the reporter for the Board of Agriculture in 1794 as in possession of a large part of the county. "The consciousness of their independence," we are told, "renders them impatient of oppression or insult." But "this class of men is daily decreasing. . . . Circumstances . . . have compelled many a statesman [a term used in Westmoreland synonymously with yeoman] to sell his property, and reduced him to the necessity of working as a laborer in those fields which perhaps he and his ancestors had for many generations cultivated as their own." Wherever a large part of the land was held in small tracts, higher wages and relative economic independence were apt to be found. Employers of farm labor in such places thought themselves disadvantaged as compared with those in regions where the small holders had been dispossessed or from some other cause had suffered decline to the status of wage laborers. The landlords and farmers, desiring on the one hand to increase their holdings and on the other to obtain cheap and dependent labor to develop their estates, found with little difficulty a moral weapon with which to make war on the small holder. To attend a horse-race or a cricket-match was dissolute and sinful. To look up their sheep, cut furzes, or till a garden plot was a mere excuse for idleness, by which their labor was "lost to the community." To refuse to toil from dawn to dark for a subsistence often partly in the form of charity was insubordination in the eyes of the landed potentates, and an intolerable menace to law and order.[29]

It is apparent that during the second half of the eighteenth century, the masses of agricultural workers suffered a progressive loss of whatever degree of economic independence they had possessed in earlier times. Their condition of dependence seems to have become more complete, indeed, than that of the industrial workers; for the former, due to their isolation, had only their individual resources; while the latter, concentrated increasingly in towns and factories, were able to mitigate their individual helplessness by a certain collective influence even before the period of effective labor organization.

The facts presented seem to justify the following conclusions concerning the status of laborers in the rural sections, whence came the mass of workers to man the new industries: They suffered loss of income auxiliary to wages; prices were at the same time rising; and yet they were able to secure virtually no increase in wages. They

[29] Sinclair, *General View*, Northern Counties, 207; [Arbuthnot], *Inquiry into the Connection between the Present Price of Provisions and the Size of Farms*, 81; Pringle, *General View*, Westmoreland, 18, 30, 40, 41; Bailey and Cully, *General View*, Cumberland, 11, 37; Wedge, *General View*, Cheshire, 11; Hasbach, *English Agricultural Laborer*, 100, n. 1, and 105, ff.; Cunningham, *Growth of English Industry and Commerce*, II, Pt. II, 554, 567; Hammond, *Village Laborer*, 103-105 (a summary of the general degradation of farm workers).

were forced, in consequence, to depend very generally on public and private charity to keep their income at the level of a most meager standard of subsistence. Their wives worked as regularly as the exigencies of giving birth to children permitted, and the children became regular workers as soon as their strength allowed. Their hours of labor, while employed, were so long and exhausting as to approach the limits of physical endurance; while at the same time, large numbers were periodically unable to secure work, and still others found it necessary to resort to one or another of the various forms of casual and shifting employment. Such leisure as fell to their lot, whether regularly employed or not, was vitiated by unwholesome housing and living conditions. Those who, by means of their plots of land and their rights of commons, had long been able to maintain a position of semi-independence were rapidly being reduced to complete dependence on wage-earning employments. These various circumstances reduced the masses of farm workers to a condition which made impossible the effective exercise of any save their physical faculties, and which required that even these be exercised in blind subservience to employing landlords and farmers. Such was the condition of the rural population, the principal reservoir for supplying the new industries with workers.

But a considerable proportion of the new industrial population was recruited from the older industries. It is necessary to keep in mind the fact that there were three main types of older industrial workers: the handicraftsmen of the shops and gilds; the miners, colliers, and associated workers; and the domestic manufacturers.

The state of the first type, the shop craftsmen, was somewhat better than that of the workers in agriculture. This was the opinion of Adam Smith, who affirmed that they received higher wages, had steadier and more uniform employment, enjoyed a superior social status, and were more independent than farm workers. As for the colliers and other miners, their status is little known, but there was no such fundamental change in the organization and conditions of labor in the mines as in other forms of industrial labor. Although the condition of the older groups of industrial workers was in general better than the condition of farm laborers, the latter were sunk in such abject poverty and helplessness that the comparison means little. Whatever may have been their status in earlier times, at the time of the origin of the factory system the handicraftsmen were no longer independent workmen, the separation between workers and employers having already become well advanced. "It sometimes happens, indeed," wrote Adam Smith, "that a single independent workman has stock sufficient both to purchase the materials of his work, and to maintain himself till it be completed. He is both master and workman, and enjoys the whole produce of his own labor, or the whole value which it adds to the materials upon which it is bestowed. . . . Such cases, however, are not very frequent, and in every part of Europe twenty workmen serve under a master for one that is independent." There are important differences, to be sure, between the status of the later shop craftsman and the modern factory worker, but the dominant characteristic of both was dependence upon an employer for income in the form of wages. The workmen of Smith's time, as he points out with his accustomed analytical keenness, were helpless before the superior strength of their employers, backed by government; for "whenever the law has attempted to regulate the wages of workmen, it has always been rather to lower them than to raise them." [30]

In addition to the economic dependence of the vast majority of craftsmen, a large proportion of them were subjected to conditions and processes which, though rela-

[30] *Wealth of Nations,* Bk. I, ch. 10, Bk. III, ch. 4.

tively simple, were unwholesome and dangerous—conditions the more serious because of ignorance and indifference as to safeguards.   But in spite of the prevailing indifference, an occasional voice was raised, as when John Howlett bewailed the victims of the older industrialism: "The collier, the clothier, the painter, the gilder, the miner, the makers of glass, the workers in iron, tin, lead, copper, while they minister to our necessities or please our tastes and fancies, are impairing their health and shortening their days.   If war can tell its dismal tale of thousands slain in the field, and give its melancholy list of mangled beings who, in the language of the poet,

> With half their limbs in battle lopped away,
> Beg bitter bread through realms their valor saved,

arts and manufactures can present as long a catalogue of our fellow creatures suffocated in mines and pits, or gradually poisoned by the noxious effluvia of metals, oils, powders, spirits, etc., used in their work, and can exhibit as mournful a scene of blinded and lame, of enfeebled, decrepit, asthmatic, consumptive wretches, panting for breath, and crawling half alive upon the surface of the earth."   The work of the miners was particularly dangerous and their condition was in some respects even inferior to that of the farm laborers.   In Scotland they were kept in the status of serfdom till the end of the eighteenth century; and in many of the mines of England, they were bound by the year, and were kept in a condition more nearly approximating serfdom than were any of the other workers.   Their mid-century condition is described in an anonymous pamphlet published in 1756 and attributed to Edmund Burke: "I suppose that there are in Great Britain upwards of an hundred thousand people employed in lead, tin, iron, copper, and coal mines; these unhappy wretches scarce ever see the light of the sun; they are buried in the bowels of the earth; there they work at a severe and dismal task, without the least prospect of being delivered from it; they subsist upon the coarsest and worst sort of fare; they have their health miserably impaired, and their lives cut short, by being perpetually confined in the close vapor of these malignant minerals." [31]

The sympathetic tone observable in these quotations was extremely exceptional. What has been said concerning the prevalent attitude toward the farm laborers applies also in the case of the older types of industrial workers. Perhaps the dominant motive in determining labor policy was simply the desire for gain on the part of employers. But in so far as a rational philosophy was formulated, it was the philosophy of mercantilism. As a recent student of the subject has pointed out,[32] labor was viewed simply as a factor in production; workhouses were built not so much to relieve distress as to make labor more productive. For the same reason, a subsistence wage was advocated as a stimulus to work. The laborer was looked upon as "merely the most important cog in the national industrial machine, a cog, moreover, which could be kept turning indefinitely, without rest and almost without lubrication." Low wages and even supplementary poor relief were considered proper methods of aiding the English industrial employers to outbid foreign competitors. Poor relief therefore came to be in a sense "a kind of bounty paid to the export industries." [33] The landlords were of course interested in the export of

[31] John Howlett, in *Gentleman's Magazine*, LII, 526; E. R. Turner, "English Coal Industry in the Seventeenth and Eighteenth Centuries," in *Am. Hist. Rev.*, XXVII, 1-23 (including the quotation attributed to Burke); Hammond, *Skilled Laborer;* Furniss, *Position of the Laborer in a System of Nationalism.*

[32] Furniss, *Position of the Laborer in a System of Nationalism.* See also Conyers Read's extensive review in *Quar. Jour. of Econ.*, XXXV, No. 2, 342-344.

[33] The quotations are from Read's review.

many of their commodities, but in this connection, it was the merchants and the master manufacturers who played the leading part in the subjection of labor. A well-nigh inexhaustible reservoir of labor for the new industries was the domestic system of manufacturing. The term has been used by different writers in different senses, but the particular type of domestic manufacturing that we are primarily concerned with was the "putting-out" system.

Among the various contemporary accounts of the "putting-out" system, there is a particularly clear-cut and interesting picture of the system in Aberdeenshire, together with the more primitive household industry preceding it. Before the middle of the eighteenth century, each farmer's family in this region spun its own wool into a coarse yarn, "which was afterwards woven by country weavers into webs of a kind of thin coarse stuff called fingrams; these were sold at fairs and country markets to traveling merchants, who made it their business to pick up things of this sort, and carry them to a market in other parts of Scotland, where they were bought for gowns by servant girls; and afforded a cheap, plain clothing." But finer tastes coming in, about the middle of the century, "the women fell into the habit of spinning worsted yarn, and knitting it into hose, chiefly for foreign sale." This required a larger quantity and a finer grade of wool, which, instead of being produced by the farmers' own flocks, was imported by merchants, who had it sorted and combed. "It was then given out by weight to the women in every corner of the county, who returned it to the merchant at a stated time in wrought hose, which he afterwards caused to be properly dressed and prepared for a market. In this way the manufacture spread wide throughout the whole county, and became an object of great importance. Many master manufacturers [the merchants or "putters-out"] thus acquired great wealth, and vast sums of money were thus brought into the country. Women of all ages were seen everywhere, walking from place to place busily employed knitting." The method of "putting out" the raw materials and collecting the manufactured articles seems to have varied from place to place. In the spinning of wool in Suffolk, for instance, we are told that "the mode of delivering this wool to the spinners is through a packman, who is employed to carry it to the houses of certain people, which are called pack-houses; to these houses the spinners repair for their wool, and there return it after it is spun into yarn." In other places, the packman or agent of the "putter-out" seems to have visited each house, as when the "discarded spinster" is made to recall how every week a load of wool had passed her home, "always stopping at the porch-house door" to supply the family with spinning.[34]

Some of the workers in the "putting-out" system, even in the rural districts, had converted their homes into handicraft shops. In some cases they depended entirely on their wages as craftsmen. In other cases their wages were supplemented by occasional rural employments, especially in harvest time, and by the cultivation of a small plot of land. In such cases, the industrial wage was the primary income, agriculture being secondary. But the most extensive development of the system was among workers whose primary dependence was an agricultural income, usually in the form of wages.

There has been a tendency to look back upon the period of domestic manufacturing as a golden age of the working classes. The earlier stages of household and community economy, while ministering crudely to crude wants, were not without important advantages, as the

[34] Anderson, *General View*, Aberdeenshire, 36, 37; *Letter to a Member of Parliament Stating the Necessity of an Amendment in the Laws Relating to the Woollen Manufactory*, 21, 22; *Discarded Spinster*, 20.

fostering of independence, self-reliance, and dexterity. But the primitive household and village economy had generally at the time of the rise of the factory system been supplanted by handicraft shops and by the "putting-out" system; and it is the latter phase of the domestic system that writers have idealized in contrast with modern industry. In the textile industries, where it was most extensively developed, the workers as a rule owned the implements, and they had the further advantage of a less rigorous discipline and oversight by their employers. But the income derived from such employments, while doubtless in some instances affording temporary aid, was in general offset by a corresponding reduction of the agricultural wage, which, for a large proportion of such workers, was the primary source of family income. As we have seen, it was regarded as entirely improper and undesirable to allow to the laborer an income in excess of a necessary subsistence; and the isolated farm laborer and his family were particularly helpless in preventing the rigorous carrying out of the subsistence doctrine. The net result, in the end, was an addition to the amount of work performed by the laborer and his family, with no increase in the family income. Indeed there is reason to believe that there was a tendency among farmers and landlords to overestimate the auxiliary earning capacity of the laborer's family in connection with industrial employments, and in consequence to press agricultural wages to such low levels as to reduce the total family income.[35] With the decline of domestic industry toward the end of the century, this tendency on the part of employers of farm workers had tragic consequences.

The real reason for idealization of the domestic system

[35] See, for instance, Arthur Young's argument for lowering farm wages on the basis of an exaggerated estimate of the earning capacity of the farmer's family. (*Farmer's Letters*, I, 194, ff.).

in contrast with the factory system is not to be found in the advantages or disadvantages accruing to the workers from either system, but rather in the fact that the domestic system afforded an auxiliary income to the farm laborer's family, which enabled employers to reduce farm wages; while the factory system took away such auxiliary employments, and at the same time tended, as will be observed later, to drive farm wages upward by the force of competition. A curious instance (curious in form and yet typical in substance) of the idealization of the domestic system is the case of *The Discarded Spinster,* published in 1791, a rimed pamphlet ostensibly by an actual "spinster" deprived of work by the new system of spinning, but written in reality by a champion of the agricultural employers:

> O happy days! when from a plenteous store,
> Encouraged Industry supply'd the poor.
> Well I remember, as from school I strayed,
> And 'cross the common to the cottage made,
> How oft the hum of whirling wheels among
> (The droning bees of many a rustic song),
> Pleased I have stood, and marked the dext'rous sleight,
> And caught the glee that renders labor light,
> Whilst Sue and Betty, and my little Ned,
> With merry movements drew the slender thread;
> Assiduous to complete their tasks that play,
> So mother promised, might complete the day;
> For then, blest times! their earnings would afford
> A leisure hour, and yet a plenteous board.

In contrast he describes the sad state of the poor since the children are "left to play,"—

> For now the jennies take all work away.
> Since when, in yonder poor house, 'cross the green,
> Where half the parish *now* are crowded in,
> We, and our mammy, who makes such a cry!—
> Tho' she don't know us if we stand just by—
> Are all thronged night times—and by day turned out
> To beg an alms, or, hungry, beat about.

But the author's concern, as revealed by his preface, is not so much for the poor as these lines would indicate. He admits that machines have not decreased work or wages in the towns, "yet this does not prove but that the circumjacent country is injured; which, to the distance of many miles, used to receive from these towns a supply of labor,"—strange words from one who is arguing that the "circumjacent country," on account of machines, has its poor houses crowded with people out of work. His bias is further shown by his naïve repetition of the idea prevalent among landlords and farmers that the chief value of manufacturing was to supplement the wages of farm workers:

> If manufactures aught a state bestead,
> 'Tis to employ the poor, and yield them bread.

Finally, he demands, on behalf of land-owning ratepayers, that the tax laws be changed so as to require manufacturers to pay rates for the support of the poor farm workers who, because of loss of spinning, are unable to subsist on their farm wages: since the new machines take away work from the farm laborer's family, the law should provide "that whom they render idle they maintain." [36]

When mechanical methods and factory organization began to encroach upon the older forms of industry, a large proportion of English laborers were primarily dependent upon agricultural employments and secondarily dependent upon manufacturing for a subsistence. This two-fold dependence forms the background of one of the major tragedies in English history. The workers were denied a subsistence wage by farmers and landlords, because their families were expected to eke out a subsistence

[36] *Discarded Spinster*, Preface, i, ii, and 4, 9, 20-22, and *passim;* *Humble Petition of the Poor Spinners;* Billingsley, *General View,* Somerset, 57; Davis, *General View,* Wiltshire, 157-159.

by spinning or some other form of industrial employment. They were denied a subsistence wage as industrial workers because they were expected to depend primarily upon agriculture. Wages, which historically by law and by custom had been kept as near the subsistence level as possible, were at the time of origin of the factory system being rapidly forced farther and farther below the subsistence level,—indeed, in many cases cut off entirely,— by the jealous competition of the two sets of employers, agrarian and industrial, in reducing wages; by the upward trend of prices; and by the agricultural processes of enclosing and engrossing.

3. Comparative well-being of old and new types of workers

On the eve of the modern system of production, the laborer, whether agrarian or industrial, was being crushed and broken by the relentless forces of an economic order from which the new system afforded temporary relief. During the early stages of industrialization, the economic well-being of the new industrial population was decidedly superior to that of the older groups. The views of contemporary observers are in remarkable accord.[37]

Employers of farm labor made frequent and long-continued complaints that wages were rising and that their laborers were being enticed from the farms. "The advance of wages," wrote the Board of Agriculture's Lancashire reporter, "and the preference given to the manufacturing employment, by the laborers in general, have

[37] Some typical general observations: Davies, *Case of Laborers in Husbandry*, 71, 149; Ruggles, *History of the Poor*, I, Preface, viii (ed. of 1797, vi, vii); Sheffield, *Remarks on the Scarcity of Grain*, 63-65; W. Young, *Observations Preliminary to a Proposed Amendment of the Poor Laws*, 41; McPherson, *Annals of Commerce*, IV, 529, note; Dyer, *Complaints of the Poor People of England*, 74.

induced many to forsake the spade for the shuttle, and have embarrassed the farmers, by the scarcity of workmen, and of course advanced the price of labor." Complaint was made, too, of "the influx of wealth amongst the laboring class" of Lancashire, which led them to form extravagant habits,—as for instance, "to indulge upon many occasions with the wheaten loaf." Such effects were felt even in the remoter villages, but it was declared that in general, "the rate of wages is in proportion to the distance of townships from the seats of manufacturers." Another champion of the agrarian employers as against the manufacturers complained that the latter "buy the hands they like best out of others' employ," with the result that "the workmen see their advantage," and he fears that this will lead to "the corruption of the workmen in their moral and civil dispositions," and to the disruption of "the internal peace of the realm." But his concern is mainly for the farmers and landlords, who, unwilling or unable to offer equal inducements, were being left without laborers. "In this part of Lancashire (the Granary) you will see in a large field of corn, shaking ripe, not above one-sixth of the number of hands . . . [needed]. Very few able-bodied men are to be seen about the harvest business, hay or corn, but the few hands are, with few exceptions, composed of females of all ages, males not come to half their strength, or such as have lost more than half of it; the farmer at the same time paying high wages for such defective means of saving his crops." [38]

[38] Holt, General View, Lancashire, 25, 53-55, 73 (ed. 1794), 179, 180, 210-213 (ed. 1795); Dickson, General View, Lancashire, 592-595, 630; Annals of Agriculture, XX, 136, 137. See also the following: Percival, in Phil. Trans., LXV, 327, LXVI, 167; Young, Northern Tour, III, 134, 135, 164, 174, 189, 193; Annals of Agriculture, XV, 564, XVIII, 571, XX, 184; European Magazine, XX, 216; Calico Printers' Assistant, Retrospect, n. 11 (referring to "herds of Lancashire boors" ·attracted into the printing industry); Manchester Mercury, Feb. 27, 1787 (advertisement of a mill for sale in Denbighshire, twenty miles from

Similar conditions existed in other industrial regions. We are told that in Staffordshire "the price of labor and the rate of wages vary in different places. They are always highest in the neighborhood of flourishing manufactures, and lowest in remote parts of the country where no such manufactures are established." Complaint is made that "our men servants often fly off into large towns where they can earn higher wages." It was the boast of Josiah Wedgwood that the potteries and other manufactures had transformed a crude, poverty-stricken and isolated region into a populous and prosperous district, with "the workmen earning near double their former wages—their houses mostly new and comfortable, and the lands, roads, and every other circumstance bearing evident marks of the most pleasing and rapid improvements." In the Warwickshire region, where enclosures seem to have resulted in an unusual amount of unemployment, farm wages were reported as about twenty-five per cent. higher in the region of the industrial centers than in remoter places. Surplus farm laborers, and even "the hardy yeomanry have been driven for employment to Birmingham, Coventry, and other manufacturing towns," and the employers of farm labor should count themselves happy, so one of their number contended in writing to the Board of Agriculture, in having near them flourishing industries to absorb their superfluous workers. "There are thousands of places within fifty miles round us," wrote William Hutton, a celebrated citizen of Birmingham, in speaking of workers putting up their labor for sale, "where such persons hawk this valuable commodity, but cannot procure a purchaser. Birmingham is a market everlastingly open for this kind of traffic." Strikingly similar is the evidence in respect

Chester, suitable for a cotton factory, an inducement being "plenty of hands at low wages, as there . . . [is] no manufactory whatever being carried on there at present").

to Cheshire, Salop, Yorkshire, and Worcestershire. "What would become of one-half of the former inhabitants of the country," asks the Board of Agriculture's Worcestershire reporter, "if our growing manufactories had not received and supported them?" [39]

In Scotland, the contrast was even more apparent. Adam Smith's grim account of the "half-starved" Scotch Highlanders seems not to have been overdrawn, nor characteristic alone of the Highlanders. With the progress of enclosures and engrossing, the condition of the masses of rural population became more critical than when Smith wrote his *Wealth of Nations*. It is not surprising, therefore, that when "manufactures dawned" on North Briton, "multitudes left the country, the abode of poverty, and fled to the town, the fountain of riches." It is not surprising that such Scotchmen as Sir John Sinclair, president of the Board of Agriculture, viewed manufacturing as the chief recourse of landlords and farmers in disposing of the surplus population without depopulating the country through emigration or starvation. Even in the regions where small holders and agricultural laborers were not being dispossessed and thrown out of employment, the comparison was in favor of the workers in the manufacturing industries. Wages were higher, as evidenced by the almost universal complaint of employers of farm workers that manufacturing had forced them to raise wages in order to retain their laborers. Hours, too, were being shortened, at least in the region of Dumbarton, where employers were said to "complain that the great

[39] Pitt, *General View*, Staffordshire, 20, 107, 161, 163 (ed. 1794), 216, 218, 237 (ed. 1808); Julia Wedgwood, *Life of Josiah Wedgwood*, 224, 225; Wedge, *General View*, Warwickshire, 21-24; Langford, *Century of Birmingham Life*, I, 445; Brown, *General View*, Derbyshire, 38-40; Holland, *General View*, Cheshire, 296; Wedge, *General View*, Cheshire, 26; Bishton, *General View*, Salop, 28, 29; Rennie, *General View*, West Riding of Yorkshire, 11, 81, 90; Pomeroy, *General View*, Worcestershire, 27, 28; *Annals of Agriculture*, XVI, 422, 423, 534, 535.

demand for workmen has raised the wages of servants for country work; has made them very scarce and shortened their hours of labor." The influence of manufacturing was felt even in remoter places, as in the region of Elgin, to the north, where "the price of labor has, in the course of the last fifteen years [since about 1780] risen to nearly double what it was before that period; and this may be accounted for, in a great measure, by the emigration of numbers of both sexes, in that class, to the manufacturing parts of the kingdom." The same writer reports that in 1794 wages, after having increased a hundred per cent in fifteen years, were, "without victuals, in winter, 6d. to 8d. and in summer 10d. a day." Characteristic of the attitude of the employers of farm labor was the complaint from Clydesdale that "the gains of manufacturing labor, and the show and appearance of greater ease and comfort, among those engaged in it, seduced the peasantry from their residence in the country and the labor of the fields to towns and manufacturing villages." [40]

Although contemporaneous records and comments, even those written from the point of view of the employers of farm labor, are in general accord as to the superior economic well-being of the industrial workers as compared with farm laborers, yet there are occasional statements which seem to qualify the conclusion. These are to the effect that the rapid rise in poor rates was attributable to manufacturing. Such an assertion is made, for instance, by John Holt, the Board of Agricul-

[40] Roger, *General View*, Angus or Forfar, 23, 24; Sinclair, *General View*, Northern Counties, 109, 110, 112, 130-132, and Appendix, 33, 41-45 (the second reference to the Appendix being to a passage entitled "Hints as to the means of preventing emigration from the Highlands of Scotland, by the establishment of manufactures there," particularly cotton manufacturing as in England); Ure, *General View*, Dumbarton, 89; Donaldson, *General View*, Elgin or Moray, 23, 24; Naismith, *General View*, Clydesdale, 74, ff.

ture's Lancashire correspondent, who has already been quoted as saying that manufacturing had led to an "influx of wealth amongst the laboring class," and had forced farmers and landlords to pay what he deemed excessive wages.[41]

It should be remembered that the incidence of the poor-law tax was being hotly debated at the time. The difficulty of rating property other than land and houses resulted in personal property and stock in trade being largely exempt; and the manufacturers, so the landlords urged, profited unduly as a result. Another grievance against the industrial employers was based on the acts of settlement, which made the laborer's home parish responsible for his support under the poor laws, unless he could secure settlement elsewhere; and it was claimed that the industrial parishes, in need of labor, were allowing laborers to come, but were refusing settlement, and whenever they seemed likely to become dependent upon the rates, were sending them back to the parishes whence they came. It is apparent that if the farm workers, dispossessed by enclosures or broken by the hard and pauperizing conditions of rural labor, could have gained settlement in the towns without the consent of the town authorities, thereby making the industrial parishes responsible for their support,—it is apparent that in such a case the employers of farm labor would have been able to escape even more largely from the results of enclosures and pauper labor, and that the newly rising industrial centers would have been overwhelmed with responsibility for veritable floods of dispossessed and broken rural workers no longer needed by their rural masters.

The poor law and the acts of settlement had long been clumsy and yet on the whole effective instruments wielded by the aristocracy and gentry for the purpose of

[41] See above, pp. 253, 254, and Holt, *General View,* Lancashire, 210, 213 (ed. 1795).

keeping the rural population in subjection and for utilizing it for their own purposes; and now these instruments were being turned against them, so agrarian employers began to feel, by the newly rising industrial masters of labor. Their resentment found expression in the charge, frequently repeated but wholly untenable in so far as it was applied to the newer industries of the period before the French wars, that manufacturing was responsible for the increase of poor rates.[42]

A keen contemporary observer, John Howlett, called attention to this "popular error." He declared that the proportion of paupers in the industrial regions was much less than in the agricultural regions. The overwhelming evidence of the greater prosperity of the industrial workers seems alone sufficient to justify such a conclusion, but Howlett's judgment was based not alone upon this reasonable inference but upon what he describes as "surveys of a sufficient number of places of every description, from almost every part of England and Wales." On the basis of this evidence, he concluded that even in the older manufacturing towns, where industry was often static or even in a declining condition, pauperism was less extensive and poor rates were lower than in the ordinary agricultural parish. He estimated that in the chief manufacturing towns, the poor rates amounted to about £1 to every six inhabitants; in smaller towns, of not more than 10,000 inhabitants, the rate was estimated at £1 to three and a half inhabitants; and in country parishes, £1 to two and three-fifths inhabitants. He found the rate lowest in Sheffield, Manchester, and Birmingham. In connection with the question of

[42] Cannan, *History of Local Rates,* 71-101; Ruggles, *History of the Poor,* I, Preface, xv, 55; W. Young, *Observations Preliminary to a Proposed Amendment of the Poor Laws,* 30-32; Wedge, *General View,* Warwickshire, 24. A passage presenting the point of view of industrial parishes is to be found in [Rose], *Observations on the Act for the Relief and Encouragement of Friendly Societies,* 14.

paupers returned by industrial towns to rural parishes, he added significantly that "the expenses for the poor in the country parishes in the immediate vicinity of these towns are not so high . . . [as in ordinary rural parishes] for this very obvious reason, that the flourishing state of their manufactures has considerably advanced the price of agricultural labor, and rendered it more adequate to the necessities of the laborer." The sums paid for the support of the poor increased rapidly, it is true, in the industrial counties such as Lancashire as well as in the older agricultural districts, but on account of the more rapid increase in population, the per capita increase was smaller. Furthermore, in spite of the acts of settlement by which the laborers' home parishes were in many cases held responsible for their support, the burden of poor rates in the industrial centers was greatly increased by the influx of workers fleeing from intolerable conditions in the country, who, from age or ignorance of industry or other causes were incapable of adjusting themselves to the new environment.[43]

A complete survey of the laboring population of England on the eve of the advent of the modern industrial system would necessitate the study of various factors not primarily economic, many of which adversely affected the workers,—as the penal code, the prison laws and practices, the game laws, the administration of the poor laws and settlement acts, and the system of apprenticing the children of paupers. These are beyond the scope and purpose of the present study. But our brief survey has sufficed to reveal conditions of pauperism, helplessness, and degradation from which the older economic society seemed to offer no way of escape. To multitudes long hopeless, the new system of production offered promise

[43] Howlett, in *Annals of Agriculture*, XI, 6, 7, XVIII, 574-581; Hasbach, *English Agricultural Laborer*, 140, 141; Troughton, *History of Liverpool*, 145-147; Langford, *Century of Birmingham Life*, I, 444, ff.

of deliverance. From the expropriated farms and commons of the cottagers and yeomen, from the shops and homes of petty manufacturers finding economic independence and often even subsistence no longer possible, from the hovels of the Scotch Highlands, the mountains of Wales, and the undulating fruitful plains of Ireland,— plains fruitful of human poverty even more than of the bounties of nature,—all roads led to the mill valleys, cities, factories and mines of the industrial regions as to the promised land. Historical veracity demands the blotting out of the idyllic pictures that have been painted of working-class conditions in agriculture and the older industries preceding the great economic change; it necessitates a modification of the judgment that the status of the workers in the new industrial centers was inherently, inevitably inferior.

During the earlier stages of industrialization, the new industries indubitably ameliorated rather than rendered harsher the conditions of life for the workers. Furthermore, certain considerations frequently overlooked must be taken into account in forming a just conclusion concerning the later effects of industrialism. The conditions prevailing in the new industrial centers were more readily observable than were the conditions of the obscure and widely scattered workers who furnished recruits for the new industries. The stimulus for criticism was less powerful earlier than when the clash of interests between the landed aristocracy and the industrialists led adherents of the former to attack the labor policies of the latter group. The economic policies of the government and of employers, and the economic well-being of the workers, were profoundly affected by the quarter-century of wars, which created economic vicissitudes bearing most heavily upon the workers, and which inevitably enabled the dominant groups and the more powerful individuals to utilize not only their natural, normal influence, but as well the irresistible war-time magic of patriotism, in directing the course of events into channels formed by their own interpretations and their own interests. The underlying, traditional conception of class relations, and the brutal and coercive spirit in which that conception was interpreted and enforced during the revolutionary wars and the reaction,—for this conception and for the manner of its enforcement alike, the agrarian more largely than the industrial employers were responsible.

This underlying, traditional conception of class relations had for centuries placed a premium upon servility among the workers. Individuals who evidenced initiative and assertiveness were discountenanced. Survival was made difficult for all except those who, with docility, adapted themselves to conditions of inferiority. A few individuals, to be sure, among the lower classes, found it possible to rise, but only at the expense of deserting their own class and becoming champions if not members of the dominant groups. Through successive generations, those who dared assert their independence within their class were repressed or eliminated, and only those who adapted themselves to the artificially created conditions of inferiority were allowed to survive, unless, perchance, in the various perverted forms of the criminal classes, seeking by different methods the same ends as the aristocracy—and chiefly the privilege of living without labor. The ruling classes attempted, unconsciously no doubt, to cheat nature of her prerogative in determining the hereditary traits of the people. The revenge of nature found expression in the driving of these hereditary traits which the rulers sought to eliminate into various channels essentially hostile to the social order recognized by the rulers. Those who sought to utilize nature as an aid in preying upon the people found nature raising up a class to prey upon them. Their policy of artificial selection, going back to the times of conquest and feudal disorder, and persistently applied for many centuries, resulted at length in the breeding of masses of people substantially inferior in hereditary traits as well as in social environment. The blight of inferiority thus created survived, and made the problem of social well-being not only environmental but also hereditary, not only a matter of the laborer's liberation from the shackles of a social order artificially weighted against him, but also the freeing of the spirit of the worker from inherited inertia and servility.

4. New conditions adverse to working-class well-being

These were the handicaps that hung heavily at the necks of the workers who fled not without hope of betterment into the newly developing industrial centers. But the hope of betterment itself became a dangerous incentive, because it moved increasing numbers to seek for similar opportunities, till the industrial workers, pressed upon by ever-augmented multitudes of their fellow-workers from the rural regions and the older, oftentimes declining industries, found themselves ultimately ensnared again in the net from which they had momentarily escaped.

The extremely degraded character and the well-nigh inexhaustible numbers of the population whence came the industrial workers are the two outstanding facts explanatory of the failure of these workers to secure for themselves any considerable share of the immense increase of wealth attending the introduction of the new system of industry. But notwithstanding the obvious advantages of that system,—advantages which, in spite of the barriers of the settlement acts, were sufficient to attract vast numbers from the farms and the craftsmen's shops,—the strains and stresses and maladjustments in the new industries were far from favorable to the workers. These strains and stresses and maladjustments were in large part, to be sure, the results of a too rapid influx of workers fleeing from pauperism and economic hopelessness; and they were aggravated by a veritable orgy of wealth-getting by industrial employers at a time when social and governmental restraints were being broken down, save in so far as these restraints promoted the domination and exploitation of the workers; but they were in part, no doubt, inevitable accompaniments of a period of novel and rapid transition. Probably most of the noxious growths that sprang up in the industrial soil were exotics which prudent husbandry could have excluded; but some were indigenous and could have been uprooted only with difficulty even under favorable circumstances.

Among the latter was congestion of population. Unwholesome conditions in respect to housing, sanitation, and health had indeed been the rule rather than the exception among the common people, in town and country alike. London, to be sure, had made considerable progress since the early years of the Stuart Restoration, due in part to the terrible stimulus of simultaneous fire and plague. As for the towns in general, their streets were narrow, crooked, and congested, their houses were crowded, dingy and dank, and their arrangements for lighting, cleaning and sewerage were primitive. The conditions of rural housing have already been described.[44]

It is true, of course, that the occupants of the wretched rural hovels, and in a measure the inhabitants of the earlier and smaller towns, had readier access to the invigorating air and sunshine of the open country; but in other respects, the state of housing was almost incredible. With this in mind, one's sensibilities are not so likely to be disturbed by descriptions of conditions

[44] See above, pp. 236, 237.

resulting from the concentration of population in the industrial towns—as when a member of the Manchester Literary and Philosophical Society told his fellow-members in 1787 that he "had too frequently had opportunities of seeing a man with his wife and three or four children all residing in one small room, in which they dress their victuals, eat, work, and sleep." The problems of housing and public health growing out of the influx of population seem early to have engaged the attention of certain public-spirited citizens of Manchester, and our knowledge of conditions there is relatively adequate as compared with other centers. As early as 1790, a local physician of note, Dr. Ferriar, described clearly the evils of over-crowding, and pointed out some of the more obvious remedies. In a paper addressed in 1790 to a committee for regulating the police,—a paper substantially repeated at a public meeting in 1796,—he stated that cellars were being used extensively as dwellings, the cellars commonly consisting of two rooms. The front room was used as a kitchen, the back room as living quarters. In this living room there was but a single small window, on a level with the ground, and near the roof of the cellar. "It is often patched with boards, and in its best state is so much covered with mud as to admit very little either of air or light. In this cell, the beds of the whole family, sometimes consisting of seven or eight, are placed. The floor of this room is often unpaved: the beds are fixed on the damp earth. But the floor, even when paved, is always damp. In such places, where a candle is required even at noonday, to examine a patient, I have seen the sick without bedsteads, lying on rags; they can seldom afford straw." Some he found living in houses located in blind alleys, in a situation "which excludes them from light and air. Consumption, distortion and idiocy are common in such resorts." In some districts, conditions were such as to maintain a continuous epidemic of fevers. "I have known nine patients confined in fevers at the same time, . . . and crammed into three small, dirty rooms, without the regular attendance of any friend, or of a nurse." The problem was complicated, he added, by the natural difficulty of newcomers in adjusting themselves to a new environment. "Persons newly arrived from the country are most liable to suffer from these causes, and . . . there arises a double injury to the town, from the loss of their labor, and the expense of supporting them in their illness." The good doctor was not without sympathy for the immediate victims, but, like his contemporaries generally, he seems to have been little moved by a sense of injustice. Such conditions were regarded in the first instance as merely furnishing occasions for a virtuous benevolence; and in so far as attempts were made to remove the causes rather than merely to relieve the resultant suffering, the moving forces were those suggested by Dr. Ferriar,—loss of the labor of the victims, and the expense of supporting them,—and in addition, the fear that the plague spots would spread without respect for persons or classes.[45]

The acuteness of the housing problem in Manchester, Birmingham, and other industrial towns was largely a result of the coming in of the new types of workers, whose labor in factories and shops was dissociated from their homes. In the factories themselves, and in the living quarters connected with the more remotely situated factories, the congested and unwholesome conditions

[45] Thomas Henry, F.R.S., in *Memoirs*, Manchester Lit. and Phil. Soc., III, 162, n. (general discussion of the problems of city growth, 159-173); Ferriar, *Medical Histories and Reflections*, II, 213-227, III, 76, 77, and *passim*; Aikin, *Description of the Country Round Manchester*, 192-196; *Reports*, Soc. for Bettering the Condition of the Poor, I, 98-115, II, 158-164; Creighton, *History of Epidemics*, II, 148-151; Brockbank, *Sketches of the Staff of the Manchester Infirmary*, 131, ff.

early attracted attention. An epidemic of fever in 1784 in the vicinity of Manchester was believed by many to have originated in the cotton factories. The justices of the peace asked a group of physicians to investigate and make recommendations. They reported that "a low, putrid fever, of a contagious nature, has prevailed many months in the cotton mills and amongst the poor in the township of Radcliffe." Robert Peel, one of the proprietors of the Radcliffe factories, claimed that it had been brought into the community and had gained headway before appearing in the factories. The committee of physicians failed to discover its origin. "But . . . we are decided in our opinion," their report stated, "that the disorder has been supported, diffused, and aggravated by the ready communication of contagion to numbers crowded together; by the accession to its virulence from putrid effluvia; and by the injury done to young persons through confinement, and too long continued labor; to which several evils the cotton mills have given occasion." The report consisted mainly of suggestions as to methods of combating the epidemic, rather than of descriptions of conditions; but in the same year was published a pamphlet entitled *A Short Essay Written for the Service of the Proprietors of Cotton Mills and the Persons Employed in Them,* in which some of the characteristic conditions of the modern factory are set forth with clearness even at that early date. "The cotton mills," we are told, "are large buildings, but so constructed as to employ the greatest possible number of persons. That no room may be lost, the several stories are built as low as possible. Most of the rooms are crowded with machines, about which it is necessary to employ a considerable quantity of oil, in order to facilitate their motion. From the nature of the manufacture, a great deal of cotton dust is constantly flying about, which, adhering to the oil, and heated by the friction, occasions a strong and disagreeable smell. The number of people who work in the mill must certainly be proportioned to the size of it. In a large one I am informed there are several hundreds; from which it is evident, a very considerable division must be allowed to each apartment. The manufacturers, in many instances, constantly labor day and night. (It should be observed that the proprietors of some cotton mills, alarmed by the consequences of obliging their servants to work incessantly, have shut up their mills in the night.) Of course a great number of candles must be used, and scarce any opportunity for ventilation afforded. From hence it is evident that there is a considerable effluvia constantly arising from the bodies of a large number of persons, . . . from the oil and cotton dust, and from the candles used in the night, without any considerable supply of fresh air. There are, indeed, trifling casements, sometimes opened, sometimes not; but totally insufficient to subserve any valuable purpose." [46]

As soon as the epidemic of 1784 had abated, interest in problems of health and sanitation lagged. In 1789, many manufacturing towns near Manchester, particularly Bury, Rochdale, and Oldham, were seriously afflicted; and in 1794, and the following year, fever again became epidemic at Manchester. Unwholesome conditions in the new manufacturing centers were unquestionably aggravated by the sudden influx of population and by the long hours, the night work, the lack of sanitation, and the poverty and ignorance of the workers in the factories.

[46] *Manchester Mercury*, Oct. 19, 1784 (report of the committee of physicians to the justices of the peace), Oct. 26, Nov. 2, 9, 16 (controversy between Robert Peel and Peter Walker concerning conditions in Peel's factories); *Short Essay Written for the Proprietors of Cotton Mills and the Persons Employed in Them*, 9, 10, and *passim*; Clerke, *Thoughts upon the Means of Preserving the Health of the Poor*, 3-7 and *passim* (contains the Physicians' report of 1784); Percival, *Essays*, II, 293, 296-300 (by the chairman of the committee of physicians).

And yet epidemics seem to have been little more destructive there than in other regions. Virulent fevers raged among the Scotch and Irish immigrants, particularly at Carlisle, from 1763 to 1780. There are many reports of epidemic conditions in Scotland. Typhus was prevalent during the 'eighties in the counties of Oxford, Gloucester, Worcester, Wilts, and Buckingham. Fever was described by Dr. John Alderson of Hull as "the constant complaint of every neighborhood," and he stated that "almost every newspaper presents us with an example of the direful consequences of infection." If in the region of Manchester the conditions were more serious than elsewhere, it was in that region that the most energetic remedial measures were undertaken. The industrial communities were probably moved by sentiments of humanitarianism and social justice no more than were other people of the time, but the general spirit of change and readjustment prevailing among them made it easier for them to break the ties of tradition and to pursue rational and experimental policies. Furthermore, the influx and shifting of population increased the danger of the spread of disease to the wealthier classes. The Board of Agriculture was informed in 1795 that exceptional health prevailed in the "large manufactories" of Lancashire, due in part to the inoculation of the workers. "Many gentlemen," the report continued, "pay for the inoculation of the poor in their own neighborhood." Concerted action for the maintenance of health was undertaken at various places, and particularly at Manchester. A board of health was there organized; "houses of recovery" and "fever wards" were established; handbills were distributed among the common people, and rewards were offered for the observance by poor families of the rules of cleanliness and health; and an attempt was made to enlist the cooperation of physicians, apothecaries, magistrates and town officials, the

Strangers' Friend Society, and the local gentry. Similar plans were adopted at Chester, Stockport, Liverpool, Bolton, and other towns in the vicinity. These activities were endorsed by the Society for Bettering the Condition of the Poor, which reported that "a board of health and a house of recovery, upon the plan of that at Manchester, would be useful in all towns, but particularly among manufacturers." It was during this period, too, that Manchester underwent a number of enlargements by the opening up of new streets and the widening of old ones.[47]

But the net results were slight. Little attention was paid, especially after the triumph of reaction accompanying the French wars, to the roots of the trouble, namely, housing facilities and conditions of labor in the factories. It is important to remember, too, that the "putting-out" system, never entirely eliminated, even after the full development of the factory system, was extensively in use; and work done in the homes of the workers, under housing conditions then prevalent, must have been a serious factor in the spread of disease. The rebuilding of towns usually meant not an improvement in the quarters occupied by the workers, but rather the building of middle-class homes often rivaling those of the gentry and

[47] Clerke, *Thoughts upon the Means of Preserving the Health of the Poor*, 7 and *passim; Gentleman's Magazine*, LX, Pt. I, 430 (a review of the pamphlet by Clerke, with incidental information of interest); Ferriar, *Medical Histories and Reflections*, III, 74, ff.; Creighton, *History of Epidemics*, II, 134, ff. (dealing with other regions as well as the manufacturing centers); Troughton, *History of Liverpool*, 179, 313; Holt, *General View*, Lancashire, 208, 210, 212 (ed. 1795); Brockbank, *Sketches of the Staff of the Manchester Infirmary*, 138, 139, 142, and *passim; Reports*, Soc. for Bettering the Condition of the Poor, I, 98-115, II, 158-164; Gisborne, *Duties of Men*, 558-561; *Report of Select Committee on Children Employed in Manufactories*, 1816, 139, 140 (containing resolutions of Manchester Board of Health, 1796. These are reprinted in Bland, Brown and Tawney, *English Economic History: Select Documents*, 495, 496). Concerning health conditions and measures of relief at Birmingham, see Langford, *Century of Birmingham Life*, I, 153-174, II, 143-145.

a mere increase in the number of working-class lodgings to enable the employers to accommodate in the crudest manner their constantly increasing numbers of workers.[48] Factory owners were gently admonished concerning the need of greater benevolence in dealing with their employees; even less was said to the owners of working-class lodgings, and it was only in respect to the latter that the local authorities could effectively take action. Many difficulties stood in the way, but the edge of initiative was dulled mainly, no doubt, by the fact that principal officials and leading private citizens alike were in most cases themselves owners cither of factories or of lodgings.

Overcrowding in unwholcsome and neglected working-class sections of the industrial centers, and long hours of labor in the carelessly constructed, unsanitary, and oftentimes dangerous factories, had obviously a devitalizing effect upon the workers, keeping their physical and mental energies at a low ebb. There was little possibility for alertness and assertiveness necessary for economic advance, or even for the maintenance of initial standards of well-being in the new industries.

Such conditions were aggravated by the burden of economic vicissitudes, which rested most heavily upon workers. Fluctuations in trade, speculation, changing tastes and fashions, the shifting of industries, overstocking of the market, violent reactions of industry and finance to wars and political changes—these and similar factors had long been operative, but they were in many instances accentuated by the new technique and organization of industry. Landlords, merchants, and industrialists, possessed of reserves, having access to extensive credit facilities, and able to reduce their expenses temporarily to a minimum, were in general prepared for such

[48] Aikin, *Description of the Country Round Manchester*, 182, 192, and *passim*.

emergencies. Not so the workers, who were the first victims. Their wages were reduced or employment entirely cut off as the first means of reducing the expenses of their employers. Without reserves and without credit, and incapable of reducing their normally meager expenditures except at the cost of urgently needed food, clothing and shelter, each recurring period of industrial depression tended to sink them to a lower level of poverty and ultimately of pauperism. Even periods of expansion and general employment brought dubious relief, for rising prices usually outran advancing rates of wages. In the view of the workers themselves, the question of prices was more serious than that of wages, giving rise to a large proportion of the riots and public disturbances of the time.

By far the most important cause of economic disturbances and the consequent burden of vicissitudes borne chiefly by the workers is to be found not in the technical changes but in the recurring wars and political upheavals —the Seven Years' War, the quarrels with the colonies culminating in the American Revolution, the disturbances on the Continent, and England's participation in the wars following the French Revolution. The wars had extremely important economic consequences, some favorable, some unfavorable, for all groups of society, but particularly for the common people—consequences which in their case were mostly unfavorable in the first instance, and which were aggravated by political reaction and repression in the name of patriotism. These effects of wars were not without contemporaneous recognition. "Inhabitants of Manchester!" exclaimed the members of the Manchester Constitutional Society, in December, 1792, in an address opposing the government's warlike attitude, "pause awhile on behalf of your own interests, and consider what class of ye can be benefited by war." The various classes are mentioned, and the dangers peculiar to each are set forth, but particular emphasis is put upon the common people. "How are the families of the poor to be maintained? If a decent subsistence cannot even now be obtained but with unwearied labor and painful exertion, what is to be done when employment ceases, when wages are sunk, and provisions rise?" The poor, it is pointed out, are denied a voice in making decisions, and citizens who make decisions should have their welfare in mind. "Ye know, or ye ought to know, that various laws, like the game laws and the combination laws, are expressly against the poor—that they are liable to be torn from their families by the violence of the press gang, while the rich and the luxurious repose in peace upon their beds of down. Headlong promoters of self-destruction, look round upon the habitations of misery, and pause for a few moments on the consequence of your proceedings." One of the ironies of history is to be found in the fact that the Manchester Constitutional Society and other champions of the popular interest, as at Birmingham, were victims of mob violence during the "church and king" riots for the defense of "the throne and the altar." Subtle forces over which the masses had no control successfully urged them into a blind and oftentimes violent loyalty, and this in turn plunged them into wars in which they were invariably the first and severest of sufferers and the last and least of beneficiaries.[49]

[49] The address of the Manchester Constitutional Society is in Thomas Walker's *Review of Some of the Political Events Which Have Occurred in Manchester during the Last Five Years,* 50, which also contains accounts of riots there. Some contemporaneous records of the Birmingham riots are in Langford, *Century of Birmingham Life,* I, 472-499, and in *An Authentic Account of the Riots of Birmingham.* The influence of wars on the well-being of the people is discussed in Daniels, *Early English Cotton Industry,* 82-91. Daniels' discussion deals mainly with the wars preceding the French Revolution. Following are some references concerned with the immediate effects of English intervention in the wars of the French Revolution: *Inquiry into the Causes of the Present Derangement of Public Credit in Great Britain;* Chalmers, *Estimate,* Dedication, xlix-liv, and *passim* (ed.

Other factors, and particularly warfare, must therefore be held responsible, even more largely than the new industrial system, for fluctuations in employment, in wages, and in prices. More directly a result of the introduction of machinery and of large-scale organization was the subjection of the workers to a deadening mechanical and administrative routine. Some of the earlier processes of production afforded the workers genuine opportunities for the expression of their personalities in their work, and some of them even permitted the embodiment of artistic conceptions affording pleasure to the craftsmen. The various processes were not so highly specialized, not so closely articulated and interdependent, and not subjected so minutely to the supervision of bosses and managers. The effects on the workers of the mechanization and super-organization of production were early recognized. The great pioneer in the manufacture of machinery, James Watt, argued as early as 1785 that the real makers of goods are the inventors and the designers of tools and machinery. Others "are to be considered in no other light than as mere acting mechanical powers; . . . it is scarcely necessary that they should use their reason." The anonymous author of *An Authentic Account of the Riots of Birmingham* (1791) explains the participation of the workers in the riots by saying that the nature of their employments is such that "they are taught to act, and not to think." Various critics of the early textile factories based their objections on the fact that the workers were forced from their homes, where the work could

1794); Griggs, *General View,* Essex, 11, 12; Billingsley, *General View,* Somerset, 90; Pitt, *General View,* Staffordshire, 161; Wedge, *General View,* Cheshire, 26; Holt, *General View,* Lancashire, 54 (ed. 1794); Wedge, *General View,* Warwickshire, 21; Donaldson, *General View,* Northamptonshire, 11; Martin, *General View,* Renfrewshire, 20; Naismith, *General View,* Clydesdale, 74-76; Belches, *General View,* Stirling, 56, 57; Ure, *General View,* Dumbarton, 88; Prentice, *Historical Sketches and Personal Recollections of Manchester,* 1, and *passim;* Owen, *Life,* I, 35.

be carried on intermittently and with some degree of initiative, into crowded quarters where they were subjected to routine and supervision. This seems to have been one of the main objections of the craftsmen to machinery.[50]

But contemporary observers outside the ranks of the workers themselves seem generally to have welcomed rather than opposed the subjection of labor to mechanical and administrative routine. Probably the most serious immediate consequences of this change were in connection with child labor, which was almost universally approved. To give employment to young children was regarded as so meritorious as to justify special favors from those in authority. Typical of numerous petitions of the time is that of the Manchester manufacturers to the government in 1788 for protection from the competition of the East India Company's cottons, partly on the ground that "your petitioners employ a great many poor persons of both sexes, particularly young children, who are rendered capable of maintaining themselves at an early period of life, and of being useful to their parents and the community." A visitor to Lancashire in 1791, upon observing the great wealth and prosperity resulting from the general employment of the poor of all ages, "from four years old to fourscore," in the operation of the new machines, is led to exclaim: "These are thy blessings, O Commerce! These are thy rewards, O Industry!" This attitude toward child labor was not confined to the eighteenth century, nor was it peculiar to manufacturing. The spirit of earlier times is illustrated by a patent granted to two gentlemen in 1678 for "a new spinning engine," one of the chief advantages claimed for it being

[50] *Min. of the Evidence, Com. of H. of L.*, 1785 (on Irish Resolutions), 252, 253 (testimony of James Watt); *Authentic Account of the Riots of Birmingham*, Preface, v; *Humble Petition of the Poor Spinners* (Leicestershire); Commons *Journals*, XLIX, 276, 277; Hammond, *Skilled Laborer*, 54, and *Town Laborer*, 21.

that by means of it "a child of three or four years of age may do as much as a child seven or eight years old." The family income of farm laborers was based alike by the intent of their employers and by stern economic necessity upon the labor of their children.[51] A benevolent Anglican clergyman having an exceptional interest in the welfare of the laboring classes [52] recommended the general adoption of the rule applied in Rutland in 1785 "that no persons be allowed any relief . . . on account of any child above six years of age who shall not be able to knit; nor on account of any child above nine years of age who shall not be able to spin either linen or woollen." He cited as worthy of emulation the case of a family where the earnings of the head of the family were duplicated by the earnings of the family, including a girl of five who could "spin adroitly." Even so philanthropic an organization as the Society for Bettering the Condition of the Poor looked with satisfaction upon the bringing up of children in cottages "half naked, and indifferently fed," because they "make hardier and better laborers than those in parish work houses"; and it recommended the general adoption of payment of agricultural laborers by piece work because it induced the father to take "his sons to the field with him as soon as they can handle a hook or raise a mattock; and they soon earn their living, besides being at an early age inured to industry and weather." [53]

With the rise of humanitarianism and utilitarianism, and with the emergence of effective working-class organizations, there developed another view of the position of the worker in society, and a new conception of the natu-

[51] See above, pp. 228, 229.

[52] David Davies. See above, pp. 224, 226.

[53] *Board of Trade Papers*, 6/140, Doc. 30; *European Magazine*, XX, 216; Woodcroft, *Titles of Patents of Invention*, I, 40; Davies, *Case of Laborers in Husbandry*, 112, 118; *Reports*, Soc. for Bettering the Condition of the Poor, I, 39, 40.

ral rights of the children of the workers. Then it was that attention was focused upon the children of the factories, partly because their concentration in factories rendered the evils of their state more conspicuous, and partly because the profit-making incentive in the exploitation of child labor was there more obvious. In consequence, there has been a tendency to ignore the prevalence of child labor in earlier times and under other circumstances, and to forget the earlier state of children in the workhouses and elsewhere. And yet it is unquestionably true that one of the most serious consequences of the reduction of labor to simpler routine processes by the introduction of machinery and of mass organization of labor forces in factories was a more harmful if not a more extensive exploitation of children. Perhaps equally serious was the more general reduction of the labor of women to the same deadening and enervating routine. The vigor, the initiative, the well-being of future generations were more directly menaced.

It is obvious that this deadening routine and decrease of opportunity for finding pleasure in their work involved a proportionately increased need of leisure and opportunity for enjoyments not connected with their daily routine. There has been much idle talk about the "dignity of labor." A large proportion of labor, especially under modern conditions of extreme specialization and monotonous routine, is inherently undignified and injurious to the personality of the worker, unless rewarded by exceptional leisure and opportunity for external enjoyments. There was obviously an increasing need for such rewards, and yet the hours of labor were little changed, except to the disadvantage of the workers by the introduction of night shifts and Sunday labor.[54] Leisure for wholesome

[54] For some early complaints, on religious grounds, of labor on Sunday in the cotton factories, see *Manchester Mercury*, July 4, 1786, April 1, 1788; *Owen MSS.*, XXXIX, 298.

recreation was usually not available, but in any case, other obstacles intervened. Public parks and other recreation centers were virtually unknown. The pleasures of hunting were forbidden by the game laws, such enjoyments being reserved for possessors of leisure and devotees to recreation who were unacquainted with the pangs of compulsory hunger. Music and the drama, even in the simpler forms, were usually beyond the financial means if not the cultural capacity of the masses. Reading was barred, if not by illiteracy, then by the stamp taxes and the prohibitive costs. Popular education for the enjoyment of leisure was unknown.

There was, to be sure, a movement of some importance for popular education—the Sunday-school movement originated by Robert Raikes of Gloucester. His initial work was in connection with the children of the poor in that town, especially among the families of workers in the pin manufactory there. Similar schools were rapidly organized in various regions, and the industrial centers were preeminent in the movement. Richard Arkwright, Robert Peel, and other manufacturers patronized Sunday schools at some of their plants. At Birmingham, it was ruled that "all persons employed in the manufactories shall have the preference as to admission." In the *Manchester Mercury* of May 30, 1786, appeared a news item saying, "It is observed in the London papers that this town has taken the lead of all the kingdom in the business of Sunday schools." Raikes himself estimated the number of Sunday-school students throughout England at the end of 1787 at 250,000, with 5,000 in the town of Manchester. The number in Manchester later became much larger.

A commendable spirit of benevolence no doubt actuated the supporters of Sunday schools, and the movement unquestionably brought to some of the workers a meager enlightenment. There was opposition on the part of some, notably Ruggles in his *History of the Poor*, because of the belief that such knowledge as was taught in the Sunday schools was "not necessary to a performance of the duties of the poor towards God or towards their neighbor, and it may lead them towards a breach of their duty towards both," their supreme duty, it was believed, being to serve as "hewers of wood and drawers of water." But the fear that Sunday-school instruction would make the poor more "dissatisfied with that low and humble situation in life which Providence has ordained to be their lot" seems to have been ill-founded. The originator of the movement, as stated by him in his correspondence, desired to teach the poor, under prudent supervision, how to read the catechism; and to instruct them in such manner as would cause them to "become more tractable and obedient" and more inclined to "decent and orderly conduct." A significant manner in which the poor of the industrial centers fell short of these virtues to be inculcated by Sunday-school instruction was in attempts at concerted action to improve their relations with their employers. The schools were generally maintained by the contributions of prominent citizens, ordinarily employers, the subscribers forming a committee to select the books to be used, to choose the teachers and assistants who were paid to carry on the actual work of instruction, and in general to supervise the work of the schools. The manner of making the students "more tractable and obedient" is illustrated by the following dialogue spoken by two scholars at Manchester, and published contemporaneously as evidence of the good effects of the Sunday schools:

FIRST [scholar]:—O happy day, appointed for reproof,
    Which brings our feet beneath this welcome roof,
    Where we may learn to read, to hear, to speak
    The paths of Virtue, which we ought to take:
    Where we can find instruction, and delight

To pass in cheerful songs the Sabbath night.
SECOND:—I too with joy this blessed day receive,
And hope we shall assemble here at eve;
Yea, gladly welcome every Sabbath day—
For we should love the school more than our play.
FIRST:—It gives me pleasure much to find that we
In these respects so happily agree;
And children yonder playing in the street
Had better here some useful task repeat.
SECOND:—I think so too; for though I love right well
To play, I love to sing, and read, and spell;
But play in school time we ought not indeed;
For if we do, how shall we learn to read?
To love our sport and not our book, at once
Displays a hopeless child, a playful dunce.
FIRST:—Hopeless indeed; and we who better know,
Should thank the hands from whom our favors flow;
For by their goodness we may here improve,
And bless the worthy labors of their love.
SECOND:—Right, and I'll join you in this Christian part,
To pay the tribute of a grateful heart.
BOTH:—Then as our thanks to all our friends are due,
We give them now to *you*, to *you*, and *you*.[55]

Later news items indicate that the Manchester Sunday schools were in a declining state, due not to lack of money but to lack of scholars; and it is a curious commentary on the prevailing state of mind that this was attributed mainly to the carelessness of parents and the natural indolence of the children. These influences did no doubt interfere with the effectiveness of the movement. But the principal obstacle, from the point of view of benefits accruing to the workers, was the conception, dominant among the supporters of Sunday schools, that the chief virtue, among the "lower orders" of society, was a meek and docile subordination to their masters. Of course such a conception was not a result of cruel or malicious motives; rather it was an expression of the

---

[55] Addressed to their benefactors.

prevalent belief that rigorous class rule was ordained by nature or by Providence and was best for all concerned. The result of this attitude on the part of the leading patrons of Sunday schools was that the one significant movement for popular education probably contributed more to the continued subjection of the workers than to their emancipation.[56]

Thrust into the crowded and miserable lodgings of the shabbiest and most neglected quarters of the towns or of the mill and mining centers; buffeted about by industrial vicissitudes; and enervated by deadening mechanical and administrative routine unrelieved by leisure or by opportunity for recreation and pleasure not connected with their work—it was under these conditions that the heterogeneous masses of workers who manned the new industries were forced to live. From these brutalizing conditions, no genuine relief was attainable. The inevitable result was resort to spurious relief in the forms of pleasures themselves more brutalizing—drunkenness and sexual excesses, giving rise to successive generations of workers each more numerous and more deeply submerged in poverty and degradation than its predecessor.

In the case of excessive propagation as well as of other noxious growths among the industrial workers, the roots ran deep into the soil of earlier generations. It was long held to be axiomatic that the wealth and power of the "nation" (the nation being characteristically confused with the possessors of the nation's wealth) depended upon a numerous laboring population, whose productive

[56] *New Annual Register*, 1785, 2d part, 212-214; *Gentleman's Magazine*, LVII, Pt. II, 948; *European Magazine*, XIV, 315, 316; Langford, *Century of Birmingham Life*, I, 409-421; *Owen MSS.*, XXXIX, 298, 301; *Manchester Chronicle*, April 11, 1789 (containing the dialogue above quoted), Sept. 26, 1789; *Manchester Mercury*, Jan. 6, 1784, Jan. 11, Feb. 15, 1785, Jan. 10, May 30, 1786, May 22, Aug. 28, Dec. 11, 1787, Aug. 19, 1788; Ruggles, *History of the Poor*, II, 180; Cowe, *Religious and Philanthropic Tracts*, 3, 26, 57-59; Davies, *Case of Laborers in Husbandry*, 123-127.

labors were to be assured by the stimulus of poverty. The more numerous were the laborers, and at the same time the poorer,—that is, the more dependent on their daily employments for a subsistence,—the richer and more powerful would be the "nation." [57] To maintain a "plentiful supply" of poor laborers was therefore the supreme end of "national" policy. This general attitude was reflected curiously in a proposal made by the Rev. Josiah Tucker, Dean of Gloucester, who was a leading economic thinker of his time as well as a prominent churchman. In order to increase the demand for woollen goods, he suggested the clearing of waste lands and the building of small cottages in which "to raise up such a generation of men, women and children as shall be obliged, by their station in life, to be clad in such garments as are made out of coarse wools, and to use such sort of goods for their bedding and furniture." [58] But the number of workers in many regions came to be viewed as excessive because of the burdensome poor rates, and in many parishes artificial restraints were imposed on the propagation of the "lower orders," by direct economic pressure or by the administration of the poor law and the acts of settlement. The poor law, however, generally tended to promote an unrestrained increase in numbers. It became a symbol of economic hopelessness and pauperism, and at the same time the assurance of a subsistence. [59]

[57] Furniss, *Position of the Laborer in a System of Nationalism,* especially ch. 1.

[58] Tucker, *Reflections on the Low Price of Coarse Wools,* 31. The Dean's proposal is also printed in Bischoff, *History of the Woollen and Worsted Manufacture,* I, 225-228.

[59] *Parl. Hist.,* XVII, 843-845; W. Young, *Observations Preliminary to a Proposed Amendment of the Poor Laws,* 31, 32; Arthur Young, *Farmer's Letters,* I, 300, ff.; Young, *Political Arithmetic,* 75, 76 (quoted by Slater, *English Peasantry and the Enclosure of the Common Fields,* 104; see also Slater, 265, 266); Townsend, *Dissertation on the Poor Laws,* 47, ff.; Brown, *General View,* West Riding of Yorkshire, 25.

Such were the earlier influences surrounding the workers who were drawn into the new industries, and who, in their new environment, were dominated by forces making continued unrestrained and reckless procreation inevitable. With the rise of the "dismal science" of political economy, their excessive multiplication was attributed to so-called laws of nature, and in particular to what was supposed to be the natural and inevitable tendency of population to outrun the means of subsistence.[60] Writers who held these views adhered rigorously to the age-old classification of society into the two groups, the laboring poor on the one hand and the owners of wealth on the other. To them, the former group was on an entirely different plane of existence; its members were naturally primitive in their traits and reactions. "The rich appear to be raised in pride and false dignity far above the rest of human beings: whilst the poor are considered as differing only from brutes in being actuated by those inclinations and propensities which disgrace humanity." An occasional voice was raised which attributed such views, and such conditions in so far as they existed, to the political system and the "atrocious laws." But such "dangerous" if not seditious criticism was for the most part anonymously expressed, and had no important place in the thought of the time.[61] Laboring under the limitations of the prevailing conception of social classes, and lacking the varied data available to later students of society, it is not surprising that these early writers failed to emphasize the demoralizing influences of a socially created environment and the restraining and refining

[60] Many writers before Malthus had expressed the same general views, as in the following instances: *Present State of Great Britain and North America*, 19, 20; Townsend, *Dissertation on the Poor Laws*, 47, ff.; Howlett, in *Gentleman's Magazine*, LII, 526.

[61] The instance quoted is from *Politics for the People*, first part, No. 10, p. 146. For the publisher's difficulties with the authorities, see Part II, No. 1, p. 1.

influences of a rising standard of living and a larger participation by the workers in the gifts of nature and the fruits of industry. Such conceptions were seldom entertained by writers, and were even more rarely adopted by rulers, either political or economic, as the basis of their policies.

Our study of the industrial workers began with the paradoxical contrast between an unparalleled increase of productive power and of the means of securing material well-being on the one hand, and on the other a mass of poverty and attendant social degradation seldom equaled in the records of history. Study of the contemporaneous forces beyond the workers' control has indicated the principal causes of the contrast. The industrial workers came from sources which were polluted, and labored in an environment which was degrading. The thought of the time, and the agencies of social control, were beyond their reach and hostile to the improvement of their economic condition. Government, in so far as it functioned, was controlled by upper-class conceptions and interests, but the new society was largely influenced by blind chance and by the brutalizing and ultimately self-destructive forces of competition. There is ample explanation of the paradox.

5. Forces favorable to group integration and organization

The historian of the beginnings of modern industrial society must paint a gloomy picture, and yet the somber tones are not entirely unrelieved. The reactions of the workers afford a remarkable instance of the powers of resistance inherent in human nature. The gloom of the picture is still more relieved if viewed in the light of the later history of the industrial workers; for out of their abysmal degradation they emerged in the face of appalling obstacles with an intelligent and comprehensive program for social reorganization. The consequences of class government, of crude individualism, of blind chance, and of brutal competition became more and more apparent, but the traditional agencies of social control demonstrated repeatedly their helplessness or their incapacity. The heirs of power, of wealth, of culture, of social position, their economic welfare being assured by inheritance and maintenance of the *status quo,* naturally in general opposed any fundamental reorganization. It fell to the lot of the industrial workers to become the principal initiators and organizers of the movement to supplant the admittedly irrational, disorderly, wasteful and inequitable processes of economic life by rational, coordinated and cooperative processes worked out on the basis of a "science of society." [62] This movement is far removed in time as well as in character from the eighteenth-century origins of modern industrial society; and yet it was during the period of origins that conditions and forces emerged which made possible the later movement for a rational, cooperative reorganization.

Perhaps the most obvious of these was the incalculable increase of productive power in the supplying of economic goods, making improvement in general well-being possible. By the older, cruder methods of producing and transporting commodities, there was often an unavoidable deficit of goods. Improvements in economic technique, involving potentially a practically unlimited productive power, meant that scarcity from this cause could largely be avoided. The causes of scarcity among any considerable part of the population were to be sought for elsewhere. Men were at first disinclined, to be sure, to give up their old fatalistic explanations of scarcity and

<hr>

[62] Perhaps the clearest formulation of the ideals of this movement is to be found in the noted document, *Labor and the New Social Order,* issued in 1918 by the Labor party—a document which has commanded world-wide interest and respect, even from those who oppose the specific policies proposed for putting the ideals into effect.

poverty, and the "dismal science" even evolved new conceptions of a fatalistic nature for putting the blame on inescapable "laws" of nature. But obvious facts began even before the end of the eighteenth century to force their way into consideration. The vastly accelerated rate of wealth production and the increasing profuseness and ostentatious display of luxury became apparent to the understandings of the workers even dulled as they were by unmitigated and stupefying poverty. The periods of acutest "scarcity" proved to be periods when machinery and men and even natural resources for producing and transporting goods were idle. Fields of rotting grain and warehouses bursting with goods, and at the same time multitudes of workers unemployed and starving—these came to be familiar phenomena. Surely not fate, surely not limitations on man's productive powers, should primarily be blamed, but what? Such questioning led ultimately to the widespread belief that men themselves were to blame, because they had allowed their productive powers and their social relations to be controlled by tradition, by the accidents of inheritance, by various irrational forces. The finding of artificial causes led naturally to the quest for corresponding remedies.

These conceptions were essentially social in character. The older handicraftsmen, even when organized in gilds, had been dominated by the ideal of economic independence by virtue of the ownership of their tools and the control in some degree of the output of their labor. This ideal had been seriously impaired, to be sure, by the relative increase in the number of apprentices and journeymen having merely the status of employees, but even they quite commonly owned their tools, maintained personal relations with their employers, and were intrigued by the hope, however vain, of becoming master craftsmen. The domestic manufacturer, the gildsman, the agricultural worker, had frequently had access to a plot of land, or had owned a cow, or had possessed other simple means for obtaining a meager but independent income. By the agrarian changes, those connected with the land were generally deprived of independent means of production. By the industrial changes, the industrial workers were even more generally divorced from the ownership of their tools and from the control of the output of their labor, and were deprived of the slightest hope of becoming masters. This general loss by the workers of independent productive resources destroyed the foundations of individualism among them, at a time when individualism was becoming dominant among the owners of the instruments of production, and especially among the rising industrialists. The individualism of the latter especially ran beyond bounds because of their unwonted wealth and power and their unrestrained acquisitive instincts. The individualistic ideal of social relations as dominated and utilized by these men speedily proved incompatible with the economic advancement of the non-possessing classes. As long as the workers could cling to the slightest hope of individual economic independence, their own individualism was an insurmountable obstacle in the way of their choosing the only possible alternative for their economic salvation, namely, the ideal of socialized, cooperative economic life. Under the conditions created by machinery and factories and large-scale production, the complete and final separation of the workers, except here and there an individual, from opportunity for economic independence became inevitable, and this fact became more and more apparent to the workers themselves. The way was therefore early being prepared for the ultimate acceptance of the new conception by the workers.

This change of attitude was naturally opposed by the individualistic possessing and ruling classes, and was by virtue of their influence long delayed. But the change was being facilitated by conditions over which employers had little and employees less control. These conditions were most apparent and most effectual in respect to industrial labor, but they were not without significance even in agriculture. The enclosures and the engrossing of farms tended to bring about a concentration of workers under the same management; the general adoption of a new agricultural technique tended to reduce the laborers to uniform conditions of work; and the improvements in means of communication and travel tended to break down the isolation of the farm workers, which had long restricted any socialized conceptions of economic life held by them to their immediate local community. As for the industrial workers, they were being concentrated in cities and in economically homogeneous groups. They were subjected to a common administrative discipline. They were reduced to a common level of wages and working conditions—a common level which was naturally and obviously contrasted with the entirely different plane of income and of living conditions on which the employing group lived. The individual worker performed over and over again some fractional and seemingly trifling act having significance only in connection with correlated acts by other members of the group. In respect alike to his work, to his living conditions, and to the promotion of his welfare, the individual worker was more and more merged in the group. The group concept was literally thrust upon him. Because of these circumstances, there was an inevitable development of group consciousness.

The natural result of a consciousness of unity and common interests was united action by the group for the promotion of group welfare. But serious obstacles were in the way. There was a certain lack of native intelligence and vigor due to the pressure of hereditary forces operating through a process of social selection which tended to weed out those individuals who were lacking in docility.[63] To this heritage was added the weight of environmental conditions making difficult the development of intelligence and the exercise of initiative. Whenever these obstacles were surmounted, further barriers were raised by a hostile government.

The government had earlier been committed to the regulation of economic life in such manner as to maintain wages and working conditions on a subsistence basis, which, however inadequate, was nevertheless stable and dependable. But this policy was by degrees given up, slowly and unintentionally at first, but during the latter part of the eighteenth century it was rapidly and at length consciously abandoned. Fundamentally, the change was the result of the transformation of economic society, which rendered the system of regulation in its older forms obsolete. The change of policy was accompanied by the rise of the doctrine of *laissez-faire*, which gave theoretical and moral sanction, and which helped to prevent the development of a new system of regulation compatible with the changes in economic life.[64] More important than the causes of the reversal of policy by the government were its effects on the workers. The government, to which they had looked not without a certain confidence for the maintenance of stable conditions on the basis of a subsistence, was now almost invariably arrayed on the side of those changes which left them at the mercy of increasingly powerful employers.[65] They naturally in consequence resorted to the processes of

[63] See above, pp. 262, 263.
[64] Webb, *History of Trade Unionism*, 48, ff.; Cheyney, *Industrial and Social History of England*, ch. 8, secs. 61-63.
[65] The Spitalfields Weavers Act, 13 Geo. III, c. 68 (quoted in Bland, Brown and Tawney, *English Economic History: Select Documents*, 547-551), was probably the most notable exception, and it was essentially an attempt to revive the old policy of the public determination of wages on the basis of changes in the cost of living.

self-help by means of organization. The government, therefore, indirectly and unintentionally stimulated the tendency, inherent in the changed economic society, toward working-class unity and organization. The intent of the government was hostile. While it abandoned its old policy of maintaining a stable standard of living, it refused to extend its newly adopted *laissez-faire* principles to its relations to working-class self-help. The common law in respect to such matters as combinations, so-called conspiracies, and the relations between "masters" and "servants" was supplemented by increasingly harsh parliamentary enactments, and the common law and the statutes were enforced with increasing rigor, and oftentimes with relentless cruelty.[66] Lawful and peaceful united action in consequence became virtually impossible.

Closely connected with the obstacles put in the way of organization and advance on the part of the working classes by the government was the hostility of employers. The employing group had long been self-conscious and active in promoting its interests, but its class consciousness and class interests were confused with social consciousness and social interests. Its domination of the various forces of social control, economic, political, cultural, religious, enabled it to denounce and suppress any manifestations of group action outside its own group. "Whoever imagines," wrote Adam Smith, "that masters rarely combine, is as ignorant of the world as of the subject. Masters are always and everywhere in a sort of tacit and uniform combination. . . . We seldom, indeed, hear of this combination, because it is the usual, and one may say, the natural state of things." The workmen, too, he continues, sometimes form combinations, and

---

[66] For a summary of legal provisions which directly or indirectly affected adversely the self-help and advancement of the working classes, see Howell, *Labor Legislation*, I, 21-42.

"they are always abundantly heard of. In order to bring the point to a speedy decision, they have recourse to the loudest clamor, and sometimes to the most shocking violence and outrage. They are desperate, and act with the folly and extravagance of desperate men, who must either starve, or frighten their masters into an immediate compliance with their demands. The masters, upon these occasions, are just as clamorous upon the other side, and never cease to call aloud for the assistance of the civil magistrate, and the rigorous execution of those laws which have been enacted with so much severity against the combination of servants, laborers, and journeymen." [67] We have already seen [68] that soon after the publication of the *Wealth of Nations,* the group consciousness of the industrial employers found more definite expression in the form of local and national employers' organizations and chambers of commerce, having among their objects the control of what were regarded as unruly tendencies among the workers. But in general, tacit informal combination of all employers, utilizing with increasing facility the government and other agencies of social control, continued to suffice for preventing serious manifestations of working-class self-consciousness, except in riots and physical demonstrations which could readily be outlawed and put down by armed force.

Riots, tumults, strikes, and underground methods are phenomena common to various periods and stages of economic life in England. But during the period of rapid change in the latter part of the eighteenth century, there was apparently an increased resort to physical demonstrations. These were often connected immediately in the minds of the workers with the introduction of labor-saving machines. To this cause has commonly been attributed a large proportion of the disturbances of

[67] *Wealth of Nations,* Bk. I, ch. VIII.
[68] Ch. III.

the late eighteenth and early nineteenth centuries. Occasional unemployment resulting from the use of machines, a frequent shifting and readjustment of labor, a natural lack of foresight as to the ultimate expansion of industry and increase of employment, and knowledge of the dubious opportunities of the workers for sharing the profits of industrial expansion,—such circumstances combined to cause many local groups of workers to fix their attention momentarily upon the machines as the cause of their distress. This attitude was sometimes fostered by the gentry and the farmers, in some cases due to the decline of domestic industry viewed as an auxiliary source of farm laborers' income, and in other cases due to the competition of the new industries in the labor market. But in explaining the frequency of riots and disturbances we must take into account causes more persistent and vital. Among these were the fluctuations of employment, of wages, and of prices, due in large part to the wars. But the most significant cause was the difficulty of uniting in associations for legally and peacefully promoting their interests.

Our knowledge of so-called riots and disturbances is almost entirely limited to accounts by hostile observers. Accounts by participants, and even by sympathizers, especially before the French Revolution, are extremely rare. But it is apparent from available records that no matter how peaceful and orderly the demonstrations, and no matter how legitimate from the point of view of redressing grievances, they were usually denounced as riots and seditions, to be put down by armed force.[69]

---

[69] Following are references to a few characteristic accounts of such activities and of the methods of dealing with them: *Annual Register,* 1761, 82, 83 (Chron.), 1776, 161, 162 (Chron.), 1779, 228, 229 (Chron.), 1787, 218, 219 (Chron.), 1788, 209, 210 (Chron.), 1789, 204, 205 (Chron.), 1790, 222 (Chron.); Julia Wedgwood, *Life of Josiah Wedgwood,* 200-202, 220; Commons *Journals,* XXXVII, 804, 882, 925, 926; *Home Office Papers,* 43/4, p. 21 (Dundas to Blundell, May 30, 1792),

In view of this fact, and in view of the increasing difficulties in the way of peaceful, permanent organization among the workers, the more frequent resort to so-called mob violence is a valid indication of the rising spirit of group consciousness and the growing desire for concerted action.

But more significant evidence of these tendencies is furnished by the rise of peaceful, permanent organizations in the face of seemingly insurmountable obstacles. The beginnings of the modern trade union movement, while not traceable, as some have believed, to the older craft gilds, are nevertheless discernible in the period preceding the age of machinery. The craft gilds were dominated by the master craftsmen, who, as industry advanced, came to perform more and more the functions not of manual workers but of employers and *entrepreneurs*. The rise of a separate and distinct class of permanent wage-earning craftsmen without tools of their own and without control of the output of their labor had been proceeding independently of the introduction of machinery; and it was among this class that embryonic trade unions are first discernible. Early instances enumerated by the Webbs in their great *History of Trade Unionism* [70] include organizations of printers, hatters, London tailors, West of England wool workers, gold beaters, stocking-frame workers, Sheffield cutlers, Liverpool shipwrights, Spitalfields silk weavers, and Newcastle keelmen. While these instances antedate the age of machinery, an examination of the groups mentioned reveals in several of the instances the existence of ex-

p. 106 (Dundas to Blundell, Oct. 3, 1792), p. 254 (Dundas to Calthorpe, June 12, 1793); Boulton and Watt MSS., *Letter Book* (*Office*), 1786-1788, 249, 251, 255, 256 (letters by Watt).

[70] Pp. 27-39. See also Heaton, *Yorkshire Woollen and Worsted Industries*, 312-321; Unwin, *Industrial Organization in the Sixteenth and Seventeenth Centuries*; Turner, "The Keelmen of Newcastle," in *Am. Hist. Rev.*, XXI, 542-545.

ceptional conditions approximating in important respects the conditions which were later to become no longer exceptional but characteristic by the revolution in technique and by its correlated administrative transformation of economic society. The shipwrights were connected with the highly capitalized shipping industry; they were obviously not typical craftsmen; and at a great port such as Liverpool, they were thrown together under conditions exceptionally favorable for organization. Somewhat similar was the status of the keelmen of Newcastle, connected with the monopolistic coal industry of that region. The gold beaters and the silk weavers, both exceptionally skilled, were dependent upon employers because of the extraordinary cost of the raw materials. Printing establishments had early assumed many of the characteristic features of modern factory groups. The stocking frame was not a typical craftsman's tool, but was in fact a forerunner of the age of machinery. The organization of the Manchester worsted small-ware weavers was largely on account of the changes growing out of the introduction of the Dutch loom or swivel loom, another significant forerunner of the mechanical revolution.

The rise of a dependent wage-earning class among the skilled handicraftsmen before the age of machinery was preparing the way in limited fields of labor for the formation of organizations similar in character to the modern trade unions. And yet this fact is insignificant in comparison with the overshadowing influence of the introduction of machinery. To a certain extent, the older tendency toward organization among the skilled handicraftsmen was checked and disrupted by the introduction of machinery, for many old forms of skill were supplanted by the new technique, and there was a certain equalizing process by which the skilled and the unskilled, the craftsman, the miner, the transport worker, the innumerable unapprenticed helpers, and even the farm laborers, tended to approach the same level. The peculiar significance of the age of machinery in relation to the organization of the working classes is to be found in the fact that it introduced conditions favorable for organization among practically all groups of workers, skilled and unskilled alike. The obstacles in the way, and in particular the increasing rigor of hostile laws, prevented these inherently favorable conditions from giving rise to effective organizations openly avowing trade-union purposes among either the older handicraftsmen or the new types of industrial workers, till long after the close of the eighteenth century.

Organizations having as their aim any participation in the determination of wages and working conditions or in the control of the processes of production were rigorously repressed; but in one direction, the tendency toward organization was allowed, and even encouraged. This was in the formation of friendly societies. The term may be used to include organizations with varying names having as a common purpose the maintenance of a fund by specified contributions of members for providing some form of insurance against sickness and other misfortunes. From practical necessity if not from inclination, their meetings were commonly held at inns and public houses. The funds were commonly kept in a box with specified arrangements for security and for access by authorized members. From this circumstance they were generally in earlier times known as box clubs.[71]

As may naturally be inferred from their humble character, their origins are obscure and probably remote in

[71] The literature on the subject of the early friendly societies is extremely meager. Baernreither, *English Associations of Working Men,* deals unsatisfactorily with their early history. The most important sources are the early rules and regulations contained in some of the older libraries, particularly the British Museum.

time. It is certain, however, that during the second half of the eighteenth century, they rapidly multiplied in number and importance, and frequently reduced their rules and regulations to printed form. By 1792, there was a movement under way for the affiliation of local groups into "united benefit societies." [72] With the passage of the friendly societies act of 1793, available information becomes somewhat more detailed and dependable. This law provided for the registration of friendly societies' rules with the justices of the peace. Reports made by the justices to the national government indicate that the dates of origin were in most cases during the two or three decades immediately preceding the passage of the law. The following table indicates the number and distribution of societies registered with the justices of the peace and approved by them by 1796 as compared with 1801:

County or Town	1796	1801
Bedfordshire	5	9
Berkshire	12	14
Bristol	..	32
Buckinghamshire	30	44
Cambridgeshire	17	20
Cheshire	50	..
Cornwall	50	69
Cumberland	67	73
Derbyshire	115	133
Devonshire	..	156
Dorsetshire	12	13
Durham	51	66
Essex	182	205
Gloucestershire	93	111
Hampshire	16	..
Herefordshire	32	32
Hertfordshire	31	33
Huntingdonshire	11	..
Kent	13	..
Kent and Canterbury	..	161

[72] Circular issued by Committee of United Benefit Societies, Feb. 24, 1792 (Br. Mus. 8275.bb.2(4)).

County or Town	1796	1801
Lancashire	452	820
Leicestershire	94	84
Lincolnshire	53	..
London	..	250
Middlesex	..	c.600
Monmouthshire	24	33
Norfolk	145	203
Northamptonshire	62	62
Northumberland	10	13
Nottinghamshire	92	141
Oxfordshire	26	15
Rutland	11	14
Shropshire	95	125
Somersetshire	114	123
Staffordshire	79	88
Suffolk	219	235
Surrey	130	188
Sussex	29	31
Warwickshire	149	188
Westmoreland	19	15
Wiltshire	19	30
Worcestershire	125	156
Yorkshire:		
East Riding	10	16
North Riding	48	48
West Riding	281	330
Hull	..	20
Wales	77	100

It will be observed from the above table [73] that the
numbers registered in counties having industrial centers
were relatively large, but a fact of greater significance
concerning the organizing tendencies of industrial workers is their hostility to the law of 1793 and their extensive
refusal to register in accordance with its provisions. It
was Sir F. M. Eden's opinion that as late as 1801, not
more than two-thirds to three-fourths of the societies had
registered, and the unregistered societies seem to have

[73] The figures for 1796 were derived from *Chatham Papers*, Vol. 309,
Reports of Clerks of Peace on Registration of Friendly Societies; for
1801, from Eden, *Observations on Friendly Societies,* 7, derived by
him from similar reports of justices of the peace.

been mostly in the manufacturing regions. He stated that nearly all of the Sheffield workers were members of friendly societies; and yet "I believe none of the [Sheffield] societies," he wrote somewhat earlier in his *State of the Poor,* "have had their rules confirmed by the magistrates, from an apprehension that in bringing forward the late act, Government were actuated by very different views from what they profess." [74] Nor was their apprehension unfounded. The law professed to be for the purpose merely of strengthening and encouraging them and protecting their members. In fact, the principal motive for regulating rural friendly societies was a more effective utilization of them as a means of reducing the poor rates. It is probable that an equally important motive for regulating the societies in manufacturing towns was to confine them to specific activities approved by the authorities.

There seems generally to have been little fear that rural friendly societies would be used for any purpose other than that of providing insurance in some form, thus promising relief to the ratepayers. Writers were well-nigh unanimous in praising the peasants for displaying the virtues of "subordination in all its native beauty" in contrast with the industrial workers, who were as widely denounced for their "insubordination," and for being "often turbulent and dissatisfied without reason." [75] The motives for public regulation were

[74] Eden, *Observations on Friendly Societies,* 5-7, and *State of the Poor,* III, 873, 874.

[75] Ruggles, *History of the Poor,* II, 224, 225 (ed. 1794), 287-289 (ed. 1797). Ruggles approves agricultural friendly societies but condemns those in the manufacturing towns because of the "bad, seditious, and turbulent purposes" to which they lend themselves. For some characteristic contrasts of the docile spirit of the peasants and the spirit of "insubordination," *i.e.,* of combination to improve their lot, evident among town workers, see, in addition to Ruggles, Fox, *General View,* Glamorganshire, 45, 46; Pearce, *General View,* Berkshire, 42; Holt, *General View,* Lancashire, 213 (ed. 1795); Fullarton, *General*

foreshadowed by John Acland, a Devonshire justice of the peace and leading advocate of friendly-society legislation. The title of his book is itself significant: *A Plan for Rendering the Poor Independent on Public Contributions.* At the outset of his discussion, he enumerated the disadvantages of allowing the societies to continue without control. He believed that "a greater drawback than all the rest" was the tendency of the societies in the towns to engage in "mutinous" disputes with their employers. Similar views were commonly expressed. In the opinion of the author of the law, George Rose, it was effective in restraining registered societies from unlawful practices. Complaints, he said, had been made "of persons assembling under the pretence of a friendly society, for bad and dangerous purposes,"—as preventing reductions in wages,—but he knew of no such cases among societies duly registered according to law. A similar distinction between registered and unregistered societies was made by the parliamentary committee which investigated the status of friendly societies in 1825.[76]

A significant illustration of the effect of the law is the case of the Friendly Associated Cotton Spinners of Manchester. Their rules as printed in 1792, the year preceding the enactment of the law, contain the customary provisions concerning the officers, the box, and the

View, Ayrshire, 87-89; Robertson, *General View,* Midlothian, 26, 27; Brown, *General View,* Derbyshire, 38-40; *Gentleman's Magazine,* LXII, Pt. II, 894, LXIII, Pt. I, 523; *Annals of Agriculture,* XX, 180-182; Ashton, *Old Times,* 115 (quoting *Times,* Sept. 5, 1794); *Letter to Sir T. C. Bunbury,* 15. The Worsted Committee (see above, p. 165) was fearful of the "prejudicial tendency" of allowing liberties to friendly societies, lest it enable "the members thereof to form illegal combinations." (Worsted Committee's *Minutes,* Apr. 2, 1792, quoted by Heaton, *Yorkshire Woollen and Worsted Industries,* 320).

[76] Rose, *Observations on Banks for Savings,* 43, 44; *Report from the Select Committee on the Laws Respecting Friendly Societies,* 1825, 7, 8, 23.

mutual benefits, and certain significant regulations in addition. One of these stated, in the unlettered language of the group, that "no member of the said Friendly Association shall learn any person to spin cotton (except his or her own child and paupers who receive relief from the overseers) until such person shall have undertaken to pay the sum of one pound and one shilling to the fund of the said society." Another article provided that "when any spinner shall come into a shop to work, the members of the said society employed therein shall require him to produce a ticket to show that he is a member." If he is not a member, they "shall deem him unworthy of notice and report his name to the committee." An article aimed evidently at the "speeding-up" tendencies of employers stated that if any member of the society shall "in a boasting manner (as hath frequently been done) acquaint every person they meet with what great quantities of cotton they have spun in a short time, and what a deal of money they have earned (which idle boasting hath tended much to the detriment of the cotton spinners)," the offender shall be fined two shillings, and for repetition of the offense be expelled. An article even more significant stated that "no person or persons who is a member of the said society shall go to any shop, or even engage in any shop to work, where there has been a lawful turnout, to prevent any arbitrary power that has been often attempted to be done by the masters in the town and neighborhood of Manchester, which has been a very great injury to the cotton spinners." Any person refusing to abide by this regulation was to be expelled. It is apparent that this organization of cotton spinners was far more than a friendly society. It was essentially a trade union of the modern type, with a mutual benefit fund. Fortunately there is available also a copy of the rules and regulations of the society for 1795, as approved by the justices of the peace in accordance with the law of 1793. The minor provisions are practically identical with those of the year 1792. The article requiring a newcomer in a shop to show his membership ticket was eliminated, as was the article forbidding members to work in shops where there had been a "turnout." Emphasis was now placed on provisions of quite another character. Any member assaulting an employer, or damaging property, or indulging in riotous conduct, or combining to raise wages contrary to law, was to be expelled.[77]

To what extent such changes in the rules of the friendly societies made at the time of registration involved corresponding changes in purposes and activities, it is impossible to say. But it is probable that with many the change in rules required for securing the approval of the justices of the peace was little more than a formality. It is impossible, too, to say to what extent the unregistered societies entered the larger field of the illegal combinations, but probably most of them refused to register because of the hope of being able thereby the more readily to evade the restraints imposed by government on action beyond the simple functions of the box clubs. Certain it is that the clear cut differentiation of working-class organizations into the two types, the friendly society and the trade union, was not generally apparent before the passage of the friendly societies act of 1793, nor was the differentiation completed till after the legalization of trade unions. That the two functions continued to be performed by organizations calling themselves friendly societies is indicated by the reports of the parliamentary committees which investigated the general subject of working-class organizations in 1824 and 1825. The committee for investigating friendly societies

[77] *Articles of Agreement of the Friendly Associated Cotton Spinners,* Manchester, 1792; *Articles, Rules, Orders, and Regulations of the Friendly Associated Cotton Spinners,* Manchester, 1795.

stated that an "abuse" that had attracted much attention was resort to illegal, that is to say, to trade-union, functions. "These clubs were, in very many instances, composed of persons working at the same trade; the habits and opportunities of association which the friendly societies gave to them doubtless afforded facilities of combination for raising wages and other purposes." The committee thought that this "abuse," in the case of the registered societies, had been slight. The committee which, in 1824, investigated the operation of the combination laws was more positive as to the widespread utilization of friendly societies for trade-union purposes. After the repeal of the combination acts in 1824, the sudden outburst of activity on the part of working-class organizations led in 1825 to another investigation. The committee printed the rules of a large number of organizations which had been particularly active along trade-union lines since the repeal of the combination acts, and in general these rules conformed substantially to the rules of friendly societies, with additional provisions incorporating trade-union functions. The committee emphasized the existence of secret rules and regulations, conflicting in some cases with the printed regulations "by which they are ostensibly governed." These revelations indicate the widespread use of friendly societies as cloaks for trade-union activities. The relaxation in law and in law enforcement in respect to combinations led to the gradual emergence of trade unions in name and formal rules as well as in functions; while the various laws favoring associations which conformed strictly to friendly-society functions still further promoted a differentiation in organization which was earlier exceptional.[78]

The policy of the government in connection with the

[78] *Report from Committee on Friendly Societies*, 1825, 7, 8, 23; *Report from Committee on Combination Laws*, 1825, 4, 24-59.

friendly societies act of 1793 was a compromise between two conflicting motives. The authorities were agreed that working-class organizations should in general be exterminated. They were in accord, also, in the eager desire to reduce the poor rates. By the action taken, the tendency toward organization, which had long been severely restricted, and which was to be dealt with so ruthlessly by the combination acts of 1799 and 1800, was allowed to survive in the friendly societies in the hope that they could be rendered relatively "harmless" to employers by supervision, and at the same time made serviceable in reducing the indirect costs of labor in the form of the poor rates. Whatever may be one's judgment concerning the wisdom or justice of the government's policy, the fact remains that the friendly-society movement, especially before the hand of authority directed its course, was a significant expression of working-class consciousness and capacity for concerted action.

There was published at Manchester in 1756 a booklet entitled *The Worsted Small-ware Weaver's Apology.* It was supposedly written by "Timothy Shuttle," member of a weavers' box club which had presumed to enter into a conflict with the employing weavers. The "Apology" was for not heeding the advice that the cobbler should stick to his last. "As it is the first time," the writer states, "that ever anything appeared in print in behalf of the worsted small-ware weavers, it is very likely to meet with a great deal of stiff censures, and scornful jeers, from those who are either enemies to the weavers, or has them in . . . contempt." The fate which the unlettered "Timothy Shuttle" bemoaned was a fate common to subordinate classes. Whenever they have found a voice, it has met rebuff in various forms, the advice that the cobbler should stick to his last being the mildest. In general they have been voiceless.

The student of the history of subordinate classes therefore finds himself confronted with the two-fold difficulty of inadequate first-hand records and of such records as exist having been written for the most part by members of dominant groups from their own point of view—a point of view obscured, however, by the fallacious identification of group interests with social interests. This we found to be measureably true even in the case of the rising and influential class represented by such men as Arkwright, Boulton and Wedgwood, in their relations to the older aristocracy. In the case of the industrial workers, the information is far less extensive, and the upper-class bias in most of the records—a bias at times obvious but more often subtle and implicit—is far more serious. In consequence, the history of the most important development in the social life of modern England—the rise of the industrial workers—must remain in its early stages a tentative and vague outline.

BIBLIOGRAPHY

1. Non-Contemporaneous Accounts and Bibliographies

Abram, W. A., *History of Blackburn, Town and Parish.* Blackburn, 1877.

Allen, G. C., "An Eighteenth-Century Combination in the Copper-Mining Industry," in *Econ. Jour.*, XXXIII, 74-85 (Mch., 1923). "Combination" refers not to employees but to capitalists.

Ansell, C., *Treatise on Friendly Societies.* London, 1835. Includes outline of legislation.

Ashbourne, Lord (E. Gibson), *Pitt: Some Chapters of His Life and Times.* London, 1898. Includes extensive but not very well discriminated extracts from correspondence.

Ashley, W. J., *Economic Organization of England.* London, 1914.

Ashton, J., *Old Times. A Picture of Social Life at the End of the Eighteenth Century.* London, 1885.

Axon, W. E. A., *Annals of Manchester.* London, 1886.

Axon, W. E. A., *Lancashire Gleanings.* Manchester, 1883.

Baernreither, J. M., *English Associations of Working Men.* Tr. from the German by Alice Taylor. London, 1893. Devoted largely to nineteenth-century friendly societies.

Bagnall, W. R., *Samuel Slater and the Early Development of the Cotton Manufacture in the United States.* Middletown, Ct., 1890. Slater was an Englishman, and the book throws light on English as well as American conditions.

Baines, E., Jr., *History of the Cotton Manufacture in Great Britain.* London, 1835. This early work is still indispensable.

Baines, E., *History of the County Palatine and Duchy of Lancaster.* 4 vols. London, 1836. The biographical portions are by W. R. Whatton.

Baines, T., and Fairbairn, W., *Lancashire and Cheshire, Past and Present.* 2 vols. London, n. d.

Beckman, J., *History of Inventions, Discoveries and Origins.* Tr. from the German by W. Johnson. 4th ed., rev. by W. Francis and J. W. Griffith. 2 vols. London, 1846. Much curious information, not altogether dependable.

BISCHOFF, J., *Comprehensive History of the Woollen and Worsted Manufactures.* 2 vols. London, 1842. A useful compilation.

BOURNE, H. R. F., *Romance of Trade.* London, n. d. Interesting but uncritical popular essays on various subjects, some of which are pertinent to the present study.

BROCKBANK, E. M., *Sketches of the Lives and Work of the Honorary Medical Staff of the Manchester Infirmary.* Manchester, 1904.

BROOKE, R., *Liverpool as It Was During the Last Quarter of the Eighteenth Century.* Liverpool, 1853.

BROWN, P. A., *French Revolution in English History.* London, 1918.

BROWNING, O., "The Treaty of Commerce between England and France" (1786), in *Trans. Roy. Hist. Soc.,* 1885, n.s., II, 349-364.

CANNAN, E., *History of Local Rates in England.* 2d ed. London, 1912.

Century of Fine Cotton Spinning. 2d ed. Manchester, 1913. History of a noted firm, with extracts from trade books, etc., going back to 1788.

CHAPMAN, S. J., *The Lancashire Cotton Industry. A Study in Economic Development.* Manchester, 1904. A careful study of the mechanical and administrative changes connected with the industry, on the side of labor as well as of capital, with a valuable bibliography.

CHEYNEY, E. P., *Industrial and Social History of England.* Rev. ed. New York, 1921.

CREIGHTON, C., *History of Epidemics in Britain.* 2 vols. Cambridge, 1894. A valuable work.

CUNNINGHAM, W., *Alien Immigrants to England.* London, 1897.

CUNNINGHAM, W., *Growth of English Industry and Commerce,* Part I, in the Middle Ages; Part II, in Modern Times. Two volumes of Part II, consecutively paged. 4th ed. Cambridge, 1912. Conservative in tone but thorough in scholarship, this most important of comprehensive works in its field is valuable alike for its interpretations and its bibliographical aids.

DANIELS, G. W., *Early English Cotton Industry.* Manchester, 1920. Introduction by Professor Unwin. A notable instance of painstaking research in the obscurer sources of economic history.

DIRCKS, H., *Life, Times, and Scientific Labors of the Second Marquis of Worcester.* London, 1865. Worcester's *Century of Inventions* is reprinted with notes; other documents are appended; and bibliographies are included.

DOBBS, A. E., *Education and Social Movements, 1700-1850.* London, 1919. Somewhat indefinite and diffuse.

DOWELL, S., *History of Taxation and Taxes in England.* 4 vols. London, 1884.

DUMAS, F., *Étude sur le traité de commerce de 1786 entre la France et l'Angleterre.* Toulouse, 1904.

DUMBELL, S., "Early Liverpool Cotton Imports and the Organization of the Cotton Market in the Eighteenth Century," in *Econ. Jour.,* XXXIII, 362-373 (Sept., 1923).

DUNLOP, O. J., and DENMAN, R. D., *English Apprenticeship and Child Labor.* London, 1912.

ELLISON, T., *Cotton Trade of Great Britain.* London, 1886.

FRENCH, G. J., *Life and Times of Samuel Crompton.* 2d ed. Manchester, 1860.

FURNISS, E. S., *Position of the Laborer in a System of Nationalism. A Study of the Labor Theories of the Later English Mercantilists.* Boston, 1920. A thorough and useful monograph.

GRINDON, L. H., *Lancashire: Brief Historical and Descriptive Notes.* New York, 1892.

GUEST, R., *Compendious History of the Cotton Manufacture.* Manchester, 1823. Contains interesting documents and plates, but the title is misleading. The author's main purpose is to disprove Arkwright's claims as an inventor.

HAMMOND, J. L., and BARBARA, *The Village Laborer, 1760-1832.* 2d ed., London, 1913. This book and the two companion volumes by the same authors (*Town Laborer,* London, 1917, and *Skilled Laborer,* London, 1919) are interestingly written studies, critical of the dominant classes. While emphasizing the early nineteenth-century period, they are useful for the latter part of the eighteenth century.

HANDS, W., *Law and Practice of Patents for Invention.* London, 1808.

HASBACH, W., *History of the English Agricultural Laborer.* London, 1908. This valuable work, originally published in Germany in 1894, was reedited by the author and translated by Ruth Kenyon. A mine of information concerning both conditions and ideas, though some of the conclusions are doubtful. Extensive bibliography.

HEATON, H., *Yorkshire Woollen and Worsted Industries from the Earliest Times up to the Industrial Revolution.* Oxford, 1920. A work of extensive learning and careful scholarship.

HELM, E., *Chapters in the History of the Manchester Chamber of Commerce.* London, [1902]. Of slight value for the eighteenth century.

HOWELL, G., *Labor Legislation, Labor Movements and Labor*

Leaders. 2d ed. 2 vols. London, 1905. Useful but not unbiased.

HULME, E. W., "Early History of the English Patent System," in *Select Essays in Anglo-American Legal History,* III, 117-147.

HULME, E. W., "History of the Patent System under the Prerogative and at Common Law," in *Law Quar. Rev.,* XII, 141-154, and XVI, 44-56.

HULME, E. W., "On the Consideration of the Patent Grant, Past and Present," in *Law Quar. Rev.,* XIII, 313-318.

HULME, E. W., "On the History of the Patent Law in the Seventeenth and Eighteenth Centuries," in *Law Quar. Rev.,* XVIII, 280-288.

HUMPHREYS, A. L., *Handbook to County Bibliography, Being a Bibliography of Bibliographies Relating to the Counties and Towns of Great Britain and Ireland.* London, 1917.

HUTCHINS, B. L., and HARRISON, A., *History of Factory Legislation.* Westminster, 1903.

JAMES, J., *History of the Worsted Manufacture in England.* London, 1857. The point of view is indicated by the fact that it was undertaken at the suggestion, and written under the patronage, of a committee of worsted manufacturers.

JEWETT, L., *The Wedgwoods.* London, 1865. Includes a history of the early potteries of Staffordshire.

LAPRADE, W. T., *England and the French Revolution, 1789-1797.* Baltimore, 1909.

McCULLOCH, J. R., *The Literature of Political Economy.* London, 1845. A "classified catalog . . . with historical, critical and biographical notes." Unless the author's preconceptions in favor of Ricardian economics are kept in mind, the criticisms are misleading, but the work contains information of value.

McLEAN, A. (ed.), *Local Industries of Glasgow and the West of Scotland.* Glasgow, 1901.

McNEILL, J. G. S., *Constitutional and Parliamentary History of Ireland till the Union.* New York, 1918.

MANTOUX, P., *La Révolution industrielle au XVIIIᵉ siècle: Essai sur les commencements de la grande industrie moderne en Angleterre.* Paris, 1905. Indispensable, but in need of revision.

MARWICK, W. H., "The Cotton Industry and the Industrial Revolution in Scotland," in *Scot. Hist. Rev.,* XXI, 207-218 (Apr., 1924).

METEYARD, E., *Life of Josiah Wedgwood.* 2 vols. London, 1865, 1866.

MUIR, R., *History of Liverpool.* Liverpool, 1907.

MUIRHEAD, J. P., *Life of James Watt, with Selections from His Correspondence.* New York, 1859.

MUIRHEAD, J. P., *Origin and Progress of the Mechanical Inventions of James Watt.* 3 vols. London, 1854. Much documentary material.

PARKER, C. S., *Sir Robert Peel. From His Private Papers.* 3 vols. London, 1891, 1899. Largely documentary, the early portion dealing with Peel's ancestors and their industrial connections.

PLAYNE, A. T., *History of the Parishes of Minchinampton and Avening.* Gloucester, 1915. Chs. 20-22 contain accounts of the woollen industry of the older type.

PRENTICE, A., *Historical Sketches and Personal Recollections of Manchester.* 2d ed. London, 1851.

PRICE, W. H., *English Patents of Monopoly.* Boston, 1906. In the appendices are several extracts from sources, including the Statute of Monopolies, 1624.

PROTHERO, R. E., *English Farming Past and Present.* London, 1912.

READ, C., "Some Recent Studies of the Industrial Revolution," in *Quar. Jour. of Econ.*, XXXV, No. 2, 341-353 (Feb., 1921).

ROGERS, J. E. T., *History of Agriculture and Prices in England,* 1259-1793. 6 vols. Oxford, 1866-1887.

ROGERS, J. E. T., *Six Centuries of Work and Wages.* New York, 1884.

ROSE, J. H., "The Franco-British Commercial Treaty" (1786), in *Eng. Hist. Rev.*, XXIII, 709-724 (1908).

ROSE, J. H., *William Pitt and National Revival.* London, 1911. Somewhat biased in favor of Pitt.

SALZMANN, L. F., *English Industries of the Middle Ages.* London, 1913. Revised and illustrated ed., 1923.

SCRIVENOR, H., *History of the Iron Trade.* New ed. London, 1854.

SHAW, W. A., *Manchester Old and New.* 3 vols. London [1894]. A work of conventional popular character, of slight value to the student of economic history.

SIMON, Sir J., *English Sanitary Institutions.* London, 1890.

SLATER, G., *English Peasantry and the Enclosure of Common Fields.* London, 1907. Valuable.

SMILES, S., *Men of Invention and Industry.* New York, 1885. Sketches of obscure figures. Useful, but evidencing the limitations characteristic of the author's biographical writings. His various other works, as *Lives of the Engineers, Lives of Boulton and Watt,* and *Industrial Biography,* while frequently uncritical and naïve, are at the same time based upon extensive research.

[STRICKLAND, M. C.], *Memoir of the Life, Writings, and Mechanical Inventions of Edmund Cartwright.* London, 1843.

TAIT, J., *Medieval Manchester and the Beginnings of Lancashire.* Manchester, 1904.

TAYLOR, R. W. COOKE, *Modern Factory System.* London, 1891.

THOMAS, P. J., "The Beginnings of Calico Printing in England," in *Eng. Hist. Rev.,* XXXIX, 206-216 (Apr., 1924).

TOYNBEE, A., *Lectures on the Industrial Revolution.* London, 1913. (First ed., 1884.)

TRAILL, H. D., and MANN, J. S., (eds.), *Social England.* 6 vols. Illus. ed. London, 1904. Useful bibliographies.

[TROUGHTON, T.], *History of Liverpool.* Liverpool, 1810.

TURNER, E. R., "English Coal Industry in the Seventeenth and Eighteenth Centuries," in *Am. Hist. Rev.,* XXVII, 1-23 (Oct., 1921).

TURNER, E. R., "The Keelmen of Newcastle," in *Am. Hist. Rev.,* XXI, 542-545 (Apr., 1916).

UNWIN, G., *Industrial Organization in the Sixteenth and Seventeenth Centuries.* Oxford, 1904.

UNWIN, G., "The Transition to the Factory System," in *Eng. Hist. Rev.,* XXXVII, 206-218 (Apr., 1922), and 383-397 (July, 1922). Superseded by the book next mentioned.

UNWIN, G., HULME, A., and TAYLOR, G., *Samuel Oldknow and the Arkwrights.* Manchester, 1924. Based on sources recently discovered in the ruins of Oldknow's eighteenth-century cotton mill. Many of the sources are quoted. A realistic illustration of the great economic transition.

URE, A., *The Cotton Manufacture of Great Britain Systematically Investigated.* 2 vols. London, 1836. Useful statistics and technical descriptions. Largely from the point of view of the manufacturers.

USHER, A. P., *Industrial History of England.* Boston, 1920. Inclined toward controversy, and particularly hostile to Marxian conceptions.

VICTORIA COUNTY HISTORIES. Elaborate works of antiquarian interest with abundant topographical and other data not without value to students of economic history.

WARE, H., *Life and Correspondence of the late Samuel Hibbert Ware.* Manchester, 1882.

WEBB, S. and B., *History of Trade Unionism.* Rev. ed. London, 1920. The extensive bibliography in the earlier edition of this book, the outstanding work of its kind, is not included in the revised edition.

WEDGWOOD, JULIA, *Personal Life of Josiah Wedgwood.* London, 1915.
WESTERFIELD, R. B., *Middlemen in English Business* (1660-1760), in *Trans.,* Conn. Acad. of Arts and Sciences, XIX, 111-445. New Haven, 1915. A mass of valuable data concerning the organization of commerce and industry before the great transition.
[WHEATLEY, H. B.], "The Society of Arts," a series of articles in *Engineering* (London), LII, 83, 134, 163, 173, 231, 278, 361, 451.
WHEELER, J., *Manchester: Its Political, Social, and Commercial History, Ancient and Modern.* London, 1836.
WHITE, G. S., *Memoir of Samuel Slater.* 2d ed. Philadelphia, 1836.
WILKINSON, J. F., *The Friendly Society Movement.* London, 1886. The first chapter, on the period before the nineteenth century, is valueless.
WOOD, H. T., *History of the Royal Society of Arts.* London, 1913.
WOOD, H. T., *Industrial England in the Middle of the Eighteenth Century.* London, 1910.
WRIGHT, G. H., *Chronicles of the Birmingham Chamber of Commerce, A.D. 1813-1913, and of the Birmingham Commercial Society, A.D. 1783-1812.* 1913. Inaccurate as to early history.

II. CONTEMPORANEOUS SOURCES OF INFORMATION

1. Unpublished materials:

Board of Trade Papers.
Boulton and Watt Collection. Letter Books, Drawings, and a variety of Letters, Documents, and Exhibits. In Birmingham Free Library.
Chatham Papers. Record Office.
Foreign Office Papers.
Home Office Papers.
Manchester Miscellaneous Papers, 1784-1791. In Manchester Free Library.
Owen Manuscripts. In Manchester Free Library. Newspaper clippings included.
Wyatt Manuscripts. In Birmingham Free Library.

2. Publications Issued by the Government:

Calendar of Home Office Papers, 1760-1775.
Factories Inquiry Commission, Supplementary Report, Part I (1834).

First Report from the Select Committee Appointed to Inquire into the Operation of the Existing Laws Affecting the Exportation of Machinery, 1841.

Journals of the House of Commons.

Journals of the House of Lords.

Minutes of the Evidence Taken before a Committee of the House of Commons, on the Adjustment of the Commercial Intercourse between Great Britain and Ireland, 1785.

Minutes of the Evidence Taken before a Committee of the House of Lords on the Adjustment of the Commercial Intercourse between Great Britain and Ireland, 1785.

Principles of Mr. Harrison's Time-Keeper, with Plates of the Same. Published by order of the Commissioners of Longitude. London, 1767.

Report from the Select Committee on Combination Laws, particularly as to Act 5 Geo. IV, c. 95, 1825.

Report from the Select Committee on the Laws Relating to the Export of Tools and Machinery, 1825.

Report from the Select Committee on the Laws Respecting Friendly Societies, 1825.

Report of the Commissioners for His Majesty's Customs to the House of Commons on an Adjustment of the Commercial Intercourse between Great Britain and Ireland, 1785.

Report of the Commissioners of Excise to the House of Commons, 1785. On Irish Resolutions.

Report of the Lords of the Committee of Council Relating to Trade and Plantations upon the Two Questions Referred to Them by His Majesty's Order in Council, 1785. On Irish Resolutions.

Report of the Minutes of Evidence Taken before the Select Committee on the State of the Children Employed in the Manufactures of the United Kingdom, 1816.

Reports from Committees of the House of Commons, 1715-1802. 15 vols. and index.

Rutland MSS., Historical MSS. Commission. 3 vols. 1894.

Second Report from the Select Committee Appointed to Inquire into the Existing Laws Affecting the Exportation of Machinery, 1841.

Statutes.

WOODCROFT, B., *Subject-matter Index of Patents of Invention from March 2, 1617 to October 1, 1852.* 2 vols. London, 1857.

WOODCROFT, B., *Titles of Patents of Invention Chronologically Arranged from March 2, 1617 to October 1, 1852.* 2 vols. London, 1854.

3. Publications of Societies and Miscellaneous Collections of Sources:

Articles of Agreement. Rules, Orders, and Regulations Made and To Be Observed by and between the Members of the Friendly Associated Cotton Spinners within the Township of Manchester, in the County of Lancaster, and in Other Townships and Places in the Neighborhood Thereof. Manchester, 1792.

Articles of the Falkirk Society. Newcastle, 1783.

Articles, Rules, Orders, and Regulations, Made and to Be Observed by and between the Members of the Friendly Associated Cotton Spinners within the Township of Manchester, and in Other Townships and Places in the Neighborhood Thereof. Manchester, 1795.

BAILEY, A. M., *One Hundred and Six Copper Plates of Mechanical Machines and Implements of Husbandry Approved and Adopted by the Society for the Encouragement of Arts, Manufactures and Commerce.* London, 1782.

BAILEY, W., *Advancement of Arts, Manufactures and Commerce; or, Descriptions of the Useful Machines and Models Contained in the Repository of the Society for the Encouragement of Arts, Manufactures and Commerce.* London, 1772.

BLAND, A. E., BROWN, P. A., and TAWNEY, R. H., *English Economic History: Select Documents.* 2d ed. London, 1915.

Catalogue of the Books, Pamphlets, and Maps belonging to the Society for the Encouragement of Arts, Manufactures and Commerce. London, 1790.

College of Arts and Sciences Instituted at Manchester, June 6, 1783. Circular dated July 9, 1783.

Correspondence between the Right Honble. William Pitt and Charles Duke of Rutland, Lord Lieutenant of Ireland, 1781-1787. Edinburgh and London, 1890.

Correspondence of Josiah Wedgwood, 1781-1794. Ed. by K. E. Farrer. London, 1906.

Correspondence of the Right Honorable Sir John Sinclair, Bart., with Reminiscences. 2 vols. London, 1831.

DAVIES, J., *A Collection of the Most Important Cases Respecting Patents of Invention.* London, 1816.

DOSSIE, R., *Memoirs of Agriculture and Other Economical Arts.* London, 1768, etc.

[FRIENDLY SOCIETIES]—A Collection of Pamphlets containing rules and regulations of a large number of friendly societies of various types of the latter part of the eighteenth and the early part of the nineteenth century. British Museum, 8275.bb. 1 to 5.

HARLAND, J., *Collectanea Relating to Manchester and Its Neighborhood.* Vols. 68 and 72, Chetham Society Publications, 1866, 1867.

HEATON, H. (ed.), *Letter Books of Joseph Holroyd (Cloth-factor) and Sam Hill (Clothier). Documents Illustrating the Organizaof the Yorkshire Textile Industry in the Early Eighteenth Century.* Halifax, 1914.

Journal and Correspondence of William Lord Auckland. [G. Hogge, ed.]. 4 vols. London, 1861.

LANGFORD, J. A., *Century of Birmingham Life.* 2 vols. Birmingham, 1868. Poorly organized but valuable extracts from local contemporaneous literature.

Letters and Papers of the Society at Bath for the Encouragement of Agriculture, Arts, Manufactures and Commerce. Bath, 1783, etc.

Memoirs of the Manchester Literary and Philosophical Society. London, 1785, etc.

Museum Rusticum et Commerciale: or, Select Papers on Agriculture, Commerce, Arts, and Manufactures. London, 1764, etc. Published by virtue of the patronage of members of the London Society of Arts.

Parliamentary History. Ed. by William Cobbett. London, 1813-1817.

Parliamentary Register. London, 1775-1791 (Vols. I-XXX). Less dependable than the *Parliamentary History,* but published contemporaneously and contains debates not included in Cobbett's work.

Philosophical Transactions of the Royal Society. The Royal Society adhered in the main to its traditional interest in abstract philosophy and pure science.

Plan of the Literary and Philosophical Society of Newcastle upon Tyne. 1793.

Plan of the Society for the Encouragement of Arts, Manufactures and Commerce. A circular dated London, Feb. 19, 1755.

Premiums Offered by the Society for the Encouragement of Arts, Manufactures and Commerce. Various circulars and pamphlets issued during the early years of the society.

Public Proceedings of the General Chamber of Manufactures of Great Britain on the French Treaty. London, 1787.

Report of the Committee of the Magistrates of the Counties of Chester and Lancaster, Appointed for Taking into Consideration the Present Mode of Maintaining, Conveying, and Shipping Vagrants in the Said Counties. [Lancaster, 1785.]

Report of the Committee of the Town Council of Glasgow, Appointed to Consider the Corn Bill at Present Pending in Parliament. Glasgow, 1791. (Bound in *Board of Trade Papers*, 6/133.)

Reports of the Society for Bettering the Condition and Increasing the Comforts of the Poor. London, 1798, etc.

Rules and Orders of the Society Instituted at Bath for the Encouragement of Agriculture, Arts, Manufactures and Commerce. Bath, 1783.

Rules and Orders of the Society Instituted at London for the Encouragement of Arts, Manufactures and Commerce. London, 1760, etc.

Transactions of the Society for the Encouragement of Arts, Manufactures and Commerce. London, 1783, and annually thereafter.

Trial of a Cause Instituted by Richard Pepper Arden, Esq., His Majesty's Attorney General, by Writ of Scire Facias, to Repeal a Patent Granted on the Sixteenth of December, 1775, to Mr. Richard Arkwright. (King's Bench, June 25, 1785.) London, 1785. Includes *Case of Mr. Richard Arkwright and Company.*

WEBSTER, T., *Reports and Notes of Cases on Letters Patent for Inventions.* 2 vols. London, 1844.

Whole Proceedings on the Trial of an Action Brought by Thomas Walker, Merchant, against William Roberts, Barrister at Law, for a Libel. Manchester, 1791.

4. Periodicals:

Annals of Agriculture.
Annual Register.
European Magazine.
Gazetteer and New Daily Advertiser. London. Chiefly valuable for the official announcements, resolutions, etc., of commercial and industrial organizations, notably the General Chamber of Manufactures. Its news items and comments are also useful if proper account is made of their political bias.
Gentleman's Magazine.
London Magazine and Monthly Intelligencer.
Manchester Chronicle.
Manchester Mercury.
New Annual Register.
Wonderful Magazine, or Marvellous Chronicle. Vols. I and II, London, 1764, 1765.

5. Works of Reference, History, Travel, and Description:

Account of the Manner in Which a Standing General Commercial Committee Was Established at Birmingham for the Purpose of Watching over and Conducting the Public Interests of that Town and Neighborhood. Birmingham, 1784.

Agricultural Reports. Each report deals ordinarily with a single county. Note in first volume, in British Museum: "This is a complete collection of all the Reports, etc., of the Board of Agriculture, from its first institution to its dissolution. It was carefully collected by the Secretary of the Board, from whom it was purchased." The reports from the several counties are bound together arbitrarily in a set of ten volumes. These are the original reports made to the Board, a semi-official body, by various persons chosen by the Board, usually residents of the counties described. Some of the reports were later revised and published for wider distribution. The titles being uniform, the full title of the first only is given. Written largely from the point of view of the country gentry, but extremely valuable. The following are the more important volumes:

> ANDERSON, J., *General View of the Agriculture and Rural Economy of the County of Aberdeen.* Edinburgh, 1794.
>
> BAILEY, J., and CULLEY, G., *Cumberland.* London, 1794.
>
> BAILEY, J., and CULLEY, G., *Northumberland.* London, 1794.
>
> BAIRD, T., *Middlesex.* London, 1793.
>
> BILLINGSLEY, J., *Somerset.* London, 1794.
>
> BISHTON, J., *Salop.* Brentford, 1794.
>
> BOYS, J., *Kent.* Brentford, 1794.
>
> BROWN, R., *West Riding of Yorkshire.* London, 1799.
>
> BROWN, T., *Derby.* London, 1794.
>
> CLARK, J., *Hereford.* London, 1794.
>
> DAVIES, T., *Wilts.* London, 1794.
>
> DONALDSON, J., *Perth.* London, 1794.
>
> DONALDSON, J., *Northampton.* Edinburgh, 1794.
>
> DRIVER, A. and W., *Hants.* London, 1794.
>
> FOOT, P., *Middlesex.* London, 1794.
>
> FRASER, R., *Cornwall.* London, 1794.
>
> FRASER, R., *Devon.* London, 1794.
>
> FULLARTON, COL., *Ayr.* Edinburgh, 1793.
>
> GRANGER, J., *Durham.* London, 1794.
>
> HOLLAND, H., *Chester.* London, 1808. Not original edition.

HOLT, J., *Lancaster*. London, 1794. Reprinted with important revisions, 1795. There was also a report for Lancashire by R. W. Dickson, revised and prepared for publication by W. Stevenson, and published London, 1815.

JOHNSTON, T., *Tweeddale*. London, 1794.

KAY, G., *North Wales*. Edinburgh, 1794.

KENT, N., *Norfolk*. London, 1794.

LEATHAM, I., *East Riding of Yorkshire*. London, 1794.

LOWE, A., *Berwick*. London, 1794.

LOWE, R., *Nottingham*. London, 1794.

MARTIN, A., *Renfrew*. London, 1794.

MONK, J., *Leicester*. London, 1794.

NAISMITH, J., *Clydesdale*. Brentford, 1794.

PITT, W. (of Pendeford), *Stafford*. London, 1794. Revised ed., 1808.

POMEROY, W. T., *Worcester*. London, 1794.

PRINGLE, A., *Westmoreland*. Edinburgh, 1794.

RENNIE, BROUN, and SHIRREF, *West Riding of Yorkshire*. London, 1794.

ROBERTSON, G., *Midlothian*. Edinburgh, 1793.

ROBERTSON, J., *Perth*. London, 1794.

SINCLAIR, SIR J., BART., *Northern Counties of Scotland*. London, 1795.

TUKE, ——, *North Riding of Yorkshire*. London, 1794.

TURNER, G., *Gloucester*. London, 1794.

VANCOUVER, C., *Cambridge*. London, 1794.

VANCOUVER, C., *Essex*. London, 1795.

WALKER, D., *Hertford*. London, 1795.

WEBSTER, J., *Galloway*. Edinburgh, 1794.

WEDGE, J., *Warwick*. London, 1794.

WEDGE, T., *Chester*. London, 1794.

YOUNG, A., *Suffolk*. London, 1794.

YOUNG, REV. A., *Sussex*. London, 1793.

AIKIN, J., *Description of the Country from Thirty to Forty Miles Round Manchester*. London, 1795. Published after prolonged and careful collection of data. The *Directory of Manchester* published in 1788 omitted a description of manufactures on the ground that this would have "anticipated in some degree another work [which has] long been preparing for the public eye, viz., *A Description of Manchester and the Country Twenty Miles Round*,"—an obvious reference to Aikin's work. Of great value.

AIKIN, J., and ENFIELD, W., *General Biography*. 10 vols. London, 1799-1815.

ANDERSON, A., *Historical and Chronological Deduction of the Origin of Commerce*. Eds. used: 1764, and 1787-1789.

Authentic Account of the Riots in Birmingham. 1791. Largely documentary. Dissenting in sympathy.

BALDWIN, T., *Airopaidia*. Chester, 1786. Described by the author as "an introduction to aerial navigation."

BELSHAM, W., *Memoirs of the Reign of George III*. 4 vols. 3d ed. London, 1796. Superficial; largely political.

BETHAM-EDWARDS, M. (ed.), *Autobiography of Arthur Young with Selections from His Correspondence*. London, 1898.

Calico Printer's Assistant. London, 1789.

CAMPBELL, J., *Political Survey of Britain*. 2 vols. London, 1774.

CAMPBELL, J. H., "Answers to Queries Relating to the Agriculture of Lancashire," in *Annals of Agriculture*, XX, 109-153. Particularly significant in connection with the relations between agriculture and the newly developing industries of the region.

CHAMBERS, E., and REES, A., *Cyclopedia: or, An Universal Dictionary of Arts and Sciences*. 4 vols. London, 1778, etc.

CLERKE, SIR W., BART., *Thoughts upon the Means of Preserving the Health of the Poor, by Prevention and Suppression of Epidemic Fevers. Addressed to the Inhabitants of the Town of Manchester*. London, 1790.

Companion to the Leasowes, Hagley, and Enville, to Which is Prefixed the Present State of Birmingham. London, 1789.

Descriptive Catalogue of the Several Superb and Magnificent Pieces of Mechanism and Jewelry Exhibited in Mr. Cox's Museum. London, 1772.

EDEN, SIR F. M., *Observations on Friendly Societies*. London, 1801.

EDEN, SIR F. M., *State of the Poor*. 3 vols. London, 1797. Very valuable.

EDWARDS, B., *History, Civil and Commercial, of the British Colonies in the West Indies*. 2 vols. 2d ed. London, 1794.

Encyclopædia Britannica. 1st, 2d, and 3d eds. Internal evidence indicates that the articles pertaining to Lancashire in the 3d edition were compiled not later than 1792.

ENFIELD, W., *Essay towards the History of Leverpool*. 2d ed. London, 1774.

FERRIAR, J., *Medical Histories and Reflections*. 3 vols. Rev. ed. London, 1810. Published originally in 1792. By a noted Manchester physician connected with the Infirmary, the Lunatic Hospital, and the public-health movement.

HOOPER, W., *Rational Recreations*. London, 1783. Evidence of popular scientific and technical interests.

McPHERSON, D., *Annals of Commerce*. 4 vols. London, 1805. Extensive statistics, legal data, etc.

Manchester Directories. Elizabeth Raffald's *Directory*, 1772, **1773**, 1781; Edmond Holme's, 1788; Scholes', 1794. Quotations from the directories are in Harland's *Collectanea*, Chetham Soc. Pubs., LXVIII, 119-154.

MARSHALL, W., *Review of the Reports to the Board of Agriculture from the Northern Department of England*. York, 1808.

MARSHALL, W., *Review of the Reports to the Board of Agriculture from the Western Department of England*. York, 1810.

MARSHALL, W., *Review of the Reports to the Board of Agriculture from the Eastern Department of England*. York, 1811.

MARSHALL, W., *Review of the Reports to the Board of Agriculture from the Midland Department of England*. York, 1815.

MARSHALL, W., *Review of the Reports to the Board of Agriculture from the Southern and Peninsular Departments of England*. York, 1817.

New and Complete Dictionary of Arts and Sciences. By a Society of Gentlemen. 4 vols. 2d ed. London, 1763, 1764.

"Observations, Natural, Economical and Literary, Made in a Tour from London to the Lakes in the Summer of 1791," in *European Magazine*, XX, 136, 216, 289, 377, 450.

[OGDEN, J.], *Description of Manchester*. Manchester, 1783. Reprinted with the title, *Manchester a Hundred Years Ago*, edited by W. E. A. Axon. Manchester, 1887. Valuable.

OWEN, ROBERT, *Life of Robert Owen Written by Himself*. 2 vols. London, 1857. Memoirs of the most interesting of the early great industrialists.

Patent, The, a Poem. London, 1776.

PERCIVAL, T., *Essays, Medical, Philosophical and Experimental*. 2 vols. 4th ed. Warrington, 1789.

PERCIVAL, T., "Observations on the State of Population in Manchester and Other Adjacent Places," in *Phil. Trans.*, LXIV (1774), 54-66, LXV, 322-335, LXVI, 160-167.

PILKINGTON, J., *View of the Present State of Derbyshire*. 2 vols. Derby, 1789.

RADCLIFFE, W., *Origin of the New System of Manufacture Commonly Called Power-Loom Weaving*. Stockport, 1828. Reminiscences of the author's early experiences, beginning about 1770. Very valuable, although colored by the author's hostility to the export of cotton twist.

RUGGLES, T., *History of the Poor: Their Rights, Duties, and the Laws Respecting Them.* 2 vols. London, 1793, 1794. Published in part in *Annals of Agriculture.* The not too enlightened point of view of a country gentleman.

Short Essay Written for the Service of the Proprietors of Cotton Mills and the Persons Employed in Them. Manchester, 1784.

SINCLAIR, J., *Account of the Origin of the Board of Agriculture, and Its Progress for Three Years after Its Establishment.* London, 1793. Documents as well as narrative.

SMOLLETT, T., *Expedition of Humphrey Clinker.* Jenson Society's ed. of Smollett's works. New York, 1911.

Tour in England and Scotland in 1785. London, 1788.

WALPOLE, G. A., *New British Traveller.* London, 1784.

WENDEBORN, F. A., *View of England towards the Close of the Eighteenth Century.* 2 vols. London, 1791. Trans. by the author from the original German edition. Written by a German who had ministered for twenty-two years to a German congregation in London.

YOUNG, A., *Farmer's Tour through the East of England.* 4 vols. London, 1771. Written from notes made during tour of 1770.

YOUNG, A., *Six Months' Tour through the North of England.* 4 vols. 2d ed. London, 1771.

YOUNG, A., *Six Weeks' Tour through the Southern Counties of England and Wales.* Dublin, 1768.

YOUNG, A., *Travels during the Years 1787, 1788 and 1789 Undertaken more Particularly with a View of Ascertaining the Cultivation, Wealth, Resources, and National Prosperity of the Kingdom of France.* 2d ed. London, 1794.

YOUNG, A., *Tour in Ireland.* Ed. by A. W. Hutton. 2 vols. London, 1892. Bibliography of Young's works, II, 348-374.

6. Books and Pamphlets Mainly Controversial and Critical:

ACLAND, J., *Plan for Rendering the Poor Independent on Public Contribution; Founded on the Basis of the Friendly Societies, Commonly Called Clubs.* Exeter, 1786. A manuscript copy of this work is in *Chatham Papers,* CCCVIII.

ANDERSON, J., *Observations on the Means of Exciting a Spirit of National Industry.* Edinburgh, 1777.

[ANSTIE, J.], *General View of the Bill Presented to Parliament during the Last Session for Preventing the Illicit Exportation of British Wool and Live Sheep.* London, 1787. By a prominent woollen manufacturer, advocating monopoly.

ANSTIE, J., *Observations on the Importance and Necessity of Introducing Improved Machinery into the Woollen Manufactory,
. . .* [especially] *of the Counties of Wilts, Gloucester and
Somerset.* London, 1803.

Answer to the Complete Investigation of Mr. Eden's Treaty.
London, 1787.

[ARBUTHNOT, J.], *Inquiry into the Connection between the Present
Price of Provisions and the Size of Farms.* London, 1773.

BELL, W., *Dissertation on the Following Subject: What Causes
Principally Contribute to Render a Nation Populous? and What
Effect Has the Populousness of a Nation on Its Trade?* Cam-
bridge, 1756.

BENTHAM, J., *Defense of Usury; to Which Is Added, A Letter to
Adam Smith, on the Discouragement of Inventive Industry.*
Philadelphia, 1796. Written in 1787.

*British Merchant for 1787. Addressed to the Chamber of Manu-
facturers.* London, 1787.

CHALMERS, G., *Estimate of the Comparative Strength of Great
Britain during the Present and Four Preceding Reigns.* London,
Several editions, those used being the editions of 1786 and 1794.
Extensively translated. Controversial, but informative.

COMBE, W., *Word in Season to the Traders and Manufacturers of
Great Britain.* 6th ed. 1792.

*Complete Investigation of Mr. Eden's Treaty, as It May Affect the
Commerce or the General Policy of Great Britain.* London,
1787. Hostile to treaty.

*Contrast, The; or, A Comparison between Our Woollen, Linen, Cot-
ton, and Silk Manufactures.* London, 1782. One of the innumerable appeals for national preference for the woollen industry.

COWE, J., *Religious and Philanthropic Tracts.* London, 1797. On
education, the state of the poor, friendly societies, etc.

CRUMPE, C., *Essay on the Best Means of Providing Employment for
the People.* London, 1793. Relating particularly to Ireland.

DAVIES, D., *Case of Laborers in Husbandry Stated and Considered.*
Dublin, 1796. Most of the information collected several years
earlier. Described by John Howlett (*Examination of Mr.
Pitt's Speech,* 45) as "an incomparable work."

*Discarded Spinster; or, A Plea for the Poor, on the Impolicy of Spin-
ning Jennies.* London, 1791. A Poem. Apparently by a country gentleman.

DYER, G., *Complaints of the Poor People of England.* 2d ed. London,
1793.

EDEN, W., *Four Letters to the Earl of Carlisle. The Third Edition, to Which Is Added a Fifth Letter on Population.* London, 1780.

[EDEN, W.], *Short Vindication of the French Treaty from the Charges Brought against It in a Late Pamphlet Entitled, A View of the Treaty of Commerce with France.* London, 1787. Written by the negotiator of the treaty.

Extravagance Supported on the Principles of Policy and Philosophy. London, n. d.

FORSTER, N., *Answer to Sir John Dalrymple's Pamphlet upon the Exportation of Wool.* Colchester, 1782.

GISBORNE, T., *Enquiry into the Duties of Men in the Higher and Middle Classes of Society in Great Britain.* London, 1794. A popular work on morals, including a discussion of the ethical bearings of industrial changes.

[HAMILTON, A.], *Enquiry into the Principles of Taxation, Chiefly Applicable to Articles of Immediate Consumption.* Dublin, 1791.

HAMILTON, J. E., *Letter to the People of England upon the Present Crisis* (the eve of the war with France). London, n. d.

HANWAY, J., *Sentimental History of Chimney Sweepers.* London, 1785.

HARTE, W., *Essays on Husbandry.* 2d ed. London, 1770.

Historical and Political Remarks upon the Tariff of the Commercial Treaty. London, 1787. An anonymous but careful analysis of the treaty of 1786, with extensive notes on earlier treaties and on industrial conditions.

HOWLETT, J., *Examination of Dr. Price's Essay on the Population of England and Wales.* Maidstone, [1781?]. A notable contribution to the population controversy. Howlett replied to critics by means of articles in the *Gentleman's Magazine*, LII, 473-475, 525, 526. Arthur Young referred to the author as a "celebrated political arithmetician," and McCulloch (*Literature of Political Economy*, 72) mentions his various tracts, "all of which are distinguished by ability, correct information, and good sense."

HOWLETT, J., *Examination of Mr. Pitt's Speech in the House of Commons on Friday, February 12, 1796, Relative to the Condition of the Poor.* London, 1796.

HOWLETT, J., *Insufficiency of the Causes to Which the Increase of Our Poor and of the Poor's Rates Have Been Commonly Ascribed.* London, 1788.

Humble Petition of the Poor Spinners (town and county of Leicester). [May 2, 1788]. An obscure pamphlet written apparently by a landed gentleman who was opposed to factories.

HUTTON, J., *Considerations on Coal and Culm.* Edinburgh, 1777.

Important Crisis in the Calico and Muslin Manufactory in Great Britain Explained. London, 1788. This noted pamphlet of 28 pages has been frequently quoted, directly and indirectly, and as frequently criticized. Its origin seems to have been as follows: On March 25, 1788, Messrs. Smith, Colquhoun, Whittaker, and Dunlop, claiming to be "delegates from the manufacturers of calicoes and muslins in England and Scotland," presented to the Board of Trade a memorandum entitled, "An Important Crisis in the Cotton Manufactory of Great Britain Explained," their purpose being to secure governmental protection against the competition of East India Company cottons. It was this memorandum, with certain minor changes, which appeared in print anonymously the next month (April) as the pamphlet herein cited. (*Board of Trade Papers*, 6/140, Docs. 25, 26).

Increase of Manufactures, Commerce and Finance, with the Extension of Civil Liberty, Proposed in Regulations for the Interest of Money. London, 1785.

Inquiry into the Causes of the Present Derangement of Public Credit in Great Britain. London, 1793.

KENRICK, W., *Address to the Artists and Manufacturers of Great Britain Respecting an Application to Parliament for the Farther Encouragement of New Discoveries and Inventions in the Useful Arts.* London, 1774.

Letter from a Manchester Manufacturer to the Right Honorable Charles James Fox on His Political Opposition to the Commercial Treaty with France. Manchester, 1787.

Letter to a Member of Parliament, Stating the Necessity of an Amendment in the Laws Relating to the Woollen Manufactory so far as Respects the Wages of the Spinners. Ipswich, 1787.

Letter to Sir T. C. Bunbury, Bart., on the Poor Rates and the High Price of Provisions, with some Proposals for Reducing Both. Ipswich, 1795.

LUSON, H., *Inferior Politics; or Considerations on the Wretchedness and Profligacy of the Poor.* London, 1787.

[MACKENZIE, J.], *A Woollen Draper's Letter on the French Treaty.* London, 1786.

Manufactures Improper Subjects of Taxation. London, 1785.

MITFORD, W., *Considerations on the Opinion Stated by the Lords of the Committee of Council upon the Corn Laws.* London, 1791.

Necessity and Policy of the Commercial Treaty with France Considered. London, 1787.

New and Old Principles of Trade Compared. London, 1788. A clear statement of commercial liberalism, by a satellite of Adam Smith.

[NICHOLSON, W.], *Observations on a Bill Relating to Wool.* Preface, by Sir Joseph Banks, dated London, 1787.

Observations on the New Corn Bill. By an Essex Farmer. London, 1793.

PALEY, W., *Reasons for Contentment; Addressed to the Laboring Part of the British Public.* Carlisle, 1792.

Papers Relative to Mr. Champion's Application to Parliament for the Extension of the Term of the Patent. 1775. Issued by Wedgwood and others, hostile to the extension of patent rights in porcelain making.

PEACOCK, J., *Proposals for a Magnificent and Interesting Establishment.* London, 1790.

PERCIVAL, T., *Short View of the Grounds and Limits of the Obligation to Pay Taxes.* Warrington, [1785]. Connected with the excise controversy.

Political Essays Concerning the Present State of the British Empire. London, 1772. Economic conditions as well as public policies are discussed with some insight.

Politics for the People; or a Salmagundy for Swine. 5th ed. London, 1794. Radical satire. The title page bears the following lines:

> Since times are bad, and solid food is rare,
> The swinish herd should learn to live on air;
> Acorns and pease, alas! no more abound,
> A feast of words is in the hog trough found.

Present State of Great Britain and North America, with Regard to Agriculture, Population, Trade, and Manufactures. London, 1767.

PRICE, R., *Essay on the Population of England from the Revolution to the Present Time.* London, 1780. A noted pamphlet, but with the erroneous conclusion that population had been declining.

Reply to a Short Review of the Political State of Great Britain at the Commencement of the Year 1787. 6th ed. London, 1787.

ROBERTS, W., *Charge to the Grand Jury of the Court Leet for the Manor of Manchester.* Manchester, 1788.

ROSE, G., *Observations on Banks for Savings.* 4th ed. London, 1817.

[ROSE, G.], *Observations on the Act for the Relief and Encouragement of Friendly Societies* (1793). By the Gentleman who framed the Bill. London, 1794.

SHEFFIELD, LORD, *Observations on the Commerce of the American States*. 6th ed. London, 1784.

SHEFFIELD, LORD, *Observations on the Corn Bill Now Depending in Parliament*. 2d ed. London, 1791. By an agrarian protectionist.

SHEFFIELD, LORD, *Observations on the Manufactures, Trade, and Present State of Ireland*. London, 1785.

Short Review of the Political State of Great Britain at the Commencement of the Year 1787. London, 1787.

"SHUTTLE, TIMOTHY," *Worsted Small-ware Weavers' Apology*. Manchester, 1756.

SINCLAIR, SIR J., BART., *Essays on Miscellaneous Subjects*. London, 1802.

SMITH, ADAM, *Wealth of Nations*.

SMITH, C., *Tracts on the Corn Trade and Corn Laws*. New ed. London, 1804. Contains as an appendix the important *Representation of the Lords of Trade on the Corn Laws*, 1790.

STEUART, SIR J., BART., *Inquiry into the Principles of Political Economy*. 2 vols. London, 1767. Somewhat pedantic, mercantilistic, and overshadowed by Adam Smith's work.

STONE, T., *Essay on Agriculture*. Lynn, 1785.

T., *Letters on the Utility and Policy of Employing Machines to Shorten Labor. To Which Are Added Some Hints for the Woollen Trade and Manufactures*. London, 1780. Occasioned by the Lancashire riots, 1779.

[TEMPLE, W.], *Vindication of Commerce and the Arts*. London, 1758. An answer to Bell's *Dissertation*.

Thoughts on the Causes of the Present Failures. 2d ed. London, 1793.

"Thoughts on the Causes and Consequences of the Present High Prices of Provisions," in *Annual Register*, 1767, 2d part, 165-172.

Thoughts on the Establishment of New Manufactures in Ireland, Occasioned by the Late Freedoms We Have Obtained, with an Account of the Manchester Manufactory Established by Mr. Brooke. Dublin, 1783.

Thoughts on the Use of Machines in the Cotton Manufacture. Addressed to the Working People in That Manufacture, and to the Poor in General. Manchester, 1780.

TOWNSEND, J., *Dissertation on the Poor Laws*. London, 1817 (reprinted from the ed. of 1786). Contains Malthusian ideas of population.

TUCKER, JOSIAH, Dean of Gloucester, *Cui Bono? or, An Inquiry, What Benefits Can Arise either to the English or the Americans, to the French, Spaniards, or Dutch, from the Greatest Victories or Successes in the Present War?* 3d ed. London, 1782.

TUCKER, J., *Four Tracts on Political and Commercial Subjects.* 3d ed. Gloucester, 1776.

TUCKER, J., *Reflections on the Present Low Price of Coarse Wools.* London, 1782.

TUCKER, J., *Reflections on the Present Matters in Dispute between Great Britain and Ireland.* London, 1785.

VANCOUVER, J., *Enquiry into the Causes and Production of Poverty and the State of the Poor.* London, 1796.

View of the Treaty of Commerce with France. London, 1787. Called forth a rejoinder by Eden.

WALES, W., *Inquiry into the Present State of Population in England and Wales.* London, 1781.

WALKER, T., *Review of Some of the Political Events Which Have Occurred in Manchester during the Last Five Years.* London, 1794.

WANSEY, H., *Wool Encouraged without Exportation; or Practical Observations on Wool and the Woollen Manufacture.* London, 1791. By a West of England woollen manufacturer, advocating monopoly of wool.

WEDGWOOD, J., *Address to the Workmen in the Pottery on the Subject of Entering into the Service of Foreign Manufacturers.* Newcastle, 1783.

WEDGWOOD, J., *Address to the Young Inhabitants of the Potteries.* Newcastle, 1783. Reprinted in Jewitt, *The Wedgwoods*, 294-306.

WILSON, J., *A Letter, Commercial and Political, Addressed to the Rt. Honorable William Pitt.* 2d ed. London, 1793. Viewed by Chalmers as of such importance as to justify a lengthy "Dedication" in the 1794 edition of his *Estimate*, for the purpose of controverting its views. The authorship was attributed by Chalmers to Dr. James Currie, Wilson being a pseudonym. (*Estimate*, ed. 1794, Dedication, p. i.)

WRIGHT, J., *Address to Parliament on the Late Tax Laid on Fustian and other Cotton Goods.* Warrington, 1785. A champion of the manufacturers in the excise controversy. The author was an army surgeon and Manchester physician.

[YOUNG, A.], *Farmer's Letters*. 2 vols. Vol. I: *To the People of England;* II: *To the Landlords of Great Britain.* London, 1771.

YOUNG, A., *Political Arithmetic.* London, 1774.

YOUNG, W., *Observations Preliminary to a Proposed Amendment of the Poor Laws.* London, 1788.

INDEX